Sexual/Textual Politics

'Neither a purely objective documentary nor a narrowly sectarian polemic ... this book exemplifies feminist theory-making at its rigorous best.'

Women's Review

What are the political implications of a feminist critical practice? How do the problems of the literary text relate to the priorities and perspectives of feminist politics as a whole?

Sexual/Textual Politics addresses these fundamental questions and examines the strengths and limitations of the two main strands in feminist criticism, the Anglo-American and the French, paying particular attention to the works of Cixous, Irigaray and Kristeva.

In the years since publication this book has rightly attained the status of a classic. Written for readers with little knowledge of the subject, *Sexual/Textual Politics* nevertheless makes its own intervention into key debates, arguing provocatively for a com-mitedly political and theoretical criticism as against merely textual or apolitical approaches.

With a new afterword in this edition, *Sexual/Textual Politics* is a brilliantly accessible must-read for all those interested in feminist literary theory.

Toril Moi is James B. Duke Professor of Literature and Romance Studies at Duke University, North Carolina. She is the author of several influential works on feminist literary theory, including *What is a Woman?* (1999).

IN THE SAME SERIES

Toril
Moi

First published 1985 by Methuen & Co. Ltd
Reprinted 1986 (three times) and 1987

Reprinted 1988 (twice), 1989, 1990, 1991 (twice),
1993, 1994, 1995, 1999, 2001, 2003
by Routledge
11 New Fetter Lane, London EC4P 4EE

Simultaneously published in the USA and Canada
by Routledge
29 West 35th Street, New York, NY 10001

This second edition first published 2002

Routledge is an imprint of the Taylor & Francis Group

© 1985, 2002 Toril Moi

Typeset in Joanna by RefineCatch Limited, Bungay, Suffolk
Printed and bound in Great Britain by
TJ International Ltd, Padstow, Cornwall

British Library Cataloguing in Publication Data
A catalogue record for this book is available from the British Library

Library of Congress Cataloging in Publication Data
A catalog record for this book has been requested

ISBN 0–415–28011–7 (Hbk)
ISBN 0–415–28012–5 (Pbk)

Til mamma og pappa

CONTENTS

GENERAL EDITOR'S PREFACE

No doubt a third General Editor's Preface to New Accents seems hard to justify. What is there left to say? Twenty-five years ago, the series began with a very clear purpose. Its major concern was the newly perplexed world of academic literary studies, where hectic monsters called 'Theory', 'Linguistics' and 'Politics' ranged. In particular, it aimed itself at those undergraduates or beginning postgraduate students who were either learning to come to terms with the new developments or were being sternly warned against them.

New Accents deliberately took sides. Thus the first Preface spoke darkly, in 1977, of 'a time of rapid and radical social change', of the 'erosion of the assumptions and presuppositions' central to the study of literature. 'Modes and categories inherited from the past' it announced, 'no longer seem to fit the reality experienced by a new generation'. The aim of each volume would be to 'encourage rather than resist the process of change' by combining nuts-and-bolts exposition of new ideas with clear and detailed explanation of related conceptual developments. If mystification (or downright demonisation) was the enemy, lucidity (with a nod to the compromises inevitably at stake there) became a friend. If a 'distinctive discourse of the future' beckoned, we wanted at least to be able to understand it.

With the apocalypse duly noted, the second Preface proceeded piously to fret over the nature of whatever rough beast might stagger portentously from the rubble. 'How can we recognise or deal with the new?', it complained, reporting nevertheless the dismaying advance of 'a host of barely respectable activities for which we have no reassuring names' and promising a programme of wary surveillance at 'the boundaries of the precedented and at the limit of the thinkable'. Its conclusion, 'the unthinkable, after all, is that which covertly shapes our thoughts' may rank as a truism. But in so far as it offered some sort of useable purchase on a world of crumbling certainties, it is not to be blushed for.

In the circumstances, any subsequent, and surely final, effort can only modestly look back, marvelling that the series is still here, and not unreasonably congratulating itself on having provided an initial outlet for what turned, over the years, into some of the distinctive voices and topics in literary studies. But the volumes now re-presented have more than a mere historical interest. As their authors indicate, the issues they raised are still potent, the arguments with which they engaged are still disturbing. In short, we weren't wrong. Academic study did change rapidly and radically to match, even to help to generate, wide reaching social changes. A new set of discourses was developed to negotiate those upheavals. Nor has the process ceased. In our deliquescent world, what was unthinkable inside and outside the academy all those years ago now seems regularly to come to pass.

Whether the *New Accents* volumes provided adequate warning of, maps for, guides to, or nudges in the direction of this new terrain is scarcely for me to say. Perhaps our best achievement lay in cultivating the sense that it was there. The only justification for a reluctant third attempt at a Preface is the belief that it still is.

TERENCE HAWKES

PREFACE

This introduction to feminist literary theory, the first full introduction to this field, I believe, to be published in English, is intended for the general reader as well as for students of literature.[1] I have aimed to present the two main approaches to feminist literary theory, the Anglo-American and the French, through detailed discussion of the most representative figures on each side. Though I hope to have given an accurate and comprehensive account of the main tendencies within the field, the book does not set out to provide a survey of the vast number of feminist critical studies published since the late 1960s. Nor does it offer a survey of different feminist readings or interpretations of literary works. Its main concern is to discuss the methods, principles and politics at work within feminist critical practice.

One of the central principles of feminist criticism is that no account can ever be neutral. My own presentation of the feminist field is therefore an explicitly critical one. Arguing as I do from a position that often leads me to disagree with other feminists, it would seem that I expose myself to accusations of lack of solidarity with other women. Should feminists criticize each other at all? If it is true, as I believe, that feminist criticism today is stifled by the absence of a genuinely critical debate about the political implications of its methodological and theoretical choices, the answer to that question is surely an unqualified affirmative. The suppression of debate within the camp has been a prominent feature of precisely the kind of male leftist politics to which feminists have objected. To let the idea of sisterhood stifle discussion of our politics is surely not a constructive contribution to the feminist struggle. When Simone de Beauvoir was asked whether one ought to criticize women as severely as men, she answered: 'I think one must be able to say, "No: no, that won't do! Write something else, try and do better. Set higher standards for yourselves! Being a woman is not enough" ' (*Simone de Beauvoir Today*, 117).

The principal objective of feminist criticism has always been political: it seeks to expose, not to perpetuate, patriarchial practices. I have therefore tried to situate my critique of the theoretical positions of other feminists clearly within the perspective of feminist politics: it is after all primarily on that terrain that we as feminists must be able to legitimate our own work. Constructive criticism should, however, indicate the position from which it is speaking; simply to say that one is speaking as a feminist is not a sufficient response to that responsibility. Like many other feminist academics, I speak as a woman with only a tenuous foothold in a male-dominated profession. I also speak as a Norwegian teaching French literature in England, as a stranger both to France and to the English-speaking world, and thus as a woman writing in a foreign language about matters to which in many ways she remains marginal. Any marginalization is of course relative: I also speak as a white European trained within the mainstream of Western thought, which is why I feel that the issues raised by continental, British and American feminism are still of crucial importance to my own critical and political practice.

A final point: the terms 'Anglo-American' and 'French' must not be taken to represent purely national demarcations: they do not signal the critics' birthplace but the intellectual tradition within which they work. Thus I do not consider the many British and American women deeply influenced by French thought to be 'Anglo-American' critics.

I would like to thank Clare Hall, Cambridge for awarding me their Hambro Fellowship for 1981/2; though I did not in fact write the book there, my year in Cambridge gave me the time to think through many of the issues raised in this text. Kate Belsey's energetic support was instrumental in getting the project off the ground in the first place. I am also grateful for the stimulating response from my many Australian audiences in the summer of 1983: they gave me much-needed encouragement and self-confidence. I would also like to thank Penny Boumelha, Laura Brown, Terry Eagleton and my editor, Terence Hawkes, for their constructive criticism.

Lady Margaret Hall
Oxford

ACKNOWLEDGEMENTS

'Who's afraid of Virginia Woolf?' appeared, in a slightly different version, in The Canadian Journal of Social and Political Theory (1985) 9, 1–2, Winter/Spring.

Sections of chapters 3 and 4 in Part One and chapter 4 in Part Two appeared in an essay entitled 'Sexual/textual politics', in Francis Barker et al. (eds) (1983) The Politics of Theory. Proceedings of the Essex Conference on the Sociology of Literature, July 1982. Colchester: University of Essex, 1–14.

A NOTE ON THE TEXT

Full bibliographical references are listed at the end of the book. Throughout the text parenthetical documentation has been limited to give only the amount of information needed to identify a work in the list of references. At times no parenthetical reference has been needed. For example, 'Janine Chasseguet-Smirgel has discussed the problem of female creativity' refers to the only work by Chasseguet-Smirgel included in the list of works cited. Parenthetical references to the actual book or article have thus only been supplied when the final list of references include more than one work by the same author.

INTRODUCTION

Who's afraid of Virginia Woolf?
Feminist readings of Woolf

On a brief survey, the answer to the question posed in the title of this chapter would seem to be: quite a few feminist critics. It is not of course surprising that many male critics have found Woolf a frivolous Bohemian and negligible Bloomsbury aesthete, but the rejection of this great feminist writer by so many of her Anglo-American feminist daughters requires further explanation. A distinguished feminist critic like Elaine Showalter, for example, signals her subtle swerve away from Woolf by taking over, yet changing, Woolf's title. Under Showalter's pen *A Room of One's Own* becomes *A Literature of Their Own*, as if she wished to indicate her problematic distance from the tradition of women writers she lovingly uncovers in her book.

In this chapter I will first examine some negative feminist responses to Woolf, exemplified particularly in Elaine Showalter's long, closely argued chapter on Woolf in *A Literature of Their Own*. Then I will indicate some points towards a different, more positive feminist reading of Woolf, before finally summing up the salient features of the feminist response to Woolf's writings. The point of this exercise will be to illuminate the relationship between feminist critical readings and the often unconscious theoretical and political assumptions that inform them.

THE REJECTION OF WOOLF

Elaine Showalter devotes most of her chapter on Woolf to a survey of Woolf's biography and a discussion of *A Room of One's Own*. The title of her chapter, 'Virginia Woolf and the flight into androgyny', is indicative of her treatment of Woolf's texts. She sets out to prove that for Woolf the concept of androgyny, which Showalter defines as 'full balance and command of an emotional range that includes male and female elements' (263), was a 'myth that helped her evade confrontation with her own painful femaleness and enabled her to choke and repress her anger and ambition' (264). For Showalter, Woolf's greatest sin against feminism is that 'even in the moment of expressing feminist conflict, Woolf wanted to transcend it. Her wish for experience was really a wish to forget experience' (282). Showalter sees Woolf's insistence on the androgynous nature of the great writer as a flight away from a 'troubled feminism' (282) and locates the moment of this flight in *Room*.

In opening her discussion of this essay Showalter claims that:

> What is most striking about the book texturally and structurally is its strenuous charm, its playfulness, its conversational surface. . . . The techniques of *Room* are like those of Woolf's fiction, particularly *Orlando*, which she was writing at the same time: repetition, exaggeration, parody, whimsy, and multiple viewpoint. On the other hand, despite its illusions of spontaneity and intimacy, *A Room of One's Own* is an extremely impersonal and defensive book.
>
> (282)

Showalter gives the impression here that Woolf's use of 'repetition, exaggeration, parody, whimsy, and multiple viewpoint' in *Room* contributes only to creating an impression of 'strenuous charm', and therefore somehow distracts attention from the message Woolf wants to convey in the essay. She goes on to object to the impersonality of *Room*, an impersonality that springs from the fact that Woolf's use of many different personae to voice the narrative 'I' results in frequently recurring shifts and changes of subject position, leaving the critic no single unified position but a multiplicity of perspectives to grapple with. Furthermore, Woolf refuses to reveal her own experience fully and clearly, but insists on disguising or parodying it in the text, obliging Showalter to point out for us that 'Fernham' really is Newnham College, that 'Oxbridge' really is Cambridge and so on.

The steadily shifting, multiple perspectives built up by these techniques evidently exasperate Showalter, who ends by declaring that 'The entire book is teasing, sly, elusive in this way; Woolf plays with her audience, refusing to be entirely serious, denying any earnest or subversive intention' (284). For Showalter, the only way a feminist can read the book properly is by remaining 'detached from its narrative strategies' (285); and if she manages to do so, she will see that *Room* is in no way a particularly liberating text:

> If one can see *A Room of One's Own* as a document in the literary history of female aestheticism, and remain detached from its narrative strategies, the concepts of androgyny and the private room are neither as liberating nor as obvious as they first appear. They have a darker side that is the sphere of the exile and the eunuch.
>
> (285)

For Showalter, Woolf's writing continually escapes the critic's perspective, always refusing to be pinned down to one unifying angle of vision. This elusiveness is then interpreted as a denial of authentic feminist states of mind, namely the 'angry and alienated ones' (287), and as a commitment to the Bloomsbury ideal of the 'separation of politics and art' (288). This separation is evident, Showalter thinks, in the fact that Woolf 'avoided describing her own experience' (294). Since this avoidance makes it impossible for Woolf to produce really committed feminist work, Showalter naturally concludes that *Three Guineas* as well as *Room* fail as feminist essays.

My own view is that remaining detached from the narrative strategies of *Room* is equivalent to not reading it at all, and that Showalter's impatience with the essay is motivated much more by its formal and stylistic features than by the ideas she extrapolates as its content. But in order to argue this point more thoroughly, it is necessary first to take a closer look at the theoretical assumptions about the relationship between aesthetics and politics that can be detected in Showalter's chapter.

Showalter's theoretical framework is never made explicit in *A Literature of Their Own*. From what we have seen so far, however, it would be reasonable to assume that she believes that a text should reflect the writer's experience, and that the more authentic the experience is felt to be by the reader, the more valuable the text. Woolf's essays fail to transmit any direct experience to the reader, according to Showalter, largely because as an upper-class woman Woolf lacked the necessary negative experience to qualify as a good feminist writer. This becomes particularly evident in *Three Guineas*, Showalter argues:

> Here Woolf was betrayed by her own isolation from female main-stream. Many people were infuriated by the class assumptions in the book, as well as by its political naiveté. More profoundly, however, Woolf was cut off from an understanding of the day-to-day life of the women whom she wished to inspire; characteristically, she rebelled against aspects of female experience that she had never personally known and avoided describing her own experience.
>
> (294)

So Showalter quotes Q. D. Leavis's 'cruelly accurate *Scrutiny* review' with approval, since 'Leavis addressed herself to the question of female experience, making it clear that from her point of view, Woolf knew damn little about it' (295).

Showalter thus implicitly defines effective feminist writing as work that offers a powerful expression of personal experience in a social framework. According to this definition, Woolf's essays can't be very political either. Showalter's position on this point in fact strongly favours the form of writing commonly known as critical or bourgeois realism, precluding any real recognition of the value of Virginia Woolf's modernism. It is not a coincidence that the only major literary theoretician Showalter alludes to in her chapter on Woolf is the Marxist critic Georg Lukács (296). Given that Showalter herself can hardly be accused of Marxist leanings, this alliance might strike some readers as curious. But Lukács was a major champion of the realist novel, which he viewed as the supreme culmination of the narrative form. For him, the great realists, like Balzac or Tolstoy, succeeded in representing the totality of human life in its social context, thus representing the fundamental truth of history: the 'unbroken upward evolution of mankind' (Lukács, 3). Proclaiming himself a 'proletarian humanist', Lukács states that 'the object of proletarian humanism is to reconstruct the complete human personality and free it from the distortion and dismemberment to which it has been subjected in class society' (5). He reads the great classical tradition in art as the attempt to sustain this ideal of the total human being even under historical conditions that prevent its realization outside art.

In art the necessary degree of objectivity in the representation of the human subject, both as a private individual and as a public citizen, can be attained only through the representation of *types*. Lukács argues that the type is 'a peculiar synthesis which organically binds together the general and the particular both in characters and situations' (6). He then goes on to insist that 'true great realism' is superior to all other art forms:

> True great realism thus depicts man and society as complete entities, instead of showing merely one or the other of their aspects. Measured by this criterion, artistic trends determined by either exclusive introspection or exclusive extraversion equally impoverish and distort reality. Thus realism means a three-dimensionality, an all-roundness, that endows with independent life characters and human relationships.
>
> (6)

Given this view of art, it follows that for Lukács any art that represents 'the division of the complete human personality into a public and private sector' contributes to the 'mutilation of the essence of man' (9). It is easy to see how this aspect of Lukács's aesthetics might appeal to many feminists. The lack of a totalizing representation of both the private and the working life of women is Patricia Stubbs's main complaint against all novels written by both men and women in the period between 1880 and 1920, and Stubbs echoes Showalter's objection to Woolf's fiction when she claims that in Woolf 'there is no coherent attempt to create new models, new images of women', and that 'this failure to carry her feminism through into her novels seems to stem, at least in part, from her aesthetic theories' (231). But this demand for new, realistic images of women takes it for granted that feminist writers should want to use realist fictional forms in the first place. Thus both Stubbs and Showalter object to what they regard as Woolf's tendency to wrap everything in a 'haze of subjective perceptions' (Stubbs, 231), perilously echoing in the process Lukács's Stalinist views of the 'reactionary' nature of modernist writing. Modernism, Lukács held, signified an extreme form of the fragmented, subjectivist, individualist psychologism typical of the oppressed and exploited human subject of capitalism.[1] For him, futurism as well as surrealism, Joyce as well as Proust, were decadent, regressive descendants of the great anti-humanist Nietzsche, and their art thus lent itself to exploitation by fascism. Only through a strong, committed belief in humanist values could art become an effective weapon in the struggle against fascism. It was this emphasis on a totalizing, humanist aesthetics that led Lukács to proclaim as late as 1938 that the great writers of the first part of the twentieth century would undoubtedly turn out to be Anatole France, Romain Rolland and Thomas and Heinrich Mann.

Showalter is not of course like Lukács, a *proletarian* humanist. Even so, there is detectable within her literary criticism a strong, unquestioned belief in the values, not of proletarian humanism, but of traditional bourgeois humanism of a liberal-individualist kind. Where Lukács sees the harmonious development of the 'whole person' as stunted and frustrated by the inhuman social conditions imposed by capitalism, Showalter examines the oppression of women's potential by the relentless sexism of patriarchal society. It is certainly true that Lukács nowhere seems to show any interest in the specific problems of *women's* difficulties in developing as whole and harmonious human beings under patriarchy; no doubt he assumed naively that once communism had been constructed everybody, including women, would become free beings. But it is equally true that Showalter in her own criticism takes no interest in the necessity of combatting capitalism and fascism. Her insistence on the need for political art is limited to the struggle against sexism. Thus she gives Virginia Woolf no credit for having elaborated a highly original theory of the relations between sexism and fascism in *Three Guineas*; nor does she appear to approve of Woolf's attempts to link feminism to pacifism in the same essay, of which she merely comments that:

> *Three Guineas* rings false. Its language, all too frequently, is empty
> sloganeering and cliché; the stylistic tricks of repetition, exaggeration,
> and rhetorical question, so amusing in *A Room of One's Own*, become
> irritating and hysterical.

(295)

Showalter's traditional humanism surfaces clearly enough when she first rejects Woolf for being too subjective, too passive and for wanting to flee her female gender identity by embracing the idea of androgyny, and then goes on to reproach Doris Lessing for merging the 'feminine ego' into a greater collective consciousness in her later books (311). Both writers are similarly flawed: both have in different ways rejected the fundamental need for the individual to adopt a unified, integrated self-identity. Both Woolf and Lessing radically undermine the notion of the unitary self, the central concept of Western male humanism and one crucial to Showalter's feminism.

The Lukácsian case implicitly advocated by Stubbs and Showalter holds that politics is a matter of the right content being represented in the correct realist form. Virginia Woolf is unsuccessful in Stubbs's eyes because she fails to give a 'truthful picture of women', a picture that would include equal emphasis on the private and the public. Showalter for her part deplores Woolf's lack of sensitivity to 'the ways in which [female experience] had made [women] strong' (285). Implicit in such criticism is the assumption that good feminist fiction would present truthful images of strong women with which the reader may identify. Indeed it is this that Marcia Holly recommends in an article entitled 'Consciousness and authenticity: towards a feminist aesthetic'. According to Holly, the new feminist aesthetic may move 'away from formalist criticism and insist that we judge by standards of authenticity' (4). Holly, again quoting Lukács, also argues that as feminists:

> We are searching for a truly revolutionary art. The content of a given
> piece need not be feminist, of course, for that piece to be humanist,

and therefore revolutionary. Revolutionary art is that which roots out the essentials about the human condition rather than perpetuating false ideologies.

(42)

For Holly, this kind of universalizing humanist aesthetic leads straight to a search for the representation of strong, powerful women in literature, a search reminiscent of The Soviet Writers' Congress's demand for socialist realism in 1934. Instead of strong, happy tractor drivers and factory workers, we are now, presumably, to demand strong, happy *women* tractor drivers. 'Realism', Holly argues, 'first of all demands a consistent (noncontradictory) perception of those issues (emotions, motivations, conflicts) to which the work has been limited' (42). Once again, we are confronted with a version of Showalter's demand for a unitary vision, with her exasperation at Woolf's use of mobile, pluralist viewpoints, with her refusal to let herself be identified with any of the many 'I's in her text; the argument has come full circle.

What feminists such as Showalter and Holly fail to grasp is that the traditional humanism they represent is in effect part of patriarchal ideology. At its centre is the seamlessly unified self – either individual or collective – which is commonly called 'Man'. As Luce Irigaray or Hélène Cixous would argue, this integrated self is in fact a phallic self, constructed on the model of the self-contained, powerful phallus. Gloriously autonomous, it banishes from itself all conflict, contradiction and ambiguity. In this humanist ideology the self is the *sole author* of history and of the literary text: the humanist creator is potent, phallic and male – God in relation to his world, the author in relation to his text.[2] History or the text become nothing but the 'expression' of this unique individual: all art becomes autobiography, a mere window on to the self and the world, with no reality of its own. The text is reduced to a passive, 'feminine' reflection of an unproblematically 'given', 'masculine' world or self.

RESCUING WOOLF FOR FEMINIST POLITICS: SOME POINTS TOWARDS AN ALTERNATIVE READING

So far we have discussed some aspects of the crypto-Lukácsian perspective implicit in much contemporary feminist criticism. The major drawback of this approach is surely signalled in the fact that it proves incapable of appropriating for feminism the work of the greatest British woman writer of this century, despite the fact that Woolf was not only a novelist of considerable genius but a declared feminist and dedicated reader of other women's writings. It is surely arguable that if feminist critics cannot produce a positive political and literary assessment of Woolf's writing, then the fault may lie with their own critical and theoretical perspectives rather than with Woolf's texts. But do feminists have an alternative to this negative reading of Woolf? Let us see if a different theoretical approach might rescue Virginia Woolf for feminist politics.[3]

Showalter wants the literary text to yield the reader a certain security, a firm perspective from which to judge the world. Woolf, on the other hand, seems to practise what we might now call a 'deconstructive' form of writing, one that engages with and thereby exposes the duplicitous nature of discourse. In her own textual practice, Woolf exposes the way in which language refuses to be pinned down to an underlying essential meaning. According to the French philosopher Jacques Derrida, language is structured as an endless deferral of meaning, and any search for an essential, absolutely stable meaning must therefore be considered metaphysical. There is no final element, no fundamental unit, no transcendental signified that is meaningful in itself and thus escapes the ceaseless interplay of linguistic deferral and difference. The free play of signifiers will never yield a final, unified meaning that in turn might ground and explain all the others.[4] It is in the light of such textual and linguistic theory that we can read Woolf's playful shifts and changes of perspective, in both her fiction and in Room, as something rather more than a wilful desire to irritate the serious-minded feminist critic. Through her conscious exploitation of the sportive, sensual nature of language, Woolf rejects the metaphysical essentialism underlying patriarchal ideology, which hails God, the Father or the phallus as its transcendental signified.

But Woolf does more than practise a non-essentialist form of writing. She also reveals a deeply sceptical attitude to the male-humanist concept of an essential human identity. For what can this self-identical identity be if all meaning is a ceaseless play of difference, if *absence* as much as presence is the foundation of meaning? The humanist concept of identity is also challenged by psychoanalytic theory, which Woolf undoubtedly knew. The Hogarth Press, founded by Virginia and Leonard Woolf, published the first English translations of Freud's central works, and when Freud arrived in London in 1939 Virginia Woolf went to visit him. Freud, we are tantalizingly informed, gave her a narcissus.

For Woolf, as for Freud, unconscious drives and desires constantly exert a pressure on our conscious thoughts and actions. For psychoanalysis the human subject is a complex entity, of which the conscious mind is only a small part. Once one has accepted this view of the subject, however, it becomes impossible to argue that even our conscious wishes and feelings originate within a unified self, since we can have no knowledge of the possibly unlimited unconscious processes that shape our conscious thought. Conscious thought, then, must be seen as the 'overdetermined' manifestation of a multiplicity of structures that intersect to produce that unstable constellation the liberal humanists call the 'self'. These structures encompass not only unconscious sexual desires, fears and phobias, but also a host of conflicting material, social, political and ideological factors of which we are equally unaware. It is this highly complex network of conflicting structures, the anti-humanist would argue, that produces the subject and its experiences, rather than the other way round. This belief does not of course render the individual's experiences in any sense less real or valuable; but it does mean that such experiences cannot be understood other than through the study of their multiple determinants – determinants of which conscious thought is only one, and a potentially treacherous one at that. If a similar approach is taken to the literary text, it follows that the search for a unified individual self, or gender identity or indeed 'textual identity' in the literary work must be seen as drastically reductive.

It is in this sense that Showalter's recommendation to remain detached from the narrative strategies of the text is equivalent to not reading it at all. For it is only through an examination of the detailed strategies of the text on all its levels that we will be able to uncover some of the conflicting, contradictory elements that contribute to make it precisely this text, with precisely these words and this configuration. The humanist desire for a unity of vision or thought (or as Holly puts it, for a 'noncontradictory perception of the world') is, in effect, a demand for a sharply reductive reading of literature – a reading that, not least in the case of an experimental writer like Woolf, can have little hope of grasping the central problems posed by pioneering modes of textual production. A 'noncontradictory perception of the world', for Lukács's Marxist opponent Bertolt Brecht, is precisely a reactionary one.

The French feminist philosopher Julia Kristeva has argued that the modernist poetry of Lautréamont, Mallarmé and others constitutes a 'revolutionary' form of writing. The modernist poem, with its abrupt shifts, ellipses, breaks and apparent lack of logical construction is a kind of writing in which the rhythms of the body and the unconscious have managed to break through the strict rational defences of conventional social meaning. Since Kristeva sees such conventional meaning as the structure that sustains the whole of the symbolic order – that is, all human social and cultural institutions – the fragmentation of symbolic language in modernist poetry comes for her to parallel and prefigure a total social revolution. For Kristeva, that is to say, there is a specific practice of writing that is itself 'revolutionary', analogous to sexual and political transformation, and that by its very existence testifies to the possibility of transforming the symbolic order of orthodox society from the inside.[5] One might argue in this light that Woolf's refusal to commit herself in her essays to a so-called rational or logical form of writing, free from fictional techniques, indicates a similar break with symbolic language, as of course do many of the techniques she deploys in her novels.

Kristeva also argues that many women will be able to let what she calls the 'spasmodic force' of the unconscious disrupt their language because of their strong links with the pre-Oedipal mother-figure. But if these unconscious pulsations were to take over the subject entirely, the subject would fall back into pre-Oedipal or imaginary chaos and develop some form of mental illness. The subject whose language lets such forces disrupt the symbolic order, in other words, is also the subject who runs the greater risk of lapsing into madness. Seen in this context, Woolf's own periodic attacks of mental illness can be linked both to her textual strategies and to her feminism. For the symbolic order is a patriarchal order, ruled by the Law of the Father, and any subject who tries to disrupt it, who lets unconscious forces slip through the symbolic repression, puts her or himself in a position of revolt against this regime. Woolf herself suffered acute patriarchal oppression at the hands of the psychiatric establishment, and Mrs Dalloway contains not only a splendidly satirical attack on that profession (as represented by Sir William Bradshaw), but also a superbly perspicacious representation of a mind that succumbs to 'imaginary' chaos in the character of Septimus Smith. Indeed Septimus can be seen as the negative parallel to Clarissa Dalloway, who herself steers clear of the threatening gulf of madness only at the price of repressing her passions and desires, becoming a cold but brilliant woman highly admired in patriarchal society. In this way Woolf discloses the dangers of the invasion of unconscious pulsions as well as the price paid by the subject who successfully preserves her sanity, thus maintaining a precarious balance between an overestimation of so-called 'feminine' madness and a too precipitate rejection of the values of the symbolic order.[6]

It is evident that for Julia Kristeva it is not the biological sex of a person, but the subject position she or he takes up, that determines their revolutionary potential. Her views of feminist politics reflect this refusal of biologism and essentialism. The feminist struggle, she argues, must be seen historically and politically as a three-tiered one, which can be schematically summarized as follows:

1   Women demand equal access to the symbolic order. Liberal feminism. Equality.
2   Women reject the male symbolic order in the name of difference. Radical feminism. Femininity extolled.
3   (This is Kristeva's own position.) Women reject the dichotomy between masculine and feminine as metaphysical.

The third position is one that has deconstructed the opposition between masculinity and femininity, and therefore necessarily challenges the very notion of identity. Kristeva writes:

In the third attitude, which I strongly advocate – which I imagine? – the very dichotomy man/woman as an opposition between two rival entities may be understood as belonging to *metaphysics*. What can 'identity', even 'sexual identity', mean in a new theoretical and scientific space where the very notion of identity is challenged?

('Women's time', 33–4)

The relationship between the second and the third positions here requires some comment. If the defence of the third position implies a total rejection of stage two (which I do not think it does), this would be a grievous political error. For it still remains politically essential for feminists to defend women *as* women in order to counteract the patriarchal oppression that precisely despises women *as* women. But an 'undeconstructed' form of 'stage two' feminism, unaware of the metaphysical nature of gender identities, runs the risk of becoming an inverted form of sexism. It does so by uncritically taking over the very metaphysical categories set up by patriarchy in order to keep women in their places, despite attempts to attach new feminist values to these old categories. An adoption of Kristeva's 'deconstructed' form of feminism therefore in one sense leaves everything as it was – our positions in the political struggle have not changed – but in another sense radically transforms our awareness of the nature of that struggle.

Here, I feel, Kristeva's feminism echoes the position taken up by Virginia Woolf some sixty years earlier. Read from this perspective, *To the Lighthouse* illustrates the destructive nature of a metaphysical belief in strong, immutably fixed gender identities – as represented by Mr and Mrs Ramsay – whereas Lily Briscoe (an artist) represents the subject who deconstructs this opposition, perceives its pernicious influence and tries as far as is possible in a still rigidly patriarchal order to live as her own woman, without regard for the crippling definitions of sexual identity to which society would have her conform. It is in this context that we must situate Woolf's crucial concept of androgyny. This is not, as Showalter argues, a flight from fixed gender identities, but a recognition of their falsifying metaphysical nature. Far from fleeing such gender identities because she fears them,

Woolf rejects them because she has seen them for what they are. She has understood that the goal of the feminist struggle must precisely be to deconstruct the death-dealing binary oppositions of masculinity and femininity.

In her fascinating book *Toward Androgyny*, published in 1973, Carolyn Heilbrun sets out her own definition of androgyny in similar terms when she describes it as the concept of an 'unbounded and hence fundamentally indefinable nature' (xi). When she later finds it necessary to distinguish androgyny from feminism, and therefore implicitly defines Woolf as a non-feminist, her distinction seems to be based on the belief that only the first two stages of Kristeva's three-tiered struggle could count as feminist strategies. She acknowledges that in modern-day society it might be difficult to separate the defenders of androgyny from feminists, 'because of the power men now hold, and because of the political weakness of women' (xvi–xvii), but refuses to draw the conclusion that feminists can in fact desire androgyny. As opposed to Heilbrun, I would stress with Kristeva that a theory that demands the deconstruction of sexual identity is indeed authentically feminist. In Woolf's case the question is rather whether or not her remarkably advanced understanding of feminist objectives prevented her from taking up a progressive political position in the feminist struggles of her day. In the light of *Three Guineas* (and of *A Room of One's Own*), the answer to this question is surely no. The Woolf of *Three Guineas* shows an acute awareness of the dangers of both liberal and radical feminism (Kristeva's positions one and two), and argues instead for a 'stage three' position; but despite her objections she ends up firmly in favour of women's right to financial independence, education and entry into the professions – all central issues for feminists of the 1920s and 1930s.

Nancy Topping Bazin reads Woolf's concept of androgyny as the union of masculinity and femininity – precisely the opposite, in fact, of viewing it as the deconstruction of the duality. For Bazin, masculinity and femininity in Woolf are concepts that retain their full essential charge of meaning. She thus argues that Lily Briscoe in *To the Lighthouse* must be read as being just as feminine as Mrs Ramsay, and that the androgynous solution of the novel consists in a *balance* of the masculine and the feminine 'approach to truth' (138). Herbert Marder, conversely, advances in his *Feminism and Art* the trite and traditional case that Mrs Ramsay must be seen as an androgynous ideal in herself: 'Mrs Ramsay as wife, mother, hostess, is the androgynous artist in life, creating with the whole of her being' (128). Heilbrun rightly rejects such a reading, claiming that:

> It is only in groping our way through the clouds of sentiment and misplaced biographical information that we are able to discover Mrs. Ramsay, far from androgynous and complete, to be as one-sided and life-denying as her husband.
>
> (155)

The host of critics who with Marder read Mrs Ramsay and Mrs Dalloway as Woolf's ideal of feminity are thus either betraying their vestigial sexism – the sexes are fundamentally different and should stay that way – or their adherence to what Kristeva would call a 'stage two' feminism: women are different from men and it is time they began praising the superiority of their sex. These are both, I believe, misreadings of Woolf's texts, as when Kate Millett writes that:

> Virginia Woolf glorified two housewives, Mrs. Dalloway and Mrs. Ramsay, recorded the suicidal misery of Rhoda in *The Waves* without ever explaining its causes, and was argumentative yet somehow unsuccessful, perhaps because unconvinced, in conveying the frustrations of the woman artist in Lily Briscoe.
>
> (139–40)

A combination of Derridean and Kristevan theory, then, would seem to hold considerable promise for future feminist readings of Woolf. But it is important to be aware of the political limitations of Kristeva's arguments. Though her views on the 'politics of the subject' constitute a significant contribution to revolutionary theory, her belief that the revolution within the subject somehow prefigures a later social revolution poses severe problems for any materialist analysis of society. The strength of Kristevan theory lies in its emphasis on the politics of language as a material and social structure, but it takes little or no account of other conflicting ideological and material structures that must be part of any radical social transformation. These and other problems will be discussed in the chapter on Kristeva (pp. 149–72). It should nevertheless be emphasized that the 'solution' to Kristeva's problems lies not in a speedy return to Lukács, but in an integration and transvaluation of her ideas within a larger feminist theory of ideology.

A Marxist-feminist critic like Michèle Barrett has stressed the materialist aspect of Woolf's politics. In her introduction to *Virginia Woolf: Women and Writing*, she argues that:

> Virginia Woolf's critical essays offer us an unparalleled account of the development of women's writing, perceptive discussion of her predecessors and contemporaries, and a pertinent insistence on the material conditions which have structured women's consciousness.
>
> (36)

Barrett, however, considers Woolf only as essayist and critic, and seems to take the view that when it comes to her fiction, Woolf's aesthetic theory, particularly the concept of an androgynous art, 'continually resists the implications of the materialist position she advances in *A Room of One's Own*' (22). A Kristevan approach to Woolf, as I have argued, would refuse to accept this binary opposition of aesthetics on the one hand and politics on the other, locating the politics of Woolf's writing *precisely in her textual practice*. That practice is of course much more marked in the novels than in most of the essays.

Another group of feminist critics, centred around Jane Marcus, consistently argue for a radical reading of Woolf's work without recourse to either Marxist or post-structuralist theory. Jane Marcus claims Woolf as a 'guerrilla fighter in a Victorian skirt' (1), and sees in her a champion of both socialism and feminism. Marcus's article 'Thinking back through our mothers', however, makes it abundantly clear that it is exceptionally difficult to argue this case convincingly. Her article opens with this assertion:

> Writing, for Virginia Woolf, was a revolutionary act. Her alienation from British patriarchal culture and its capitalist and imperialist forms and values, was so intense that she was filled with terror and determination

as she wrote. A guerrilla fighter in a Victorian skirt, she trembled with fear as she prepared her attacks, her raids on the enemy.

(1)

Are we to believe that there is a causal link between the first and the following sentences – that writing was a revolutionary act for Woolf *because* she could be seen to tremble as she wrote? Or should the passage be read as an extended metaphor, as an image of the fears of *any* woman writing under patriarchy? In which case it no longer tells us anything specific about Woolf's particular writing practices. Or again, perhaps the first sentence is the claim that the following sentences are meant to corroborate? If this is the case, the argument also fails. For Marcus here unproblematically evokes biographical evidence to sustain her thesis about the nature of Woolf's writing: the reader is to be convinced by appeals to biographical circumstances rather than to the texts. But does it really matter whether or not Woolf was in the habit of trembling at her desk? Surely what matters is what she wrote? This kind of emotion-alist argument surfaces again in Marcus's extensive discussion of the alleged parallels between Woolf and the German Marxist critic Walter Benjamin ('Both Woolf and Benjamin chose suicide rather than exile before the tyranny of fascism' (7)). But surely Benjamin's suicide at the Spanish frontier, where as an exiled German Jew fleeing the Nazi occu-pation of France he feared being handed over to the Gestapo, must be considered in a rather different light from Woolf's suicide in her own back garden in unoccupied England, however political we might wish her private life to be? Marcus's biographical analogies strive to establish Woolf as a remarkable individual, and so fall back into the old-style historical-biographical criticism much in vogue before the American New Critics entered the scene in the 1930s. How far a radical feminist approach can simply take over such traditional methods untransformed is surely debatable.

We have seen that current Anglo-American feminist criticism tends to read Woolf through traditional aesthetic categories, relying largely on a liberal-humanist version of the Lukácsian aesthetics, against which Brecht so effectively polemicized. The anti-humanist reading I have advocated as yielding a better understanding of the political nature of

Woolf's aesthetics has yet to be written. The only study of Woolf to have integrated some of the theoretical advances of post-structuralist thought is written by a man, Perry Meisel, and though it is by no means an anti-feminist or even an unfeminist work, it is nevertheless primarily concerned with the influence on Woolf of Walter Pater. Meisel is the only critic of my acquaintance to have grasped the radically deconstructed character of Woolf's texts:

> With 'difference' the reigning principle in Woolf as well as Pater, there can be no natural or inherent characteristics of any kind, even between the sexes, because all character, all language, even the language of sexuality, emerges by means of a difference from itself.

(234)

Meisel also shrewdly points out that this principle of difference makes it impossible to select any one of Woolf's works as more representative, more essentially 'Woolfian' than any other, since the notable divergence among her texts 'forbids us to believe any moment in Woolf's career to be more conclusive than another' (242). It is a mistake, Meisel concludes, to 'insist on the coherence of self and author in the face of a discourse that dislocates or decentres them both, that skews the very categories to which our remarks properly refer' (242).

The paradoxical conclusion of our investigations into the feminist reception of Woolf is therefore that she has yet to be adequately welcomed and acclaimed by her feminist daughters in England and America. To date she has either been rejected by them as insufficiently feminist, or praised on grounds that seem to exclude her fiction. By their more or less unwitting subscription to the humanist aesthetic categories of the traditional male academic hierarchy, feminist critics have seriously undermined the impact of their challenge to that very institution. The only difference between a feminist and a non-feminist critic in this tradition then becomes the formal political perspective of the critic. The feminist critic thus unwittingly puts herself in a position from which it becomes impossible to read Virginia Woolf as the progressive, feminist writer of genius she undoubtedly was. A feminist criticism that would do both justice and homage to its great mother and sister: this, surely, should be our goal.

Part I

Anglo-American Feminist Criticism

1

TWO FEMINIST CLASSICS

In the 1960s, for the first time since the women's vote was won, feminism again surfaced as an important political force in the Western world. Many women now see Betty Friedan's book *The Feminine Mystique*, published in 1963, as the first sign that American women were becoming increasingly unhappy with their lot in affluent post-war society. The early initiatives towards a more specific organization of women as feminists came from activists in the civil rights movement, and later also from women involved in protest actions against the war in Vietnam.[1] Thus the 'new' feminists were politically committed activists who were not afraid to take a stand and fight for their views. The link between feminism and women's struggle for civil rights and peace was not a new one, nor was it coincidental. Many nineteenth-century American feminists, women like Elizabeth Cady Stanton and Susan B. Antony, were first active in the struggle for the abolition of slavery. Both in the nineteenth and twentieth centuries women involved in campaigns against racism soon came to see that the values and strategies that contributed to keeping blacks in their place mirrored the values and strategies invoked to keep women subservient to men. In the civil rights movement, women rightly took offence when both black and white male liberationists aggressively refused to extend their ideals to the oppression of women. Remarks like those of Stokely Carmichael:

'The only position for women in the SNCC is prone' (1966), or Eldridge Cleaver: 'Women? I guess they ought to exercise Pussy Power' (1968),[2] contributed to the alienation of many women from the male-dominated civil rights groups. In other politically progressive movements (the anti-war movements, various Marxist groups), women were experiencing the same discrepancy between male activists' egalitarian commitment and their crudely sexist behaviour towards female comrades. In the late 1960s, women were increasingly starting to form their own liberation groups, both as a supplement and an alternative to the other forms of political struggle in which they were involved.

By 1970, there were already many different strands of political thought in the 'new' women's movement. Robin Morgan clearly characterizes NOW (National Organization of Women), the organization founded by Betty Friedan, as middle-class, liberal and reformist, declaring that the 'only hope of a new feminist movement is some kind of only now barely emerging politics of *revolutionary feminism*' (xxiii). Though Morgan is hazy about the definition of 'revolutionary' in this statement (does it mean anti-capitalist, separatist, or both?), it is clear that two major brands of modern feminism were already crystallizing as conflicting tendencies within the broad spectrum of the women's movement. The bibliography and contact addresses in *Sisterhood is Powerful: An Anthology of Writings from the Women's Liberation Movement*, edited by Robin Morgan and published in 1970, run to 26 pages, amply documenting the fact that by 1970 the women's movement as we now know it was well-established in the USA.

What then, was the role of literary criticism in this movement? The densely printed pages of bibliography in *Sisterhood is Powerful* yield only five references to works wholly or partly concerned with literature: Virginia Woolf's *A Room of One's Own* (1927), Simone de Beauvoir's *The Second Sex* (1949), Katharine M. Rogers's *The Troublesome Helpmate* (1966), Mary Ellmann's *Thinking About Women* (1968) and Kate Millett's *Sexual Politics* (1969). These works, then, form the basis for the explosive development of Anglo-American feminist criticism. *Sisterhood is Powerful* carries only one article on literature (the first chapter of Kate Millett's essay).

If we are to judge by Robin Morgan's selection, then, literary criticism was hardly a central factor in the early period of the new women's movement. Much like any other radical critic, the feminist critic can be seen as the product of a struggle mainly concerned with social and political change; her specific role within it becomes an attempt to extend such general political action to the cultural domain. This cultural/political battle is necessarily two-pronged: it must work to realize its objective both through institutional changes and through the medium of literary criticism. For many feminist critics, a central problem has therefore been that of uniting political engagement with what is conventionally regarded as 'good' literary criticism. For if the existing criteria of what counts as 'good' are laid down by white bourgeois males, there seems little chance of feminist work satisfying the very criteria it is trying to challenge and subvert. The aspiring feminist critic, then, has apparently only two options: to work to reform those criteria from within the academic institution, producing a judicious critical discourse that strives to maintain its feminism without grossly upsetting the academic establishment, or to write off the academic criteria of evaluation as reactionary and of no importance to her work.

In the early stages of feminist criticism in particular, some feminists, such as Lillian S. Robinson, consciously chose the second option:

> Some people are trying to make an honest woman out of the feminist critic, to claim that every 'worthwhile' department should stock one. I am not terribly interested in whether feminist criticism becomes a respectable part of academic criticism; I am very much concerned that feminist critics become a useful part of the women's movement.
>
> (35)

This has not, however, been the most typical response to the apparent dilemma. Like all other literary critics, the overwhelming majority of feminist critics in the 1980s work within academic institutions, and are thus inevitably caught up in the professional struggle for jobs, tenure and promotion. This professionalization of feminist criticism is not necessarily a negative phenomenon, but, as we shall see later, the real or apparent conflict between critical standards and political engagement recurs in various guises in the writings of feminist critics throughout the 1970s and early 1980s. One of the reasons for Kate Millett's success may be that she, as no other feminist critic, managed to bridge the gap between institutional and non-institutional criticism: *Sexual Politics* must surely be the world's best-selling PhD thesis. The book earned Millett an academic degree at a reputable university, and also had a powerful political impact on a world-wide audience both inside and outside the women's movement.

KATE MILLETT

Sexual Politics is divided into three parts: 'Sexual politics', 'Historical background' and 'The literary reflection'. The first part presents Millett's thesis about the nature of power relationships between the sexes, the second surveys the fate of feminist struggle and its opponents in the nineteenth and twentieth centuries and the final section sets out to show how the sexual power-politics described in her preceding chapters is enacted in the works of D. H. Lawrence, Henry Miller, Norman Mailer and Jean Genet. The book established the feminist approach to literature as a critical force to be reckoned with. Its impact makes it the 'mother' and precursor of all later works of feminist criticism in the Anglo-American tradition, and feminists of the 1970s and 1980s have never been reluctant to acknowledge their debt to, or disagreement with, Millett's path-breaking essay. Her criticism represented a striking break with the ideology of American New Criticism, which at that time still retained a dominant position within the literary academy. In courageous opposition to the New Critics, Millett argued that social and cultural contexts must be studied if literature was to be properly understood, a view she shares with all later feminist critics regardless of their otherwise differing interests.

The most striking aspect of Millett's critical studies, though, is the boldness with which she reads 'against the grain' of the literary text. Her approach to Miller or Mailer is devoid of what was in 1969 a conventional respect for the authority and intentions of the author. Her analysis openly posits another perspective from the author's, and shows how precisely such *conflict* between reader and author/text can expose the underlying premises of a work. Millett's importance as a literary critic lies in her relentless defence of the reader's right to posit her own viewpoint, rejecting the received hierarchy of text and reader. As a reader, Kate Millett is thus neither submissive nor lady-like: her style is that of a hard-nosed street kid out to challenge the author's authority at every turn. Her approach destroys the prevailing image of the reader/critic as passive/feminine recipient of authoritarian discourse, and as such is exactly suited to feminism's political purposes.

Unfortunately for later feminist critics, the positive aspects of Millett's study are entangled with a series of less-successful tactics, which seriously flaw *Sexual Politics* as a feminist literary study. While readily acknowledging Millett's importance, many feminists have noticed with dismay her extreme reluctance to acknowledge any debt to her own feminist precursors. Her views of patriarchal politics are obviously deeply influenced by Simone de Beauvoir's pioneering analysis in *The Second Sex*, but this debt is never acknowledged by Millett, who makes only two tangential references to Beauvoir's essay. Though Mary Ellmann's *Thinking About Women* contains many discussions of Norman Mailer's work, often quoting the very passages that Millett later selects for her own book, the latter only briefly mentions Ellmann's 'witty essay' (329), and acknowledges no direct influence. Katharine M. Rogers's study of misogyny in literature is mentioned in a general footnote (45), but though her thesis about the cultural causes of male misogyny is strikingly similar to Millett's own, it is passed over in silence.

This astonishing absence in a feminist writer of due recognition of her feminist precursors is also evident in Millett's treatment of women authors. We have already seen that she dismisses Virginia Woolf in one brief passage; in fact, with the sole exception of Charlotte Brontë, *Sexual Politics* deals exclusively with male authors. It is as if Millett wishes consciously or unconsciously to suppress the evidence of earlier antipatriarchal works, not least if her precursors were women: she discusses John Stuart Mill at length, for example, but not Mary Wollstonecraft. That she chooses to read the French homosexual Jean Genet's texts as representations of a subversive perception of gender roles and sexual politics, but never even mentions women writers like Edith Wharton or Doris Lessing, reinforces this impression. It is as if Millett, to give birth to her own text, must at all cost reject any possible 'mother-figures'.

There are, however, more concrete reasons for Millett's superficial treatment of other women writers and theoreticians. Millett defines the 'essence of politics' as power, seeking to prove that 'However muted its present appearance may be, sexual dominion obtains nevertheless as perhaps the most pervasive ideology of our culture and provides its most fundamental concepts of power' (25). Her definition of sexual politics is simply this: the process whereby the ruling sex seeks to maintain and extend its power over the subordinate sex. Her book as a whole is the elaboration of this single statement, rhetorically structured so as to demonstrate the persistence and pervasiveness of this process throughout cultural life. All of Millett's topics and examples are chosen for their capacity to illustrate this thesis. As a rhetorical statement, the book is therefore remarkably unified, a powerful fist in the solar plexus of patriarchy. Every detail is organically subordinated to the political message, and this, one might claim, is the real motive for Millett's reluctance to acknowledge her forceful female precursors. For to devote much of her book to analyzing patterns of subversion in women writers would unwittingly undermine her own thesis about the remorseless, all-encompassing, monolithic nature of sexual power-politics. Millett's view of sexual ideology cannot account for the evident fact that throughout history a few exceptional women have indeed managed to resist the full pressure of patriarchal ideology, becoming conscious of their own oppression and voicing their opposition to male power. Only a concept of ideology as a *contradictory* construct, marked by gaps, slides and inconsistencies, would enable feminism to explain how even the severest ideological pressures will generate their own lacunae.

Millett's limited theory of patriarchal oppression also explains her unwillingness to acknowledge Katharine M. Rogers's contribution to the study of sexism in literature. In her study of male misogyny, Rogers lists a variety of cultural reasons for the phenomenon: 1) rejection of or guilt about sex; 2) a reaction against the idealization with which men have glorified women; 3) patriarchal feeling, the wish to keep women subject to men. This last reason, Rogers claims, is the 'most important cause of misogyny, because the most widely and firmly entrenched in society' (272). Millett's own thesis comes extremely close to Rogers's third proposition, a fact that one might expect her to acknowledge. Instead, Millett does not refer to this part of Rogers's work, and persists in arguing her own theory of one single cause of patriarchal oppression. Her reductionist approach leads her to explain all cultural phenomena purely in terms of power politics, as for instance in her account of the courtly love tradition:

> One must acknowledge that the chivalrous stance is a game the master group plays in elevating its subject to pedestal level. . . . As the sociologist Hugo Beigel has observed, both the courtly and the romantic versions of love are 'grants' which the male concedes out of his total power. Both have had the effect of obscuring the patriarchal character of Western culture and in their general tendency to attribute impossible virtues to women, have ended by confining them in a narrow and often remarkably conscribing sphere of behavior.
>
> (37)

The rhetorical requirements of Millett's thesis also force her into sometimes inaccurate or truncated accounts of opposing theories. Her widely influential presentation of Freudian and post-Freudian theory sets out to prove that 'Sigmund Freud was beyond question the strongest individual counterrevolutionary force in the ideology of sexual politics during the period' (178). But any rhetorical reduction of contradiction is bound to have particularly damaging effects in the case of Freud, whose texts are notoriously difficult to pin down to a single, unified position – not only because of his theory of the unconscious, but also because of his constant revisions of his own standpoint. Millett's brusque technique is to discard all Freud's own confessions of tentativeness and uncertainty as mere 'moments of humble confusion' (178), before proceeding to what she sees as a savage demolition of psychoanalytical theory – a demolition that can now be demonstrated to be based on misreadings and misunderstandings on Millett's part. Her final diatribe against Freud and psychoanalytic theory claims without nuance or reservation that psychoanalysis is a form of biological essentialism – that is, a theory that reduces all behaviour to inborn sexual characteristics:

> Now it can be said scientifically that women are inherently subservient, and males dominant, more strongly sexed and therefore entitled to sexually subjugate the female, who enjoys her oppression and deserves it, for she is by her very nature vain, stupid, and hardly better

> than barbarian, if she is human at all. Once this bigotry has acquired the cachet of science, the counterrevolution may proceed pretty smoothly.
>
> (203)

Millett's rejection of Freud rests largely on her distaste for what she takes to be his theories of penis envy, female narcissism and female masochism. But these readings of Freud have now been powerfully challenged by other feminists. Juliet Mitchell and Jacqueline Rose have persuasively argued that Freud does not take sexual identity to be an in-born, biological essence, and that Freudian psychoanalysis in fact sees sexual identity as an unstable subject position which is culturally and socially constructed in the process of the child's insertion into human society. As for Millett's interpretation of penis envy and female narcis-sism and masochism, these too have all been challenged by other women: Sarah Kofman and Ulrike Prokop have both in different con-texts read Freud's account of the narcissistic woman as a representation of female power, and Janine Chasseguet-Smirgel has argued a cogent case for seeing female penis envy as a manifestation of the little girl's need to establish a sense of her own identity as separate from the mother, a process which for Chasseguet-Smirgel is crucial for the later development of the woman's creativity.

Another interesting aspect of Millett's account of Freud is that she effectively suppresses all references to Freud's arguably most funda-mental insight: the influence of unconscious desire on conscious action. As Cora Kaplan has convincingly argued, Millett's theory of sexual ideology as a set of false beliefs deployed against women by a conscious, well-organized male conspiracy ignores the fact that not all misogyny is conscious, and that even women may unconsciously internalize sexist attitudes and desires. In her discussion of *Sexual Politics*, Kaplan emphasizes the consequences of this view for Millett's selection of authors to be discussed:

> Gender renegades such as Mill and Engels, are allowed to espouse contradictions, but Feminism itself must be positivistic, fully con-scious, morally and politically correct. It must know what it wants, and since what many women wanted was full of contradictions and

confusions, still entangled in what patriarchy wanted them to be or
wanted for them, Millett does not let them reveal too much of their
'weakness'.

(10)

During the first part of the 1970s, at least until the publication in
1974 of Juliet Mitchell's Psychoanalysis and Feminism, Millett's unremit-
tingly negative account of psychoanalysis remained mostly unchallenged among feminists in England and America. As late as 1976,
Patricia Meyer Spacks (35) praised the account of psychoanalysis in
Sexual Politics as one of the book's strong points. Though, as we have
seen, there exists today a varied, highly developed body of feminist
readings and appropriations of Freudian theory, Millett's denunciation
of psychoanalysis is still widely accepted by feminists both inside and
outside the women's movement. The continuing effectiveness of her
views on this point may be linked to the fact that her theory of sexual
oppression as a conscious, monolithic plot against women leads to a
seductively optimistic view of the possibilities for full liberation. For
Millett, woman is an oppressed being without a recalcitrant
unconscious to reckon with; she merely has to see through the false
ideology of the ruling male patriarchy in order to cast it off and be
free. If, however, we accept with Freud that all human beings – even
women – may internalize the standards of their oppressors, and that
they may distressingly identify with their own persecutors, liberation
can no longer be seen solely as the logical consequence of a rational
exposure of the false beliefs on which patriarchal rule is based.

Millett's literary criticism is flawed by the same relentless rhetorical
reductionism that mars her critique of more general cultural theories.
A case in point is her reading of Charlotte Brontë's Villette. As Patricia
Spacks has pointed out, this contains some serious and elementary
misreadings: Millett states that 'Lucy will not marry Paul even after the
tyrant has softened' (146), even though Brontë has Lucy accept Paul
Emmanuel's offer of future marriage; she also comments that 'The
keeper turned kind must be eluded anyway; Paul turned lover is
drowned' (146), when in fact Brontë leaves the question of Paul's
possible death unsettlingly open so that the reader may construct her
own conclusion to the text. One might agree with Spacks, however, that

what Millett's readings lack in style and accuracy they make up for in passion and engagement. The force of Millett's eloquent, angry indictments indeed lends considerable authority to her survey of male sexual violence against women as displayed in modern literature: there can be no doubt that the writers she attacks (principally Henry Miller and Norman Mailer) do exhibit an offensive interest in male degradations of female sexuality. But Millett's critical readings, like her cultural analysis, are guided by a monolithic conception of sexual ideology that renders her impervious to nuances, inconsistencies and ambiguities in the works she examines. For Millett, it appears, everything is dichotomy or opposition, utterly black or untaintedly white. Though she recognizes that Lucy Snowe in *Villette* is trapped in the sexual and cultural contradictions of her time, she nevertheless lambasts Brontë for the 'deviousness of her fictional devices, her continual flirtation with the bogs of sentimentality which period feeling mandates she sink in' (146). She rejects as a purely conventional device the irruption of romantic ('sentimental') discourse into the predominantly realist *Villette*, whereas later feminist critics, particularly Mary Jacobus ('The buried letter'), have shown that it is precisely in the fissures and dislocations created by this irruption that we can locate some of the deeper implications of sexuality and femininity in the novel.

As a literary critic, Millett pays little or no attention to the formal structures of the literary text: hers is pure content analysis. She also unproblematically assumes the identity of author, narrator and hero when this suits her case, and statements like 'Paul Morel is of course Lawrence himself' (246) abound. The title of the main literary section of *Sexual Politics* is 'The literary reflection', which would seem to imply a somewhat mechanical, simplistic theory of the relationship between literature and the social and cultural forces she has previously discussed. But Millett does not in fact succeed in showing exactly what literature is a reflection of, or precisely how it reflects. The title keeps us suspended in mid-air, positing a relationship between the literary and some other region, a relationship which is neither explicitly stated nor detailedly explored.

Sexual Politics, then, can hardly be taken as a model for later generations of feminist critics. Indeed even Millett's radical assault on hierarchical modes of reading, which posit the author as a god-like authority to be humbly hearkened to by the reader/critic, has its limits. She can produce this admirably iconoclastic form of reading only because her study treats of texts that she rightly finds deeply distasteful: those written by male authors positing and parading male sexual supremacy. Feminist criticism in the 1970s and 1980s, by contrast, has focused mainly on women's texts. Since Millett avoids any feminist or female-authored text (except *Villette*), she is not confronted with the problem of how to read women's texts. Can they be read in the same splendidly anti-authoritarian fashion? Or must women reading women's texts take up the old, respectfully subordinate stance in relation to the author? Kate Millett's criticism, wholly preoccupied as it is with the abominable male, can give us no guidance on these matters.

MARY ELLMANN

Mary Ellmann's *Thinking About Women* (1968) was published before Kate Millett's *Sexual Politics*. If I choose to discuss it after Millett's essay, this in part reflects the fact that Ellmann's brilliant book never became as influential as Millett's among feminists at large. The more narrow appeal of Ellmann's essay is probably in large measure due to the fact that *Thinking About Women* does not deal with the political and historical aspects of patriarchy independently of literary analysis. As Ellmann herself puts it in her preface: 'I am most interested in women as *words*' (xv), an approach that gives her book a direct appeal to feminists with literary interests, though it is quite clearly written for a general readership rather than for a specialized academic one. Where Millett's text abounds in footnotes and bibliography, Ellmann's relatively few footnotes are mostly sardonic or satirical, and she gives her more academic readers no bibliography to peruse. Together with Millett's essay, Ellmann's book constitutes the basic source of inspiration for what is often called 'Images of Women' criticism, the search for female stereotypes in the work of male writers and in the critical categories employed by male reviewers commenting on women's work. This type of criticism will be discussed in greater detail in the next chapter.

The main thesis of *Thinking About Women* is that Western culture at all levels is permeated by a phenomenon Ellmann labels 'thought by sexual analogy'. According to Ellmann, this can best be described as our general tendency to 'comprehend all phenomena, however shifting, in terms of our original and simple sexual differences; and . . . classify almost all experience by means of sexual analogy' (6). This intellectual habit deeply influences our perception of the world: 'Ordinarily, not only sexual terms but sexual opinions are imposed upon the external world. All forms are subsumed by our concept of male and female temperament' (8). The purpose of Ellmann's essay is to expose the ludicrous and illogical nature of this sexual mode of thought. She therefore sets out to give us an example of the kind of society in which thinking by sexual analogy might be justified, before contrasting this with our own situation:

> Men are stronger than women, and the reproductive role of women is more prolonged and more arduous than men. An utterly practical (though not an ideal) society would be one in which these facts were of such importance that all men and women were totally absorbed in their demonstration – that is in the use of strength and the completion of pregnancies. Both sexes would live without intermissions in which to recognize their own monotony or, more often, to describe the complex fascination in which their senses disguised it . . .

> But leisure is primarily mindful, and as we escape the exigency of sexual roles, we more fully indulge the avocation of sexual analogies. The proportions of the two seem particularly grotesque now when the roles themselves have taken on an unprecedented irrelevance. It is strangely as though we had come upon circumstances which render the physiology of sex nearly superfluous, and therefore comic in its eager and generous self-display.
>
> (2–3)

In our modern world the reproductive capacity of women has become socially almost obsolescent, and the physical strength of men gratuitous. We should therefore no longer feel the need to think in sexual stereotypes of the 'male = strong and active' and 'female = weak and passive' kind. But, as Thinking About Women amply documents, these and similar sexual categories influence all aspects of human life, not least so-called intellectual activities, where, as Ellmann points out, the metaphors of fertilization, gestation, pregnancy and birth are of central importance.

Ellmann's second chapter, 'Phallic criticism', deals with sexual analogy in the field of literary criticism. Her analysis of this phenomenon can be gleaned from the following passage:

> With a kind of inverted fidelity, the discussion of women's books by men will arrive punctually at the point of preoccupation, which is the fact of femininity. Books by women are treated as though they themselves were women, and criticism embarks, at its happiest, upon an intellectual measuring of busts and hips.
>
> (29)

One of the most comic instances of 'phallic criticism' is Ellmann's spoof of a male reviewer's treatment of Françoise Sagan; for the sake of brevity, I first quote the male review and then immediately juxtapose Ellmann's countermove:

> Poor old Françoise Sagan. Just one more old-fashioned old-timer, bypassed in the rush for the latest literary vogue and for youth. Superficially, her career in America resembles the lifespan of those medieval beauties who flowered at 14, were deflowered at 15, were old at 30 and crones at 40.

> From a review of a new novel by the popular French novelist, François Sagan:

> Poor old François Sagan.... Superficially, his career in America resembles the life-span of those medieval troubadours who masturbated at 14, copulated at 15, were impotent at 30 and prostate cases at 40.
>
> (30)

In the largest single section of her book, Ellmann then sums up the eleven major stereotypes of femininity as presented by male writers and critics: formlessness, passivity, instability, confinement, piety, materiality, spirituality, irrationality, compliancy, and finally 'the two incorrigible figures' of the Witch and the Shrew. The fourth chapter, entitled 'Differences in tone', discusses the assertion that 'the male body lends credence to assertions while the female takes it away' (148). Ellmann's point is that men have traditionally chosen to write in an assertive, authoritarian mode, whereas women have been confined to the language of sensibility. Since the 1960s, however, much modern literature has sought to resist or subvert authoritarian modes of writing, and this has created the conditions for a new kind of writing by women:

> I hope to define the way in which it is now possible for women to write well. Quite simply, having not had physical or intellectual authority before, they have no reason to resist a literature at odds with authority.
>
> (166)

Since Ellmann's own favourites among modern women writers are Dorothy Richardson, Ivy Compton-Burnett and Nathalie Sarraute (but oddly enough not Virginia Woolf), we can see where her distaste for authority and also of traditional realism takes her.

Ellmann's point about the authority we consciously or unconsciously accord to male over female voices has been beautifully illustrated by the Danish feminist critic Pil Dahlerup in an article entitled 'Unconscious attitudes of a reviewer', published in Sweden in 1972. Here Dahlerup discusses the response of one particular male reviewer to the Danish poet Cecil Bødtker's poetry. Cecil being an ungendered name in Danish, the critic automatically assumed that he was dealing with a male poet in his review of her first collection of poetry (1955). This glowing review abounds in active verbs and has relatively few adjectives, though the ones that do occur are powerfully positive ones: 'joyous', 'enthusiastic', 'rich', and so on. A year later the same critic reviewed Cecil Bødtker's second collection of poetry. By now he had discovered that she was a woman, and though he still was warmly enthusiastic about her poetry the vocabulary of praise has undergone an interesting transformation: now Cecil Bødtker's poetry is no more than 'pleasant', there are three times as many adjectives, and these have not only changed in nature ('pretty', 'healthy', 'down to earth'), but also show an alarming propensity for taking on modifiers ('somewhat', 'a certain', 'probably' – none of which occurred in the first review). Furthermore, the adjectives 'little' or 'small' suddenly become central in the critic's discourse, whereas they only made one appearance in the 'male' review. As Dahlerup puts it: 'the male poet apparently did not write a single "small" poem'. Her conclusion is that the critic's attitude unconsciously reveals the fact that, as Mary Ellmann suggests, male reviewers just cannot attach the same degree of authority to a voice they know to be female. Even when they do give a good review to a woman they automatically select adjectives and phrases that tend to make the woman's poetry charming and sweet (as women should be), as opposed to serious and significant (as men are supposed to be).

Ellmann's final chapter, entitled 'Responses', deals with the various strategies employed by women writers to cope with the patriarchal onslaught described in her first four chapters. She shows how women writers have known how to exploit, for their own subversive purposes, the stereotypes of them and their writing created by men. Jane Austen, for instance, undermines the authoritarian voice of the writer by her wit and irony – or, as Ellmann puts it, 'We assume that authority and responsibility are incompatible with amusement' (209). But Ellmann's praise of Jane Austen's prose is also highly relevant to her own way of writing. *Thinking About Women* is an ironic masterpiece, and the wit Ellmann displays throughout her book (though less in the 'Responses' section), is, as we shall see, an important part of her argument. Ellmann's sardonic humour contributed significantly to the warm critical reception of her book, though ironically enough some critics were unable to resist the temptation to couch their praise in precisely the stereotypical terms that Ellmann denounces. The back of the Harvest edition of *Thinking About Women*, for instance, displays the following example of fervent praise: 'The sexual silliness which warps our thinking about women has never been so well exposed. But the best and most fervent accolade last: Mary Ellmann has written a funny feminist book.' In other words: we all know that feminists are dreary puritans, so all the more reason for praising Ellmann as an exception to the rule. Or as Ellmann herself puts it, when discussing the way in which sexual analogy infects the praise of work that deserves 'asexual' approval:

> In this case, enthusiasm issues in the explanation of the ways in which the work is free of what the critic ordinarily dislikes in the work of a woman. He had despaired of ever seeing a birdhouse built by a woman; now *here* is a birdhouse built by a woman. Pleasure may mount even to an admission of male envy of the work examined: an exceptionally sturdy birdhouse at that!
>
> (31)

But what exactly is the effect on her own arguments of Ellmann's lavish use of irony? Patricia Meyer Spacks feels that Ellmann writes 'in the distinctive voice of a woman' (23), and that the specific femininity of her discourse consists in its display of 'a particularly feminine sort and function of wit' (24). Spacks continues:

> A new category suggests itself for her: not the passivity of formlessness or the purposelessness of instability, but the feminine resource of evasiveness. The opponent who would presume to attack her finds her not where she was when he took aim. She embodies woman as quicksilver, always in brilliant, erratic motion.
>
> (24)

Spacks here evades the concept of irony perhaps because this has never been considered a specifically feminine mode. Instead she centres on the accusation of 'evasiveness', and tries to invent a new feminine stereotype that would accommodate Ellmann's way of writing. But this is surely to miss the point of her style. I will attempt to show that it is precisely through the use of satirical devices that Ellmann manages to demonstrate first that the very concepts of masculinity and femininity are social constructs which refer to no real essence in the world, and second that the feminine stereotypes she describes invariably deconstruct themselves. The point can be made through a closer look at her presentation of the stereotype of 'the Mother';

> The Mother is particularly useful as an illustration of *the explosive tendency*: each stereotype has a limit; swelled to it, the stereotype explodes. Its ruin takes two forms: (1) total vulgarization and (2) a reorganization of the advantage, now in fragments, about a new

center of disadvantage. In this second form, the same elements which had constituted the previous ideal make up the present anathema.

(131)

This is also one of the very few passages where Ellmann explicitly sums up the theory behind the rhetorical strategy of her book. For most of the time she is content to show through practical illustrations how the stereotype is both ideal and horror, inclusive as well as exclusive – as for instance where she first demonstrates how 'the Mother' as a stereotype slides from venerated idol to castrating and aggressive bitch, and then continues:

But our distrust of maternity is an innocuous preoccupation in contrast to our resentment of those who do not take part in it. Nothing is more reliable than the irritability of all references to prolonged virginity: behind us, and undoubtedly before us, stretch infinite tracts of abuse of *maiden ladies, old maids, schoolmarms, dried-up spinsters*, etc., etc.

(136)

Here the use of the plural pronouns 'our' and 'us' comfortably suggest that the narrator is doing no more than pointing out something 'we all' indulge in, whereas the implication of her first sentence, with its powerful paradox, is that 'we' must be either mad or stupid to pursue such an illogical practice. The narrative devices deployed here work to make the reader ('we') reject the stupidity described, while at the same time softening the blow with the reassuring use of 'us' and 'our'. If the narrator includes herself in this example of malpractice, 'we' at least don't have to feel *alone* in our stupidity. But this is not the only effect of Ellmann's tactical use of the first person plural here. It also makes it impossible for the reader to reject the implications of the paradox of the first sentence: since the narrator does not position herself at a different level from us, but on the contrary is to be found among us, 'we' are deprived of a convenient external target for our aggression. In these sentences there is simply no single instance we can choose to attack as a man-hating, castrating bitch if we feel thus inclined. Thus the reader's nagging suspicion that the narrator *after all* may be pulling his (or her) leg, that she might just not entirely count herself as one of 'us', can find no target, and her or his mounting aggression is therefore defused in the very act that kindles it.

This narrative technique cannot in my view be labelled 'feminine elusiveness', since it is an integral part of a general rhetorical enterprise that seeks to deconstruct our sexual categories in exactly the same way as the reader's aggression here is both fostered and defused. The effect of Ellmann's irony is to expose two different aspects of patriarchal ideology. In the first passage quoted above, she states abstractly the way in which any stereotype is self-destructive, easily transformed into its own unstable contradiction, and thereby demonstrates that such stereotypes' only existence is as verbal constructs in the service of ruling patriarchal ideology. But unlike Millett, Ellmann does not for a moment fall prey to the fiction that this ruling ideology forms a consistent and unified whole. On the contrary, both passages amply illustrate the self-contradictory tangles that emerge as soon as one aspect of this ideology is confronted with another.

Thinking About Women abounds in examples of this deconstructive, decentring style. Ellmann's favourite method is to juxtapose contradictory statements while depriving the reader of any authorial comment, as for instance in the following passage: 'When men are searching for the truth, women are content with lies. But when men are searching for diversion or variety, women counter with their stultifying respect for immediate duty' (93–4). The absence of an identifiable narrator's voice here fulfils a role similar to the consoling presence of the possibly treacherous 'us' in the passage discussed above: deprived of authoritative commentary as to which of the positions advanced the narrator wishes the reader to accept, she is kept reading on in the hope of finding such a guideline for interpretation. Such 'anchoring points' can in fact be found in *Thinking About Women* – indeed the paragraph just quoted is preceded by a fairly straightforward statement: 'At any rate, the incongruity of deceit and piety represents only another of the necessary sacrifices of logic to contrast' (93). Though it seems obvious here that the narrator finds such oppositions incongruous and that they represent a sacrifice of logic, this evaluation is not allowed to stand wholly unchallenged: the sacrifice of logic is characterized as 'necessary', and this single adjective is enough to throw the reader back into uncertainty. Necessary for whom? Or for what higher purpose? Does the narrator endorse this evaluation of necessity or not? The irony here is weaker because of the evaluative 'incongruity' that is allowed to dominate the first part of the sentence, but it is still not wholly absent. Even when Ellmann allows her discourse to be fixed to a certain position, she takes care to avoid total paralysis: there is always a trace of unsettling wit somewhere in her sentences.

When Patricia Spacks characterizes Ellmann's style as essentially feminine, as an example of the way in which 'the woman critic demonstrates how feminine charm can combat masculine forcefulness' (26), she falls into the very metaphysical trap that Ellmann seeks to deconstruct. Thinking About Women is, after all, a book about the insidious effects of thinking by sexual analogy, not a recommendation that we should continue the practice. In order to ensure that the reader gets this point, Ellmann first proclaims quite unequivocally that 'it seems impossible to determine a sexual sentence' (172), and quotes Virginia Woolf to reinforce her view. For Ellmann, then, sexuality is not visible at the level of sentence construction or rhetorical strategies. She therefore praises Jane Austen's irony precisely for its capacity to enable us to think outside of (or elsewhere than) the field of sexual analogy: 'Jane Austen . . . had available to her imagination a scene which must now seem to us singularly monistic: neither sex appears to be good or bad for much' (212).

As part of her deconstructive project, Ellmann therefore recommends exploiting the sexual stereotypes for all they are worth for our own political purposes. This, at least, is her own practice in Thinking About Women. When Patricia Spacks holds that Ellmann's style is elusive, it is because she believes that behind the 'charming' facade her text hides a good deal of 'feminine anger' (27). The implication is that whereas Kate Millett, according to Spacks, lets her anger show through in passionate if muddled and obfuscating sentences, Mary Ellmann conceals the same anger somewhere under her elegant wit. This argument is based on two assumptions: that feminists must at all costs be angry all the time, and that all textual uncertainty such as that created by irony must be explained in the end by reference to an underlying, essential and unitary cause. But, as the Russian theorist Mikhail Bakhtin has shown in his influential study of Rabelais (Rabelais and His World), anger is not the only revolutionary attitude available to us. The power of laughter can be just as subversive, as when carnival turns the old hierarchies upside-down, erasing old differences, producing new and unstable ones.

Ellmann's suavely polished wit makes us laugh. But it may not, after all, make us laugh in quite the carnivalesque way of a Rabelais. How then should we evaluate the effects of her book? Politically speaking, the ironist is extremely hard to assail precisely because it is virtually impossible to fix her or his text convincingly. In the ironic discourse, every position undercuts itself, thus leaving the politically engaged writer in a position where her ironic discourse might just come to deconstruct her own politics. Mary Ellmann's solution to this dilemma is to furnish enough non-ironic 'anchoring-points' in her own text to make the position from which she is speaking reasonably clear. This method, however, carries the obvious danger of undermining the satire it seeks to preserve. Ellmann chooses to write the last section, 'Responses', from a fairly 'direct' point of view, thus leaving irony to the sections dealing with male discourse on women. Since the more conventionally written final section does not deal with the same problems as the ironic parts of the book, this still leaves a gap, a space for the necessary uncertainty of ironic discourse.[3]

There is, then, no reason to argue that Mary Ellmann's sardonic prose should be *inherently* less unsettling than Kate Millett's explicit anger. The best-selling British competitor to Millett's book, Germaine Greer's *The Female Eunuch* (1970), also relies on irony, and has been none the less influential in the women's movement for all that.[4] Patricia Spack's reaction to Ellmann's essay – on the one hand taking stereotypes for essentialist categories, on the other hand stipulating anger as the fundamental feminist emotion – is paradigmatic of the general feminist reception of *Thinking About Women*. For though the feminist critics who in the early 1970s took up the brand of feminist criticism known as 'Images of Women' criticism often invoke Ellmann as one of their precursors, they invariably proceed to adopt the very categories Ellmann tries to deconstruct as models for their own readings.

2

'IMAGES OF WOMEN' CRITICISM

The 'Images of Women' approach to literature has proved to be an extremely fertile branch of feminist criticism, at least in terms of the actual number of works it has generated: specialist bibliographies list hundreds if not thousands of items under this heading. In order to limit the amount of bibliographical references in the following account of its aims and methods, I will refer mainly to the articles printed in one central collection of essays, suitably enough entitled *Images of Women in Fiction: Feminist Perspectives*. In American colleges in the early 1970s, the great majority of courses on women in literature centred on the study of female stereotypes in male writing (Register, 28). *Images of Women in Fiction* was published in 1972 as the first hardback textbook aimed at this rapidly expanding academic market. The book obviously corresponded to a deeply felt need among teachers and students, since it was reprinted several times in rapid succession.[1] What kind of perspectives, then, does this book present as 'feminist'? In her preface, the editor, Susan Koppelman Cornillon, states that the idea for the book came from her own experience in teaching women's studies:

> In all courses I felt the desperate need for books that would study literature as being writings about *people*. This volume is an effort to

> supply that need. . . . These essays lead us into fiction and then back
> out again into reality, into ourselves and our own lives. . . . This book
> will be a useful tool for raising consciousness not only in classrooms,
> but for those not involved in the academic world who are committed
> to personal growth.

(x)

The new field of feminist literary studies is here presented as one
essentially concerned with nurturing personal growth and raising the
individual consciousness by linking literature to life, particularly to the
lived experience of the reader. This fundamental outlook is reflected in
the essays of all the 21 contributors (19 women, 2 men). Both male
and female authors, mostly from the nineteenth and twentieth centuries, are studied in these essays, and both sexes come in for harsh
criticism for their creation of 'unreal' female characters. Indeed, the
editor, in her essay 'The fiction of fiction', accuses women writers of
being *worse* than male writers in this respect, since they, unlike the men,
are betraying their own sex.

In 'Images of Women' criticism the act of reading is seen as a communication between the life ('experience') of the author and the life of
the reader. When the reader becomes a critic, her duty is to present an
account of her own life that will enable *her* readers to become aware of
the position from which she speaks. In one of the essays in *Images of
Women in Fiction*, Florence Howe succinctly presents this demand for
autobiography in criticism:

> I begin with autobiography because it is there, in our consciousness
> about our own lives, that the connection between feminism and litera-
> ture begins. That we learn from lives is, of course, a fundamental
> assumption of literature and of its teacher-critics.

(255)

Such an emphasis upon the reader's right to learn about the writer's
experience strongly supports the basic feminist contention that no
criticism is 'value-free', that we all speak from a specific position
shaped by cultural, social, political and personal factors. It is authoritarian and manipulative to present this limited perspective as 'universal',

feminists claim, and the only democratic procedure is to supply the reader with all necessary information about the limitations of one's own perspective at the outset. The importance of this principle cannot be overestimated: it remains one of the fundamental assumptions of any feminist critic to date.

Problems do however arise if we are too sanguine about the actual possibility of making one's own position clear. Hermeneutical theory, for instance, has pointed out that we cannot fully grasp our own 'horizon of understanding': there will always be unstated blindspots, fundamental presuppositions and 'pre-understandings' of which we are unaware. Psychoanalysis furthermore informs us that the most powerful motivations of our psyche often turn out to be those we have most deeply repressed. It is therefore difficult to believe that we can ever fully be aware of our own perspective. The prejudices one is *able* to formulate consciously are precisely for that reason likely to be the least important ones. These theoretical difficulties are not just abstract problems for the philosophers among us: they return to manifest themselves quite evidently in the texts of the feminist critic who tries to practise the autobiographical ideal in her work. In trying to state her own personal experience as a necessary background for the understanding of her research interests, she may for instance discover, to her cost, that there is no obvious end to the amount of 'relevant' detail that might be taken into account in such a context. She then runs the risk of reading like a more or less unwilling exhibitionist rather than a partisan of egalitarian criticism. One such extreme case can be found in a feminist study of Simone de Beauvoir, where, in the middle of the book, the critic suddenly decides to spend sixteen pages on an autobiographical account of her own life and her feelings about Beauvoir.[2] This kind of narcissistic delving into one's own self can only caricature the valuable point of principle made by feminist critics: that no criticism is neutral, and that we therefore have a responsibility to make our position reasonably apparent to our readers. Whether this is necessarily always best done through autobiographical statements about the critic's emotional and personal life is a more debatable point.

As one reads on in *Images of Women in Fiction*, one quickly becomes aware of the fact that to study 'images of women' in fiction is equivalent to studying *false* images of women in fiction written by both sexes.

The 'image' of women in literature is invariably defined in opposition to the 'real person' whom literature somehow never quite manages to convey to the reader. In Cornillon's volume, 'reality' and 'experience' are presented as the highest goals of literature, the essential truths that must be rendered by all forms of fiction. This viewpoint occasionally leads to an almost absurd 'ultra-realist' position, as when, for instance, Cornillon points out that a significant part of the modern American woman's life is spent shaving her legs and removing hairs from various other parts of her body. She rightly emphasizes the degrading and oppressive nature of the male demand for well-shaved women, but then goes on to make her main literary point: 'And yet, with all that attaches itself to female leg-shaving slavery, I have never seen any fictional character either shave or pluck a hair' (117).

I would not be surprised if Cornillon turned out to be right – toe-nail clipping and the disposal of sanitary towels also seem neglected as fictional themes – but her complaint rests on the highly questionable notion that art can and should reflect life accurately and inclusively in every detail. The extreme reflectionism (or 'naturalism' in Lukács's sense of the word) advocated in *Images of Women in Fiction* has the advantage of emphasizing the way in which writers constantly *select* the elements they wish to use in their texts; but instead of acknowledging this as one of the basic facts of textual creativity, reflectionism posits that the artist's selective creation should be measured against 'real life', thus assuming that the only constraint on the artist's work is his or her perception of the 'real world'. Such a view resolutely refuses to consider textual production as a highly complex, 'over-determined' process with many different and conflicting literary and non-literary determinants (historical, political, social, ideological, institutional, generic, psychological and so on). Instead, writing is seen as a more or less faithful *reproduction* of an external reality to which we all have equal and unbiased access, and which therefore enables us to criticize the author on the grounds that he or she has created an *incorrect* model of the reality we somehow all know. Resolutely empiricist in its approach, this view fails to consider the proposition that the real is not only something we construct, but a controversial construct at that.

Literary works can and should of course be criticized for having selected and shaped their fictional universe according to oppressive and objectionable ideological assumptions, but that should not be confused with failing to be 'true to life' or with not presenting 'an authentic expression of real experience'. Such an insistent demand for authenticity not only reduces all literature to rather simplistic forms of autobiography, it also finds itself ruling the greater part of world literature out of bounds. What these critics fail to perceive is the fact that though Shakespeare probably never in his life found himself mad and naked on a heath, *King Lear* nevertheless reads 'authentically' enough for most people. It is significant that all the contributors to Cornillon's volume (with the notable exception of Josephine Donovan) adhere to a rather simple form of content analysis when confronted with the literary text. Extreme reflectionism simply cannot accommodate notions of formal and generic constraints on textual production, since to acknowledge such constraints is equivalent to accepting the inherent impossibility of ever achieving a total reproduction of reality in fiction.

The wider question at issue here is clearly the problem of realism as opposed to modernism. Predictably enough, several essays in the volume lash out against modernism, and its somewhat vaguely termed 'formalist' fellow-traveller. The modernist is accused of neglecting the 'exclusions based on class, race and sex' in order to 'take refuge in his formalist concerns, secure in his conviction that other matters are irrelevant' (286). But this is not all:

> Modernism, by contrast, seeks to intensify isolation. It forces the work of art, the artist, the critic, and the audience outside of history. Modernism denies us the possibility of understanding ourselves as *agents* in the material world, for all has been removed to an abstract world of ideas, where interactions can be minimized or emptied of meaning and real consequences. Less than ever are we able to interpret the world – much less change it.
>
> (300–1)[3]

In another essay, feminist criticism is succinctly defined as 'a materialist approach to literature which attempts to do away with the formalist illusion that literature is somehow divorced from reality' (326).[4] The 'formalist' critics referred to in this passage seem to be identifiable as the American New Critics, concerned as they were with the formal aspects of the literary work at the expense of historical and sociological factors. At this point, however, it is worth noting that though American feminist critics from Kate Millett onwards have consistently argued against the New Critics' ahistoricism, this has not prevented them from uncritically adopting the *aesthetic* ideals of the very same New Critics.

In *Images of Women in Fiction*, the double rejection of 'modernist' literature and 'formalist' criticism highlights the deep realist bias of Anglo-American feminist criticism. An insistence on authenticity and truthful reproduction of the 'real world' as the highest literary values inevitably makes the feminist critic hostile to non-realist forms of writing. There is nevertheless no automatic connection between demands for a full reproduction of the totality of the 'real' and what is known as a 'realist' fiction. At least two famous literary attempts at capturing reality in its totality, *Tristram Shandy* and *Ulysses*, end up by mischievously transgressing traditional realism in the most radical fashion precisely *because of* their doomed attempt to be all-inclusive. And some feminist critics have for instance objected to Joyce's portrayal of Molly Bloom's chamberpot and menstrual cycle (there is no reference to leg-shaving) on the grounds that, in spite of their undeniable realism, these factors contribute precisely to presenting her as a biologically determined, earthbound creature that no woman reader can really *admire*.

In this case the demand for realism clashes with another demand: that for the representation of female role-models in literature. The feminist reader of this period not only wants to see her own experiences mirrored in fiction, but strives to identify with strong, impressive female characters. Cheri Register, in an essay published in 1975, succinctly sums up this demand: 'A literary work should provide *role-models*, instill a positive sense of feminine identity by portraying women who are "self-actualizing, whose identities are not dependent on men"' (20).[5] This might however clash with the demand for authenticity (quite a few women are 'authentically' weak and unimpressive); on this point Register is unambiguous: 'It is important to note here that although female readers need literary models to emulate, characters should not be idealized beyond plausibility. The demand for authenticity supercedes all other requirements' (21).

Register's choice of words here ('should', 'demand', 'requirements') reflects the strong normative (or prescriptive, as she prefers to call it) aspect of much of this early feminist criticism. The 'Images of Women' critics downgrade literature they find lacking in 'authenticity' and 'real experience' according to their own standards of what counts as 'real'. In case of doubt about the degree of authenticity in a work, Register recommends several tests: 'One obvious check the reader might make on authenticity would be to compare the character's life with the author's' (12), she suggests. One may also use sociological data in order to check up on the social aspects of the author's work, though inner emotions must be subjected to a different form of control:

> While it is useful to compile statistical data on a collection of works from a limited time period to see how accurately they mirror female employment, educational attainment, marital status, birthrate, and the like, it is impossible to measure the authenticity of a single female protagonist's inner turmoil. The final test must be the subjective response of the female reader, who is herself familiar with 'female reality'. Does she recognize aspects of her own experience?
>
> (13)

Though Register hastens to warn us against too simplistic conclusions, since 'female reality is not monolithic, but has many nuances and variations' (13) such a governess mentality (the 'Big-Sister-is-watching-you' syndrome) must be considered one of the perhaps inevitable excesses of a new and rapidly expanding branch of research. In the 1970s, this approach led to a great number of published and unpublished papers dealing with literature from a kind of inverted sociological perspective: fiction was read in order to compare the empirical sociological facts in the literary work (as for instance the number of women working outside the home or doing the dishes) to the corresponding empirical data in the 'real' world during the author's lifetime.

It is easy today to be reproving of this kind of criticism: to take it to task for not recognizing the 'literariness' of literature, for tending towards a dangerous anti-intellectualism, for being excessively naive about the relationship between literature and reality and between author and text, and for being unduly censorious of the works of women writers who often wrote under ideological conditions that made it impossible for them to fulfil the demands of the feminist critics of early 1970s. Though it is impossible not to deplore the wholesale lack of theoretical (or even literary) awareness of these early feminist critics, their enthusiasm and commitment to the feminist cause are exemplary. For a generation educated within the ahistorical, aestheticizing discourse of New Criticism, the feminists' insistence on the *political* nature of any critical discourse, and their will to take historical and sociological factors into account must have seemed both fresh and exciting; to a large extent those are precisely the qualities present-day feminist critics still strive to preserve.

3

WOMEN WRITING AND WRITING ABOUT WOMEN

TOWARDS A WOMAN-CENTRED PERSPECTIVE

It soon became evident, however, that the simplistic, undiscriminating approach of 'Images of Women' criticism was losing its inspirational force. From about 1975, interest started to focus exclusively on the works of women writers. As early as 1971, Elaine Showalter had advocated the study of women writers as a group:

> Women writers should not be studied as a distinct group on the assumption that they write alike, or even display stylistic resemblances distinctively feminine. But women do have a special history susceptible to analysis, which includes such complex considerations as the economics of their relation to the literary marketplace; the effects of social and political changes in women's status upon individuals, and the implications of stereotypes of the woman writer and restrictions of her artistic autonomy.[1]

Showalter's view gradually gained acceptance. *Images of Women in Fiction* has two male contributors, contains more analyses of male writers than of female writers and often takes a negative attitude to works of women writers. By 1975, the situation had decisively changed. When in that year Cheryl L. Brown and Karen Olson began to compile their anthology *Feminist Criticism: Essays on Theory, Poetry and Prose* they felt surprised (and upset) that 'what women critics were writing about women's literature was not being published in respectable numbers and not readily accessible to concerned students and teachers' (preface, xiii). To compensate for this bias, their anthology (which remained unpublished until 1978) has no male contributors, and all its essays deal either with theoretical questions or with the work of women writers. This woman-centred approach has now become the dominant trend within Anglo-American feminist criticism.

Before studying more closely the major works of this powerful 'second phase' of feminist research, it should be pointed out that not all books by women critics on women writers are examples of feminist criticism. In the early years of feminist criticism, many non-feminist works enjoyed considerable influence due to the confusion of these categories, as did for example Patricia Beer's *Reader, I Married Him* from 1974. In her preface, the author clearly distances herself from other writings 'on the subject of Women's Lib' (ix), since these all share a serious flaw:

> Whatever they may claim to do, in fact they treat literature as if it were a collection of tracts into which you dip for illustrations of your own polemic, falsifying and omitting as necessary, your argument being of more moment than the other person's work of art. This rhetorical approach seems a pity as novels and plays are so much more illuminating if they are not used as a means to an end, either by writer or reader.
>
> (ix)

Beer's own book is going to be free from this deplorable bias, since 'The novel in particular, without benefit of anyone's argument, can show quite precisely how things are or were' (ix). The author, in other words, trusts precisely the sort of 'value-free' scholarship that feminists denounce as always subservient to existing hierarchies and power structures. Beer also seems convinced that *she* can capture true reality through the novels she is studying, particularly since she herself is free from feminist leanings. Other sorts of political engagement apparently have no power to distort the true representation of reality Beer seeks, or if they do she does not mention them. Her book is not written for fanatics, but for the discerning reader: '[I felt] that the subject might be of interest to readers who, without being necessarily either students of English literature or supporters of Women's Lib, had a concern in the novel and the cause of female emancipation' (ix).

The author is both fascinated and repelled by the 'women's lib' label, clearly wanting to banish it from her book yet at the same time eager to mention it (twice in half a page), since she knows that it is among the supporters of this 'rhetorical approach' that she will find many of her readers. If feminist criticism is a political criticism, sustained by a commitment to combat all forms of patriarchy and sexism, Patricia Beer's book is evidently not a work of feminist criticism. Dominant in her preface (and in her arguments throughout the book) is the desire to exercise a kind of liberal brinkmanship. Positioning herself somewhere in the middle ground 'good liberals' pursue, she is neither a supporter of 'women's lib' nor an opponent of it; on the contrary, she will acknowledge a deep 'concern' both in the novel and in the 'cause of female emancipation'. This kind of 'pseudo-feminist' criticism is of no substantial interest to students of feminist approaches to literature.

In the late 1970s, three major studies appeared on women writers seen as part of a specifically female literary tradition or 'subculture': Ellen Moers, *Literary Women* (1976), Elaine Showalter, *A Literature of Their Own* (1977) and Sandra Gilbert and Susan Gubar, *The Madwoman in the Attic* (1979). Taken together, these three books represent the coming-of-age of Anglo-American feminist criticism. Here at last were the long awaited major studies of women writers in British and American literary history. Competent and committed, illuminating and inspiring, these works immediately found a deservedly large and enthusiastic audience of women scholars and students. Today it is clear that the works of Moers, Showalter, Gilbert and Gubar have already taken their places among the modern classics of feminist criticism.

All three books strive to define a distinctively female tradition in literature on the grounds that, as Elaine Showalter puts it, 'the female literary tradition comes from the still-evolving relationships between women writers and their society' (12). For these critics, it is in other words *society*, not *biology*, that shapes women's different literary perception of the world. This basic similarity of approach should not, however, prevent us from noticing the often interesting divergences and differences among these three influential works.

'LITERARY WOMEN'

Ellen Moers's *Literary Women* was the result of a long process of reflection on women and literature, a process that started in 1963, the year in which Betty Friedan's *The Feminine Mystique* was published, a book which brought Moers to change her views on the need to treat women writers as a separate group. 'At one time', she writes, 'I held the narrow view that separating major writers from the general course of literary history on the basis of sex was futile, but several things have changed my mind' (xv). The reasons for this change of heart were, first, the convincing results of such a separation, then the fact that 'we already practice a segregation of major women writers unknowingly' (xv), and, finally, a deeper understanding of the real nature of women's history. Moers thus mirrors the development of many academic women: from suspecting all attempts at segregating women from the mainstream of historical development as a form of anti-egalitarianism, they came, during the 1960s, to accept the political necessity of viewing women as a distinctive group if the common patriarchal strategy of subsuming women under the general category of 'man', and thereby silencing them, was to be efficiently counteracted.

Literary Women was the first attempt at describing the history of women's writing as a 'rapid and powerful undercurrent' running under or alongside the main male tradition, and, because it mapped a relatively unknown territory for the first time, it received wide acclaim (63). Tillie Olsen saw *Literary Women* as a 'catalyst, a landmark book [which] authoritatively establishes the scope, depth, variety of literature written by women . . . no one can read it unchanged'.[2] Ellen Moers surely deserved this praise in 1977, but it is indicative of the pace with which feminist criticism has developed that the reader who picks up *Literary Women* in 1985 may not quite share Tillie Olsen's elation. *Literary Women*

remains a well-written and interesting book, though at times somewhat given to sentimental hyperbole, as when Moers enthuses over
George Sand and Elizabeth Barrett Browning:

> What positively miraculous beings they were. A magnetism emanates
> from their life stories, some compelling power which drew the world
> to them – and all the goods and blessings of the kind that facilitate
> and ornament the woman's life in letters.
>
> (5)

Nevertheless, the first enthusiasm over the discovery of new terrain is
now fading, and the 1985's reader may feel that Ellen Moers's book is
not really satisfactory either as literary history or as literary criticism. It
is too engrossed in circumstantial details, too unaware of any kind of
literary theory to function well as criticism, and far too limited in its
conception of history and its relations to literature to be convincing as
historiography.

Moers sees history first and foremost as a good story, or as a
compelling plot with which to identify and sympathize:

> The main thing to change my mind about a history of literary women
> has been history itself, the dramatically unfolding, living literary his-
> tory of the period of my work on this book. Its lesson has been that
> one must know the history of women to understand the history of
> literature.
>
> (xvi)

For her, history is a chronicle in the medieval sense: a careful noting
down of everything the chronicler feels is relevant to his or her particular perspective. In this sense, the chronicler believes that her version of
events, often presented as raw and unstructured 'facts', constitute 'history'. Similarly, Ellen Moers believes that she, as the author of her
history, has had no influence on it: 'The literary women themselves,
not any doctrine of mine, have done the organizing of the book – their
concerns, their language' (xii). This belief in the possibility of a neutral
registration of events sounds strangely out of place in a work that is,
after all, avowedly feminist in its approach.

Moers's trust in conventional aesthetic and literary categories, notably her belief that we just *know* which writers are 'great' (the subtitle of *Literary Women* is 'The Great Writers'), avoids confronting the fact that the category of 'greatness' has always been an extremely contentious one for feminists, given that the criteria for 'greatness' militate heavily against the inclusion of women in the literary canon. As an overview of the field of English, American and French writing by women in the period stretching from the late-eighteenth to the twentieth century, *Literary Women*, with its plot summaries, emphasis on personal details and biographical anecdotes serves a useful purpose as a preliminary introduction, but it can hardly now be read as anything but a pioneer work, a stepping-stone for the more mature feminist literary histories that emerged within a year or two of its publication.

'A LITERATURE OF THEIR OWN'

Elaine Showalter disagrees with Moers's emphasis on women's literature as an international movement 'apart from, but hardly subordinate to the mainstream: an undercurrent, rapid and powerful' (quoted in Showalter, *A Literature of Their Own*, 10), stressing instead, with Germaine Greer, the 'transience of female literary fame' or the fact that women writers celebrated in their own lifetimes seem to vanish without trace from the records of posterity. Showalter comments:

> Thus each generation of women writers has found itself, in a sense, without a history, forced to rediscover the past anew, forging again and again the consciousness of their sex. Given this perpetual disruption and also the self-hatred that has alienated women writers from a sense of collective identity, it does not seem possible to speak of a 'movement'.
>
> (11–12)

In *A Literature of Their Own*, Showalter sets out to 'describe the female literary tradition in the English novel from the generation of the Brontës to the present day, and to show how the development of this tradition is similar to the development of any literary subculture' (11). In her efforts to fill in the terrain between the 'literary landmarks' of the 'Austen peaks, the Brontë cliffs, the Eliot range and the Woolf hills' (vii), she uncovers three major phases of historical development claimed to be common to all literary subcultures:

> First, there is a prolonged phase of *imitation* of the prevailing modes of the dominant tradition, and *internalization* of its standards of art and its views on social roles. Second, there is a phase of *protest* against these standards and values, and *advocacy* of minority rights and values, including a demand for autonomy. Finally, there is a phase of *self-discovery*, a turning inward freed from some of the dependency of opposition, a search for identity. An appropriate terminology for women writers is to call these stages, *Feminine, Feminist* and *Female*.
>
> (13)

The Feminine period starts with the appearance of male pseudonyms in the 1840s and lasts until the death of George Eliot in 1880; the Feminist phase lasts from 1880 until 1920 and the Female phase starts in 1920 and is still continuing, though it took a new turn in the 1960s with the advent of the women's movement.

This, then, is the general perspective that informs Showalter's guided tour of the female literary landscape in Britain since the 1840s. Her major contribution to literary history in general, and to feminist criticism in particular, is the emphasis she places on the rediscovery of forgotten or neglected women writers. It is in no small part due to Showalter's efforts that so many hitherto unknown women writers are beginning to receive the recognition they deserve; *A Literature of Their Own* is a veritable goldmine of information about the lesser-known literary women of the period. This epochal book displays wide-ranging scholarship and an admirable enthusiasm and respect for its subject. Its flaws must be located elsewhere: in its unstated theoretical assumptions about the relationship between literature and reality and between feminist politics and literary evaluation, questions that already have been dealt with in the context of Showalter's chapter on Virginia Woolf in *A Literature of Their Own*. Since Showalter, as opposed to Moers and Gilbert and Gubar, has also written several articles on the theory of feminist criticism, I have found it unnecessary to elucidate further the theoretical implications of her *practice* of criticism in *A Literature of Their*

Own. Her theoretical perspectives will instead be discussed more fully in chapter 4's discussion of 'Theoretical reflections'.

'THE MADWOMAN IN THE ATTIC'

Sandra M. Gilbert and Susan Gubar's massive volume presents the feminist reader with an impressive set of probing, incisive studies of the major women writers of the nineteenth century: Jane Austen, Mary Shelley, the Brontës (particularly Charlotte), George Eliot, Elizabeth Barrett Browning, Christina Rossetti and Emily Dickinson are all exhaustively studied by the two critics. But *The Madwoman in the Attic* is more than 'just' a set of readings. If on the one hand it aims to provide us with a new understanding of the nature of the 'distinctively female literary tradition' (xi) of the nineteenth century, it also aspires to elaborate an ambitious new theory of women's literary creativity. The first substantial section, entitled 'Towards a feminist poetics', presents the authors' efforts to 'provide models for understanding the dynamics of female literary response to male literary assertion and coercion' (xii).

Gilbert and Gubar's enquiry shows that in the nineteenth century (as still today) the dominant patriarchal ideology presents artistic creativity as a fundamentally male quality. The writer 'fathers' his text; in the image of the Divine Creator he becomes the Author – the sole origin and meaning of his work. Gilbert and Gubar then ask the crucial question: 'What if such a proudly masculine cosmic Author is the sole legitimate model for all early authors?' (7). Their answer is that since this is indeed the case under patriarchy, creative women have a rough time coping with the consequences of such a phallocentric myth of creativity:

> Since both patriarchy and its texts subordinate and imprison women, before women can even attempt that pen which is so rigorously kept from them they must escape just those male texts which, defining them as 'Cyphers', deny them the autonomy to formulate alternatives to the authority that has imprisoned them and kept them from attempting the pen.

(13)

Since creativity is defined as male, it follows that the dominant literary images of femininity are male fantasies too. Women are denied the right to create their own images of femaleness, and instead must seek to conform to the patriarchal standards imposed on them. Gilbert and Gubar clearly demonstrate how in the nineteenth century the 'eternal feminine' was assumed to be a vision of angelic beauty and sweetness: from Dante's Beatrice and Goethe's Gretchen and Makarie to Coventry Patmore's 'Angel in the House', the ideal woman is seen as a passive, docile and above all *selfless* creature. The authors stingingly comment that:

> To be selfless is not only to be noble, it is to be dead. A life that has no story, like the life of Goethe's Makarie, is really a life of death, a death-in-life. The ideal of 'contemplative purity' evokes, finally, both heaven and the grave.
>
> (25)

But behind the angel lurks the monster: the obverse of the male idealization of women is the male fear of femininity. The monster woman is the woman who refuses to be selfless, acts on her own initiative, who *has* a story to tell – in short, a woman who rejects the submissive role patriarchy has reserved for her. Gilbert and Gubar mention characters like Shakespeare's Goneril and Regan and Thackeray's Becky Sharp, as well as the traditional array of such 'terrible sorceress-goddesses as the Sphinx, Medusa, Circe, Kali, Delilah, and Salome, all of whom possess duplicitous arts that allow them both to seduce and to steal male generative energy' (34). The monster woman for Gilbert and Gubar is *duplicitous*, precisely because she has something to tell: there is always the possibility that she may choose *not* to tell – or to tell a different story. The duplicitous woman is the one whose consciousness is opaque to man, whose mind will not let itself be penetrated by the phallic probings of masculine thought. Thus Lilith and the Queen in *Snow-White* become paradigmatic instances of the monster woman in the male imagination.

The authors of *The Madwoman in the Attic* then turn to the situation of the woman artist under patriarchy: 'For the female artist the essential process of self-definition is complicated by all those patriarchal definitions that intervene between herself and herself' (17). The dire consequence of this predicament is that the woman writer inevitably comes to suffer from a debilitating anxiety of authorship. If the author is defined as male and she finds herself already defined by him as his creature, how can she venture to take up the pen at all? Gilbert and Gubar raise, but do not answer, this question. They do, however, go on to posit what they see as the fundamental problems of feminine literary criticism:

> Since his is the chief voice she hears, does the Queen try to sound like the King, imitating his tone, his inflections, his phrasing, his point of view? Or does she 'talk back' to him in her own vocabulary, her own timbre, insisting on her own viewpoint? We believe these are basic questions feminist literary criticism – both theoretical and practical – must answer, and consequently they are questions to which we shall turn again and again, not only in this chapter but in all our readings of nineteenth-century literary women.
>
> (46)

Gilbert and Gubar's answer to their own question is a complex one. Tracing as they do 'the difficult paths by which nineteenth-century women overcame their "anxiety of authorship", repudiated debilitating patriarchal prescriptions, and recovered or remembered the lost fore-mothers who could help them find their distinctive female power' (59), they apparently believe that there is such a thing as a 'distinctive female power', but that this power, or voice, would have to take a rather round-about route to express itself through or against the oppressive effects of the dominant patriarchal modes of reading. This, then, is the main thesis of *The Madwoman in the Attic*: women writers have, in Emily Dickinson's words, chosen to 'Tell all the Truth but tell it slant', or as Gilbert and Gubar put it in perhaps the most crucial passage of their book:

> Women from Jane Austen and Mary Shelley to Emily Brontë and Emily Dickinson produced literary works that are in some sense palimpses-tic, works whose surface designs conceal or obscure deeper, less accessible (and less socially acceptable) levels of meaning. Thus these authors managed the difficult task of achieving true female literary

authority by simultaneously conforming to and subverting patriarchal literary standards.

(73)

For Gilbert and Gubar, in other words, the female voice is a duplicitous, but nevertheless true, and truly female voice. The female textual strategy, as they see it, consists in 'assaulting and revising, deconstructing and reconstructing those images of women inherited from male literature, especially . . . the paradigmatic polarities of angel and monster' (76). And this is where the eponymous madwoman makes her entrée into their argument. The madwoman, like Bertha Mason in *Jane Eyre*, is:

Usually in some sense the *author*'s double, an image of her own anxiety and rage. Indeed, much of the poetry and the fiction written by women conjures up this mad creature so that female authors can come to terms with their own uniquely female feelings of fragmentation, their own keen sense of the discrepancies between what they are and what they are supposed to be.

(78)

The 'mad double' or the 'female schizophrenia of authorship' (78) is the common factor in all the nineteenth-century novels studied in this book, and Gilbert and Gubar claim that she is an equally crucial figure in twentieth-century fiction by women (78). The figure of the madwoman is then *literally* the answer to the questions raised about female creativity:

In projecting their anger and dis-ease into dreadful figures, creating dark doubles for themselves and their heroines, women writers are both identifying with and revising the self-definitions patriarchal culture has imposed on them. All the nineteenth-and-twentieth-century literary women who evoke the female monster in their novels and poems alter her meaning by virtue of their own identification with her. For it is usually because she is in some sense imbued with inferiority that the witch-monster-madwoman becomes so crucial an avatar of the writer's own self.

(79)

The figure of the madwoman becomes emblematic of a sophisticated literary strategy that, according to Gilbert and Gubar, gives nineteenth-century female fiction its *revolutionary* edge: 'Parodic, duplicitous, extra-ordinarily sophisticated, all this female writing is both revisionary and revolutionary, even when it is produced by writers we usually think of as models of angelic resignation' (80). The angel and the monster, the sweet heroine and the raging madwoman, are aspects of the author's self-image, as well as elements of her treacherous anti-patriarchal strat-egies. Gilbert and Gubar expand this series of binary oppositions by stressing the recurrent use of imagery of confinement and escape, dis-ease and health and of fragmentation and wholeness in the fiction they study. Their often truly inventive and original readings and their com-plex theory of women's creativity has already inspired many feminist critics to continue the subtle textual work they have begun.[3]

Gilbert and Gubar are theoretically aware. Their own brand of feminist critical theory is seductively sophisticated, particularly when contrasted with the general level of theoretical debate among Anglo-American feminist critics. But what kind of theory are they really advocating? And what are the political implications of their theses? The first troubling aspect of their approach is their insistence on the identity of author and character. Like Kate Millett before them, Gilbert and Gubar repeatedly claim that the character (particularly the madwoman) is the *author's* double, 'an image of her own anxiety and rage' (78), maintaining that it is

> through the violence of the double that the female author enacts her own raging desire to escape male houses and male texts, while at the same time it is through the double's violence that this anxious author articulates for herself the costly destructiveness of anger repressed until it can no longer be contained.
>
> (85)

Their critical approach postulates a *real* woman hidden behind the patriarchal textual facade, and the feminist critic's task is to uncover her truth. In an incisive review of *The Madwoman in the Attic*, Mary Jacobus rightly criticizes the authors' 'unstated complicity with the auto-biographical "phallacy", whereby male critics hold that women's writing is somehow closer to their experience than men's, that the female text *is* the author, or at any rate a dramatic extension of her unconscious' (520). Though the two critics avoid oversimplistic conclusions, they nevertheless end up at times in a dangerously reductionist position: under the manifest text, which is nothing but a 'surface design' which 'conceals or obscures deeper, less accessible . . . levels of meaning' (73), lies the *real* truth of the texts.

This is reminiscent of reductionist varieties of psychoanalytic or Marxist criticism, though it is no longer the author's Oedipus complex or relation to the class struggle that counts as the only truth of the text, but her constant, never-changing *feminist rage*. This position, which in less sophisticated guises is perhaps the most recurrent theme of Anglo-American feminist criticism, manages to transform *all* texts written by women into feminist texts, because they may always and without exception be held to embody somehow and somewhere the author's 'female rage' against patriarchal oppression. Thus Gilbert and Gubar's readings of Jane Austen lack the force of their readings of Charlotte Brontë precisely because they persist in defining anger as the *only* positive signal of a feminist consciousness. Austen's gentle irony is lost on them, whereas the explicit rage and moodiness of Charlotte Brontë's texts furnish them with superb grounds for stimulating exegesis.

Quite apart from the reductive aspects of this approach, the insistence on the female author as the instance that provides the only true meaning of the text (that meaning being, in general, the author's anger) actually undermines Gilbert and Gubar's anti-patriarchal stance. Having quoted Edward Said's *Beginnings* with its 'miniature meditation on the word *authority*' (4) as a description of 'both the author and the authority of any literary text' (5), they quote Said's claim that 'the unity or integrity of the text is maintained by a series of genealogical connections: author-text, beginning-middle-end, text-meaning, reader-interpretation, and so on. *Underneath all these is the imagery of succession, of paternity, of hierarchy*' (5).[4] But it seems inconsistent, to say the least, to accept with Said that the traditional view of the relationship between author and text is hierarchical and authoritarian, only to proceed to write a book of over 700 pages that never once questions the authority of the *female* author. For if we are truly to reject the model of the author as God the Father of the text, it is surely not enough to reject the patriarchal ideology implied in the paternal metaphor. It is equally necessary to reject the *critical practice* it leads to, a critical practice that relies on the author as the transcendental signified of his or her text. For the patriarchal critic, the author is the source, origin and meaning of the text. If we are to undo this patriarchal practice of *authority*, we must take one further step and proclaim with Roland Barthes the death of the author. Barthes's comments on the role of the author are well worth quoting in this context:

> Once the Author is removed, the claim to decipher a text becomes quite futile. To give a text an Author is to impose a limit on that text, to furnish it with a final signified, to close the writing. Such a conception suits criticism very well, the latter then allotting itself the important task of discovering the Author (or its hypostases: society, history, psyché, liberty) beneath the work: when the Author has been found, the text is 'explained' – victory to the critic.
>
> ('The death of the Author', 147)

The relevance of Barthes's critique of the author(ity)-centred critic for *The Madwoman in the Attic* should be clear. But what then is the alternative? According to Barthes, it is to accept the *multiplicity* of writing where 'everything is to be *disentangled*, nothing *deciphered*' ('The death of the Author', 147):

> The space of writing is to be ranged over, not pierced; writing ceaselessly posits meaning ceaselessly to evaporate it, carrying out a systematic exemption of meaning. In precisely this way literature (it would be better from now on to say *writing*), by refusing to assign a 'secret', an ultimate meaning, to the text (and to the world as text), liberates what may be called an anti-theological activity, an activity that is truly revolutionary since to refuse to fix meaning is, in the end, to refuse God and his hypostases – reason, science, law.
>
> ('The death of the Author', 147)

Gilbert and Gubar's belief in the true female authorial voice as the essence of all texts written by women masks the problems raised by their theory of patriarchal ideology. For them, as for Kate Millett,

ideology becomes a monolithic unified totality that knows no contradictions; against this a miraculously intact 'femaleness' may pit its
strength. If patriarchy generates its own all-pervasive ideological structures, it is difficult to see how women in the nineteenth century could
manage to develop or maintain a feminist consciousness untainted by
the dominant patriarchal structures. As Mary Jacobus has pointed out,
Gilbert and Gubar's emphasis on the deceitful strategies of the woman
writer makes her 'evasive at the cost of a freedom which twentieth-
century women poets have eagerly sought: the freedom of being read
as more than exceptionally articulate victims of a patriarchally
engendered plot' ('Review of *The Madwoman in the Attic*', 522).

In other words: how did women manage to write at all, given the
relentless patriarchal indoctrination that surrounded them from the
moment they were born? Gilbert and Gubar avoid this question,
blandly stating as the conclusion of their first chapter that 'Despite the
obstacles presented by those twin images of angel and monster, despite
the fears of sterility and the anxieties of authorship from which
women have suffered, generations of texts *have* been possible for female
writers' (44). Indeed, but why? Only a more sophisticated account of
the contradictory, fragmentary nature of patriarchal ideology would
help Gilbert and Gubar to answer this question. In this context, Cora
Kaplan's arguments against Kate Millett are still relevant.[5]

Feminists must be able to account for the paradoxically productive
aspects of patriarchal ideology (the moments in which the ideology
backfires on itself, as it were) as well as for its obvious oppressive
implications if they are to answer the tricky question of how it is that
some women manage to counter patriarchal strategies despite the odds
stacked against them. In the nineteenth century, for instance, it would
seem true to say that bourgeois patriarchy's predilection for liberal
humanism as a 'legitimizing ideology' lent ammunition and arguments to the growing bourgeois feminist movement. If one held that
the rights of the individual were sacred, it became increasingly difficult
to argue that women's rights somehow were not. Just as Mary Wollstonecraft's essay on the rights of woman was made possible by the
emancipatory if bourgeois-patriarchal ideas of *liberté*, *égalité* and *fraternité*,
so John Stuart Mill's essay on the subjection of women was the product
of patriarchal liberal humanism. Gilbert and Gubar overlook these

points, referring to Mill only twice *en passant*, and both times as a parallel to Mary Wollstonecraft. Their theory of covert and inexpressed rage as the essence of nineteenth-century 'femaleness' cannot comfortably cope with a 'male' text that *openly* tackles the problem of women's oppression.

This *impasse* in Gilbert and Gubar's work is both accentuated and compounded by their persistent use of the epithet 'female'. It has long been an established practice among most feminists to use 'feminine' (and 'masculine') to represent *social constructs* (patterns of sexuality and behaviour imposed by cultural and social norms), and to reserve 'female' and 'male' for the purely biological aspects of sexual differ-ence. Thus 'feminine' represents nurture and 'female' nature in this usage. 'Femininity' is a cultural construct: one isn't born a woman, one becomes one, as Simone de Beauvoir puts it. Seen in this perspective, patriarchal oppression consists of imposing certain social standards of femininity on all biological women, in order precisely to make us believe that the chosen standards for 'femininity' are *natural*. Thus a woman who refuses to conform can be labelled both *unfeminine* and *unnatural*. It is in the patriarchal interest that these two terms (femininity and femaleness) stay thoroughly confused. Feminists, on the con-trary, have to disentangle this confusion, and must therefore always insist that though women undoubtedly are *female*, this in no way guar-antees that they will be *feminine*. This is equally true whether one defines femininity in the old patriarchal ways or in a new feminist way.

Gilbert and Gubar's refusal to admit a separation between nature and nurture at the lexical level renders their whole argument obscure. For what *is* this 'female creativity' they are studying? Is it a natural, essential, inborn quality in all women? Is it 'feminine' creativity in the sense of a creativity conforming to certain social standards of female behaviour, or is it a creativity typical of a feminine subject position in the psychoanalytical sense? Gilbert and Gubar seem to hold the first hypothesis, though in a slightly more historicized form: in a given patriarchal society all women (because they are biologically female) will adopt certain strategies to counter patriarchal oppression. These strategies will be 'female' since they will be the same for all women submitted to such conditions. Such an argument relies heavily on the assumption that patriarchal ideology is homogeneous and all-encompassing in its effects. It also gives little scope for an understanding of how genuinely difficult it is for women to achieve anything like 'full femininity', or of the ways in which women can come to take up a masculine subject position – that is to say, become solid defenders of the patriarchal *status quo*.

In the last chapter of their theoretical preamble ('The parables of the cave'), Gilbert and Gubar discuss Mary Shelley's 'Author's introduction' to The Last Man (1826) where the author tells us how she found the scattered leaves of the Sibyl's messages during a visit to her cave.[6] Mary Shelley then decides to spend her life deciphering and transmitting the message of these fragments in a more coherent form. Gilbert and Gubar use this story as a parable of their understanding of the situation of the woman writer under patriarchy:

> This last parable is the story of the woman artist who enters the cavern of her own mind and finds there the scattered leaves not only of her own power but of the tradition which might have generated that power. The body of her precursor's art, and thus the body of her own art lies in pieces around her, dismembered, dis-remembered, disinte-grated. How can she remember it and become a member of it, join it and rejoin it, integrate it and in doing so achieve her own integrity, her own selfhood?
>
> (98)

This parable is also a statement of Gilbert and Gubar's feminist aesthetics. The emphasis here is on wholeness – on the *gathering* of the Sibyl's leaves (but nobody asks why the Sibyl of the myth chose to *scatter* her wisdom in the first place): women's writing can only come into existence as a structured and objectified whole. Parallel to the wholeness of the text is the wholeness of the woman's self; the integrated humanist individual is the essence of all creativity. A fragmented conception of self or consciousness would seem to Gilbert and Gubar the same as a sick or dis-eased self. The good text is an organic whole, in spite of the sophisticated apparatus the authors of The Madwoman in the Attic bring to bear on the works they study.

But this emphasis on integrity and totality as an ideal for women's writing can be criticized precisely as a patriarchal or – more accurately – a phallic construct. As Luce Irigaray and Jacques Derrida have argued, patriarchal thought models its criteria for what counts as 'positive' values on the central assumption of the Phallus and the Logos as transcendental signifiers of Western culture.[7] The implications of this are often astonishingly simplistic: anything conceived of as analogous to the so-called 'positive' values of the Phallus counts as good, true or beautiful; anything that is not shaped on the pattern of the Phallus is defined as chaotic, fragmented, negative or non-existent. The Phallus is often conceived of as a whole, unitary and simple form, as opposed to the terrifying chaos of the female genitals. Now it can be argued that Gilbert and Gubar's belief in unitary wholes plays directly into the hands of such phallic aesthetic criteria. As we have seen in the case of the feminist reception of Virginia Woolf, a certain feminist preference for realism over modernism can be interpreted in the same way. To this extent, some Anglo-American feminism – and Gilbert and Gubar are no exceptions – is still labouring under the traditional patriarchal aesthetic values of New Criticism.

Gilbert and Gubar's final hope that their book will contribute to recreate a lost 'female' unity bears out this assumption:

> There is a sense in which, for us, this book is a dream of the rising of Christina Rossetti's 'mother country'. And there is a sense in which it is an attempt at reconstructing the Sibyl's leaves, leaves which haunt us with the possibility that if we can piece together their fragments the parts will form a whole that tells the story of the career of a single woman artist, a 'mother of us all', as Gertrude Stein would put it, a woman whom patriarchal poetics dismembered and whom we have tried to remember.
>
> (101)

The passage continues with a rough outline of the story of this single woman artist from Jane Austen and Maria Edgworth to George Eliot and Emily Dickinson. The concern with wholeness, with the woman writer as the *meaning* of the texts studied, is here pressed to its logical conclusion: the desire to write the narrative of a mighty 'Ur-woman'.

From one viewpoint this is a laudable project, since feminists obviously wish to make women speak; but from another viewpoint it carries some dubious political and aesthetic implications. For one thing it is not an unproblematic project to try to speak for the other woman, since this is precisely what the ventriloquism of patriarchy has always done: men have constantly spoken for women, or in the name of women. Is it right that women now should take up precisely that masculine position in relation to other women? We might argue, in other words, that Gilbert and Gubar arrogate to themselves the same authorial authority they bestow on all women writers. As for 'telling a story', this can in itself be constructed as an autocratic gesture. As we have seen, Gilbert and Gubar quote Edward Said approvingly when he writes that underneath 'beginning-middle-end' is the 'imagery of succession, of paternity, of hierarchy' (5). But a story is precisely that which ever since Aristotle has been the very model of a beginning, a middle and an end. Perhaps it isn't such a good feminist idea to start telling the whole, integrated and unified story of the Great Mother-Writer after all? As Mary Jacobus has remarked:

> This enormously energetic, often witty, shrewd and resourceful book is, it seems to me, limited in the end precisely by its preoccupation with plot; though its arts are not the traditionally female ones of the wicked Queen, they risk in their own way being as reductive. They become a form of tight lacing which immobilizes the play of meaning in the texts whose hidden plots they uncover. What they find there, again and again, is not just 'plot' but 'author', the madwoman in the attic of their title. . . . Like the story of Snow White, this is a plot doomed to repetition; their book (ample partly because it can only repeat) reenacts endlessly the revisionary struggle, unlocking the secrets of the female text again and again with the same key.
>
> ('Review of The Madwoman in the Attic', 518–19)

In the end, Jacobus argues, this eternal return to the 'original and originating "story" of women's repression by patriarchy' occurs at the cost of ignoring precisely the political implications of the critics' own stance: 'If culture, writing, and language are inherently repressive, as they may be argued to be, so is interpretation itself; and the question which arises for the feminist critic is, How are they specifically repressive for the woman writer?' ('Review', 520). Jacobus concludes that 'the story between the lines may be feminist criticism's problematic relation to the patriarchal criticism it sets out to revise' ('Review', 522). At this point, surely, we should ask ourselves if it is not time to revise a feminist aesthetics that seems in these particular respects to lead to the same patriarchal and authoritarian dead end. In other words, it is time for us to confront the fact that the main problem in Anglo-American feminist criticism lies in the radical contradiction it presents between feminist politics and patriarchal aesthetics.

4

THEORETICAL REFLECTIONS

Anglo-American feminist critics have been mostly indifferent or even hostile towards literary theory, which they have often regarded as a hopelessly abstract 'male' activity. This attitude is now beginning to change, and it seems likely that the 1980s will mark the breakthrough of theoretical reflections within the field of feminist criticism. In this section I will examine some of the precursors of this evolution towards a greater degree of feminist reflection on the purpose and function of literature and literary criticism. I have chosen for this purpose to concentrate on the theoretical work of what I take to be three fairly representative Anglo-American feminist critics: Annette Kolodny, Elaine Showalter and Myra Jehlen.

ANNETTE KOLODNY

One of the first texts to break the theoretical silence among feminist critics was Annette Kolodny's 'Some notes on defining a "feminist literary criticism" ', first published in the journal *Critical Inquiry* in 1975. The opening passage declares the freshness of Kolodny's approach: 'As yet, no one has formulated any exacting definition of the term "feminist criticism" ' (75). After a brief survey of the varieties of feminist criticism, Kolodny turns to her main subject: the study of women's

writing as a separate category. While showing that this kind of criticism is based on the 'assumption that there is something unique about
women's writing' (76), she is anxious that this approach might lead to
over-hasty conclusions about women's nature, or to endless debates
over 'the relative merits of nature versus nurture' (76). She is also
concerned about what she sees as the 'abiding commitment [in feminist criticism] to discover what, if anything, makes women's writing
different from men's' (78); since gender is a *relational* entity, it is clearly
impossible to locate a difference of style or content without comparison. 'If we insist on discovering something we can clearly label as a
"feminine mode", then we are honor-bound, also, to delineate its
counter-part, the "masculine mode"' (78). Kolodny thus advocates a
kind of feminist comparativism, much as Myra Jehlen was to do six
years later.

In spite of such cautionary warnings, Kolodny nevertheless believes
that we may arrive inductively at a number of conclusions about
feminine style in literature if we

> begin by treating each author and each separate work by each author
> as itself unique and individual. Then, slowly, we may over the course of
> time and much reading discover what kind of things recur and, more
> important still, *if* things recur.
>
> (79)

This method, however, is somewhat contradictory. For though Kolodny
wants us to jettison all preconceived notions about women's writing
('We must . . . begin not with assumptions (acknowledged or not) but
with questions' (79)), it is difficult to see how these more or less
unconscious preconceptions can be prevented from influencing our
reading of each 'unique and individual' author, as well as our selection
of features to be isolated and compared. Kolodny herself locates several
typical stylistic patterns in female fiction, of which the two most
important are 'reflexive perception' and 'inversion'. Reflexive perception occurs when a character 'discover[s] herself or find[s] some part
of herself in activities she had not planned or in situations she cannot
fully comprehend' (79), and inversion occurs when the 'stereotyped,
traditional literary images of women . . . are being turned around in

women's fiction, either for comic purposes, . . . to reveal their hidden reality [or] . . . come to connote their opposites' (80). Inversion thus comes to sound like an early version of Gilbert and Gubar's theory of the subversive strategies located beneath the surface of women's fiction.

Singling out 'the fear of being fixed in false images or trapped in inauthentic roles' as 'the most compelling fear in women's fiction today' (83), Kolodny immediately acknowledges that this is hardly a theme peculiar to women, but insists that the critic's job is to look for the *difference of experience* underlying women's use of such imagery. Feminist critics, according to Kolodny, always seek the *reality* behind the fiction and therefore must 'tread very carefully before asserting that the sometimes grotesque or apparently outré perceptions of reality granted us by women writers and their female characters *are* a distortion of any kind' (84). Her preoccupation with the experience 'behind' the text emerges with particular force in the following passage, dealing as it does with possible differences between male and female use of the same imagery:

> A man's sense of entrapment on the job and a woman's in the home may both finally share the same psychiatric label, but the language of literature, if it is honest, will reveal to us the building blocks, the minute-by-minute experience of what it *feels like* to be trapped in those very different settings.
>
> (85)

In general, Kolodny's programme for feminist criticism remains firmly planted on New Critical ground:

> The overriding task of an intellectually vigorous feminist criticism as I see it, therefore, must be to school itself in rigorous methods for analyzing style and image and then without preconception or preconceived conclusions to apply those methodologies to individual works. Only then will we be able to train our students, and our colleagues, to read women writers properly, with greater appreciation for their individual aims and particular achievements (goals which I am convinced must structure any legitimate literary criticism, regardless of its subject).
>
> (87)

Quite apart from its use of the somewhat masculinist-sounding adjectives 'vigorous' and 'rigorous' to describe the 'right' kind of feminist criticism, this insistence on analysis *without preconception* (as if that were possible) as the basis for *proper* readings of women writers betrays the traditionalism of Kolodny's approach. The rebel feminist who might want to study literature *improperly* (as Kate Millett did), to read 'against the grain' and question the established structures of 'legitimate literary criticism' (why should feminists reject illegitimacy?), can find little foothold in the space opened up by critics like Kolodny, Showalter and Jehlen. Kolodny even recommends that feminist criticism should be 'obliged to separate political ideologies from aesthetic judgments' (89), since, as she puts it, political commitment may make 'dishonest' critics of us.[1] She ends her essay by claiming that the aim of feminist criticism must be 'the reenfranchising of women writers into the mainstream of our academic curriculum through fairer, non sex biased, and more judicious appraisals of their work' (91). Though few are likely to disagree violently with this, it remains an unusually modest framework for the feminist struggle within academia. It is worth pondering whether such reformism may be the inevitable outcome of a feminist analysis based on an unquestioned acceptance of so many aspects of New Critical doctrine.

Five years later, in an article entitled 'Dancing through the minefield: some observations on the theory, practice and politics of a feminist literary criticism', published in *Feminist Studies*, Kolodny returns to some of the questions she raised in 1975, complaining that after a decade energetically developing a whole new field of intellectual enquiry, feminist criticism had still not been granted 'an honored berth on that ongoing intellectual journey which we loosely term in academia, "critical analysis". Instead of being welcomed onto the train . . . we've been forced to negotiate a minefield' (6). According to Kolodny, the academic establishment's hostile reactions to feminist criticism might be 'transformed into a true dialogue' (8) if we made our own methodological and theoretical assumptions *explicit*; and this, precisely, is what she then sets out to do. Arguing that feminist criticism is a fundamentally 'suspicious' approach to literature, Kolodny sees the principal task of the feminist critic as that of examining the validity of our aesthetic judgments: 'What ends do those judgments serve, the feminist asks; and what conceptions of the world or ideological stances do they (even if unwittingly) help to perpetuate?' (15). This is surely one of her most valuable insights.

The problem arises when she proceeds from this to a wholesale recommendation of *pluralism* as the appropriate feminist stance. Feminist criticism lacks systematic coherence, she argues, and this fact ('the fact of our diversity'), should 'place us securely where, all along, we should have been: camped out, on the far side of the minefield, with the other pluralists and pluralisms' (17). Feminists cannot and indeed should not provide that 'internal consistency as a system' that Kolodny ascribes to psychoanalysis and Marxism. In her discourse, these two theoretical formations come to figure as monolithically oppressive blocks towering over the diversified, anti-authoritarian feminist field. But it is not only untrue that Marxism and psychoanalysis offer such a unified theoretical field; it is also surely doubtful that feminist criticism is *that* diversified.[2] Kolodny acknowledges that feminist politics is the basis for feminist criticism; so that though we may argue over what constitutes proper feminist politics and theory, that debate nevertheless takes place within a feminist political framework, much like debates within contemporary Marxism. Without common political ground, there can simply be no recognizable *feminist* criticism. In this context, Kolodny's 'pluralist' approach risks throwing the baby out with the bathwater:

> Adopting a 'pluralist' label does not mean, however, that we cease to disagree; it means only that we entertain the possibility that different readings, even of the same text, may be differently useful, even illuminating, within different contexts of inquiry.
>
> (18)

But if we wax pluralistic enough to acknowledge the feminist position as just one among many 'useful' approaches, we also implicitly grant the most 'masculinist' of criticism the right of existence: it just might be 'useful' in a very different context from ours.

Kolodny's intervention in the theoretical debate pays too little attention to the role of politics in critical theory. When she states, correctly, that 'If feminist criticism calls anything into question, it must be that dog-eared myth of intellectual neutrality' (21), she still seems not to recognize that even critical theory carries with it its own political implications. Feminist criticism cannot just

> initiate nothing less than a playful pluralism, responsive to the possibilities of multiple critical schools and methods, but captive of none, recognizing that the many tools needed for our analysis will necessarily be largely inherited and only partly of our own making.
>
> (19)

Feminists must surely also conduct a political and theoretical evaluation of the various methods and tools on offer, to make sure that they don't backfire on us.

ELAINE SHOWALTER

Elaine Showalter is rightly acknowledged as one of the most important feminist critics in America. Her theoretical observations are therefore of particular interest to us. I want now to examine two of her articles on feminist literary theory, 'Towards a feminist poetics' (1979) and 'Feminist criticism in the wilderness' (1981).[3]

In the first article, Showalter distinguishes between two forms of feminist criticism. The first type is concerned with woman as reader, which Showalter labels 'feminist critique'. The second type deals with woman as writer, and Showalter calls this 'gynocritics'. 'Feminist critique' deals with works by male authors, and Showalter tells us that this form of criticism is a 'historically grounded inquiry which probes the ideological assumptions of literary phenomena' (25). This sort of 'suspicious' approach to the literary text seems however to be largely absent from Showalter's second category, since among the primary concerns of 'gynocritics' we find 'the history, themes, genres and structures of literature by women' as well as the 'psychodynamics of female creativity' and 'studies of particular writers and works' (25). There is no indication here that the feminist critic concerned with women as writers should bring other than sympathetic, identity-seeking approaches to bear on works written by women. The 'hermeneutics of suspicion', which assumes that the text is not, or not only, what it pretends to be, and therefore searches for underlying contradictions and conflicts as well as absences and silences in the text, seems to be reserved for texts written by men. The feminist critic, in other words, must realize that the woman-produced text will occupy a totally different status from the 'male' text.

Showalter writes:

> One of the problems of the feminist critique is that it is male-oriented. If we study stereotypes of women, the sexism of male critics, and the limited roles women play in literary history, we are not learning what women have felt and experienced, but only what men have thought women should be.
>
> (27)

The implication is not only that the feminist critic should turn to 'gynocritics', the study of women's writings, precisely in order to learn 'what women have felt and experienced', but also that this experience is directly available in the texts written by women. The text, in other words, has disappeared, or become the transparent medium through which 'experience' can be seized. This view of texts as transmitting authentic 'human' experience is, as we have seen, a traditional emphasis of Western patriarchal humanism. In Showalter's case, this humanist position is also tinged by a good portion of empiricism. She rejects theory as a male invention that apparently can only be used on men's texts (27–8). 'Gynocritics' frees itself from pandering to male values and seeks to 'focus . . . on the newly visible world of female culture' (28). This search for the 'muted' female culture can best be carried out by applying anthropological theories to the female author and her work: 'Gynocritics is related to feminist research in history, anthropology, psychology and sociology, all of which have developed hypotheses of a female subculture' (28). The feminist critic, in other words, should attend to historical, anthropological, psychological and sociological aspects of the 'female' text; in short, it would seem, to everything but the text as a signifying process. The only influences Showalter appears to recognize as constitutive of the text are of an empirical, extra-literary sort. This attitude, coupled with her fear of 'male' theory and general appeal to 'human' experience, has the unfortunate effect of drawing her perilously close to the male critical hierarchy whose patriarchal values she opposes.

In 'Feminist criticism in the wilderness', Showalter tends to repeat the same themes. The new component of this article is a lengthy presentation of what she takes to be the four main directions of present-day feminist criticism: biological, linguistic, psychoanalytic and cultural criticism. Though her particular division of the field may be queried, it does as a whole reveal that Showalter has come to recognize that necessity of theory. She still employs a division between 'feminist critique' (which she here also calls 'feminist reading') and 'gynocritics'. The feminist critique or reading is, we are told, 'in essence a mode of interpretation'. Showalter continues: 'It is very difficult to propose theoretical coherence in an activity [i.e. interpretation] which by its nature is so eclectic and wide-ranging, although as a critical practice feminist reading has certainly been very influential' (182). In this way she attempts to escape intractable 'male' questions like: What is interpretation? What does it mean to read? What is a text? Showalter once more rejects all meddling with 'male critical theory', since it 'keeps us dependent upon it and retards our progress in solving our own theoretical problems' (183). Her dichotomy between 'male critical theory' and 'our own theoretical problems' is not argued or elaborated in detail, which leaves us to discover for ourselves that while she denounces the 'white fathers', Lacan, Macherey and Engels (183–4), she ends up by extolling as particularly suitable for 'gynocritical' activity the cultural theory developed by Edwin Ardener and Clifford Geertz. Despite a token excuse for this glaring inconsistency ('I don't mean ... to enthrone Ardener and Geertz as the new white fathers in place of Freud, Lacan and Bloom' (205)), she nevertheless manages by this gesture to bemuse the reader who has followed her so far. Should the aspiring 'gynocritic' use 'male' theory or should she not? Showalter's final answer to this question is frankly evasive, based as it is on a dubious contrast between 'theory' and 'knowledge': 'No theory, however suggestive, can be a substitute for the close and extensive knowledge of women's texts which constitutes our essential subject' (205). But what 'knowledge' is ever uninformed by theoretical assumptions?

And so we are back where we started: the lack of a suitable theory of feminist criticism has become a virtuous necessity, since too much theoretical study would prevent us from achieving that 'close and extensive knowledge of women's texts' that Showalter herself has so richly displayed in *A Literature of Their Own*. Her fear of the text and its problems is well-justified, since any real engagement with this field of enquiry would lead to the exposure of the fundamental complicity between this empiricist and humanist variety of feminist criticism and the male academic hierarchy it rightly resists.

I will try briefly to show how this complicity works. The humanist believes in literature as an excellent instrument of education: by reading 'great works' the student will become a finer human being. The great author is great because he (occasionally even she) has managed to convey an authentic vision of life; and the role of the reader or critic is to listen respectfully to the voice of the author as it is expressed in the text. The literary canon of 'great literature' ensures that it is this 'representative experience' (one selected by male bourgeois critics) that is transmitted to future generations, rather than those deviant, unrepresentative experiences discoverable in much female, ethnic and working-class writing. Anglo-American feminist criticism has waged war on this self-sufficient canonization of middle-class male values. But they have rarely challenged the very notion of such a canon. Showalter's aim, in effect, is to create a separate canon of women's writing, not to abolish all canons. But a new canon would not be intrinsically less oppressive than the old. The role of the feminist critic is still to sit quietly and listen to her mistress's voice as it expresses authentic female experience. The feminist reader is not granted leave to get up and challenge this female voice; the female text rules as despotically as the old male text. As if in compensation for her obedience, the feminist critic is allowed to launch sceptical critiques of 'male' literature, provided she keeps this critical stance well separate from her concern with women writers. But if texts are seen as signifying processes, and both writing and reading grasped as textual production, it is likely that even texts written by women will be subjected to irreverent scrutiny by feminist critics. And if this were to happen, it is clear that the Showalterian 'gynocritic' would face a painful dilemma, caught between the 'new' feminists with their 'male' theories and the male humanist empiricists with their patriarchal politics.

The limitations of this mode of feminist criticism become

particularly clear when it is confronted with a woman's work that refuses to conform to the humanistic expectations of an authentic, realistic expression of 'human' experience. It is not accidental that Anglo-American feminist criticism has dealt overwhelmingly with fiction written in the great period of realism between 1750 and 1930, with a notable concentration on the Victorian era. Monique Wittig's Les guérillères (1969) is an example of an altogether quite different sort of text. This utopian work consists of a series of fragments depicting life in an Amazonian society involved in a war against men. The war is finally won by the women, and peace is celebrated by them and the young men who have been won over to their cause. This fragmented work is interrupted at regular intervals by a different text: a series of women's names printed in capital letters in the middle of a blank page. In addition to the hundreds of names contained in this series, the text also comprises a couple of poems and three large circles representing the vulva, a symbolism that is rejected as a form of inverted sexism at a later stage in the book. Wittig's book offers no individual characters, no psychology and no recognizable 'experience' to be strongly felt by the reader. But it is evident that the work is a deeply feminist one, and as such Anglo-American feminist critics have often tried to engage with it.

Nina Auerbach's *Communities of Women* offers these comments on the women's names intervening in the text:

> The women's names that are ritualistically chanted seem a human joke, since they are attached to no characters we come to know:
>
> DEMONA EPONINA GABRIELA
> FULVIA ALEXANDRA JUSTINE (p. 43)
>
> and so on. Though these names take on their own incantatory life, the empty resonance of their sound is also the death of the real people we used to read novels to meet.
>
> (190–1)

Wittig's text in fact nowhere indicates that the names are spoken by anyone: the 'ritualistic chanting' represents Auerbach's own attempt to attribute the fragmented text to a unitary human voice. When the text no longer offers an individual grasped as the transcendental origin of language and experience, humanist feminism must lay down its arms. Auerbach therefore wistfully hopes for better days in a human-feminist future: 'Perhaps once women have proved their strength to themselves, it will be possible to return to the individuality of Meg, Jo, Beth, and Amy, or to the humanly interdependent courtesy of Cranford' (191). If a nostalgic reversion to Cranford or Little Women is all this brand of criticism can yearn for, the urgent examination of other, more theoretically informed critical practices must surely be a pressing item on the agenda of Anglo-American feminist critics.

MYRA JEHLEN

Myra Jehlen's article 'Archimedes and the paradox of feminist criticism' seems to have voiced central concerns among many American feminists: first published in the summer of 1981, it has already been anthologized twice.[4] Her essay does indeed engage with important issues, devoted as it is to a discussion of the contradiction between what she calls 'appreciative and political readings' (579). Jehlen confronts this fundamental problem not only in feminist criticism, but argues the case for 'radical comparativism' (585) in feminist studies as a whole. According to her, the woman-centred works by Spacks, Moers, Showalter, Gilbert and Gubar suffer from their exclusive focus on the female tradition in literature. Deploring the feminist tendency to create 'an alternative context, a sort of female enclave apart from the universe of masculinist assumptions' (576), Jehlen wants women's studies to become the 'investigation, from women's viewpoint, of everything' (577). This project in itself is both ambitious and energetic. Feminist criticism actually began by examining the dominant male culture (Ellmann, Millett) and there is no reason for women today to reject this aspect of feminist work. But Jehlen takes a step further. In recommending comparison in order to locate 'the difference between women's writing and men's that no study of only women's writing can depict' (584), she points to Kate Millett's Sexual Politics as being 'all about comparison' (586). But this is clearly untrue: Millett's book, as we have seen, is all about men's writing.

There is a dangerous sliding in Jehlen's argument from a much-needed insistence on the *relational* nature of gender, to a recommendation that feminists return to studying the traditional patriarchal canon of literature. The ambiguity of her argument at this point reflects her conviction that a 'standpoint from which we can see our conceptual universe whole but which nonetheless rests firmly on male ground, is what feminists really need' (576). This ambiguity is caused in no small part by certain highly confusing rhetorical manoeuvres around the image of Archimedes and his fulcrum. Arguing that feminist thinking is a 'radical skepticism' (575) that creates unusual difficulties for its practitioners, Jehlen writes:

> Somewhat like Archimedes, who to lift the earth with his lever required someplace else on which to locate himself and his fulcrum, feminists questioning the presumptive order of both nature and history – and thus proposing to remove the ground from under their own feet – would appear to need an alternative base.
>
> (575–6)

Jehlen alludes here to a central paradox of feminism: given that there is no space *outside* patriarchy from which women can speak, how do we explain the existence of a feminist, anti-patriarchal discourse at all? Jehlen's insistence on the fulcrum image ('What Archimedes really needed was a terrestrial fulcrum' (576)) has the unfortunate effect of implying that such an effort is doomed to failure (a terrestrial fulcrum will *never* shift the earth). Instead of shifting the earth, Jehlen wants to shift feminism back on to 'male ground' – but that is, of course, precisely where feminism, both woman-centred and otherwise, has always been. If there is no space uncontaminated by patriarchy from which women can speak, it follows that we really don't need a fulcrum at all: there is simply nowhere else to go.

In her response to Jehlen, Elaine Showalter opposes her recommendation of a shift towards 'radical comparativism' on the grounds that 'such a shift might mean an abandonment of a feminist enterprise which still frightens us by its audacity' ('Comment on Jehlen', 161). Showalter defends the study of a female tradition in literature as a 'methodological choice rather than a belief', declaring that:

No woman, we know, is ever cut off from the real male world; but in the world of ideas we can draw boundaries that open up new vistas of thought, that allow us to see a problem in a new way.

(161)

But the study of a female tradition in literature, while not necessarily an attempt to create 'a female enclave', is surely *more* than a methodo-logical choice: it is an urgent *political* necessity. If patriarchy oppresses women *as* women, defining us all as 'feminine' regardless of individual differences, the feminist struggle must both try to undo the patriarchal strategy that makes 'femininity' intrinsic to biological femaleness, and at the same time insist on defending women precisely *as* women. In a patriarchal society that discriminates against women writers because they are *women*, it is easy enough to justify a discussion of them as a separate group. The problem, more urgently, is how to avoid bringing patriarchal notions of aesthetics, history and tradition to bear on the 'female tradition' we have decided to construct. Showalter herself did not avoid these pitfalls in *A Literature of Their Own*, and Jehlen seems hardly to be aware of the problem: her acceptance of the most tradi-tional patriarchal aesthetic categories is, as we shall see, little short of astonishing in a critic who calls herself a feminist.

Jehlen approaches the problem of 'critical appreciation' as opposed to 'political readings' by stating that:

What makes feminist literary criticism especially contradictory is the peculiar nature of literature as distinct from the objects of either phys-ical or social scientific study. Unlike these, literature is itself already an interpretation that it is the critic's task to decipher. It is certainly not news that the literary work is biased: indeed that is its value. Critical objectivity enters in only at a second level to provide a reliable reading, though even here many have argued that reading too is an exercise in creative interpretation.

(577)

This statement takes for granted that the literary text is an object to be deciphered. But as Roland Barthes has argued: 'Once the Author is removed, the claim to decipher a text becomes quite futile' ('The death of the Author', 147). Jehlen believes that texts are the encoded message of the author's voice: 'critical objectivity' then presumably consists in faithfully reproducing this encoded message in a more accessible form. The status of the author and the text is initially left somewhat unclear in Jehlen's essay. While rightly stating that feminism as the 'philosophy of the Other' has had to reject the Romantic belief that 'to be a great poet was to tell the absolute truth, to be the One prophetic voice for all Mankind' (579), she nevertheless goes on to state that the aim of criticism is to 'do justice' to – precisely – the author in order to reproduce 'the distinct vision' of the literary subject. Or in her own words:

> We should begin therefore, by acknowledging the separate wholeness of the literary subject, its distinct vision that need not be ours – what the formalists have told us and told us about: its integrity. We need to acknowledge, also, that to respect that integrity by not asking questions of the text that it does not ask itself, to ask the text what questions to ask, will produce the fullest, richest reading.

> (579)

It follows from this that Jehlen must take Kate Millett to task, since her 'intentionally tangential approach violated the terms of Henry Miller's work' (579) and did 'damage to his architecture' (580). For Jehlen, Millett's approach was *improper* and *violent*; her reading becomes the rape of the virginal integrity of Henry Miller's text. It is as if there was a set of objective facts about the work in question that anybody could see if they just tried hard enough and that at all costs must dominate the critic's – *any* critic's – approach. Jehlen's insistence on the *proper* reading to which feminists must submit, or else suffer expulsion into the outer darkness of 'improper' or 'dishonest' critical approaches, here echoes Annette Kolodny's views. Sue Warrick Doederlein is right when she argues that:

> New insights in linguistics and anthropology have surely given the lie to any view of autonomous works of art whose sanctity we must not violate and whose space we only enter (in our abject objectivity) 'to provide a reliable reading'. Feminist critics can (carefully) take certain

postulates from current masculinist-endorsed hypotheses that will allow us never to apologize for 'misreading' or 'misinterpreting' a text again.

(165–6)

Patrocinio Schweickart, also taking issue with Jehlen on this point, demonstrates the complicity of her theory with the doctrines of New Criticism, and comments:

It is worth noting that the formalist basis of Jehlen's argument – the notion of the autotelic art object and the concomitant notion that to read literature *qua* literature (rather than, say, as a sociological document) one must stay within the terms intrinsic to (i.e. authorized by) the text – has been seriously contested by structuralism, by deconstruction, and by some reader-response-theories. I am not saying that we should follow critical fashion blindly. My point is simply that, at the very least, the basic tenets of New Criticism have been rendered problematical. We should not take them as axiomatic.

(172)

But if Jehlen's distinction between 'critical appreciation' and 'political reading' is based on a traditionalist definition of the former, from a feminist perspective it is her desire to maintain such an absolute distinction in the first place that raises the more difficult political questions. For the difference between feminist and non-feminist criticism is not, as Jehlen seems to believe, that the former is political and the latter is not, but that the feminist openly declares her politics, whereas the non-feminist may either be unaware of his own value-system or seek to universalize it as 'non-political'. That Jehlen, writing as she does after 15 years of feminist criticism in America, should apparently have no qualms in abandoning one of the most fundamental political insights of former feminist analysis, is particularly bizarre.

Jehlen argues for the separation of politics and aesthetics in an attempt to solve a perennial problem for radical critics: the problem of how to evaluate a work of art that one finds aesthetically valuable but politically distasteful. If she nevertheless ends up arguing herself out of any recognizable feminist position on this problem, it is because she

refuses to see both that aesthetic value judgements are historically relative and also that they are deeply imbricated in political value judgements. An aesthetics recommending organic unity and the harmonic
interaction of all parts of the poetic structure for example, is not politically innocent. A feminist might wonder why anybody would want to
place such an emphasis on order and integration in the first place, and
whether it could have something to do with the social and political
ideals of the exponents of such critical theories. It would of course be
hopelessly reductive to argue that all aesthetic categories carry *automatic*
political overtones. But it is just as reductive to argue that aesthetic
structures are always and unchangingly politically neutral, or 'non-
political' as Jehlen puts it. The point is, surely, that the same aesthetic
device can be politically polyvalent, varying with the historical, political and literary context in which it occurs. Only a non-dialectical
mode of thought can argue, as Jehlen does, that Pierre Macherey's view
of cultural products as 'relatively autonomous' in relation to the historical and social context in which they are produced is inherently contradictory: to require a simple and uncomplicated answer to the highly
complex problem of the relationship between politics and aesthetics is
surely the most reductive approach of all.

Jehlen believes that 'ideological criticism' (which to her is identical
with 'political' or 'biased' criticism) is reductive. Modern critical
theory tells us that *all* readings are in some sense reductive, in that they
all impose some kind of closure on the text. If all readings are *also* in
some sense political, it will hardly do to maintain the New Critics'
binary opposition between reductive political readings on the one
hand and rich aesthetic appraisal on the other. If aesthetics raises the
question of whether (and how) the text works effectively with an
audience, it obviously is bound up with the political: without an aesthetic effect there will be no political effect either. And if feminist
politics is about, among other things, 'experience', then it is already
related to the aesthetic. It should be clear by now that one of the chief
contentions of this book is that feminist criticism is about deconstructing such an opposition between the political and the aesthetic: as a
political approach to criticism, feminism must be aware of the politics
of aesthetic categories as well as of the implied aesthetics of political
approaches to art. This is why Jehlen's views seem to me to undermine

some of the most basic tenets of feminist criticism. If feminism does not revolt against patriarchal notions of cultural criticism as a 'value-free' exercise, it is in imminent danger of losing the last shreds of its political credibility.[5]

Some feminists might wonder why I have said nothing about black or lesbian (or black-lesbian) feminist criticism in America in this survey. The answer is simple: this book purports to deal with the theoretical aspects of feminist criticism. So far, lesbian and/or black feminist criticism have presented exactly the same *methodological* and *theoretical* problems as the rest of Anglo-American feminist criticism. In her valuable survey of lesbian criticism, Bonnie Zimmerman emphasizes the parallels between feminist and lesbian criticism. Lesbian critics are engaged in establishing a lesbian literary tradition, analysing images and stereotypes of lesbians, and problematizing the concept of 'lesbian'. As far as I can judge, they thus encounter precisely the same *theoretical* problems as do 'straight' feminist critics. It is the *contents* of her work that make the lesbian critic's study different, not her method. Instead of focusing on 'women' in literature, the lesbian critic focuses on 'lesbian women', as the black feminist critic will focus on 'black women' in literature.[6]

My point, then, is simply that *in so far as textual theory is concerned* there is no discernible difference between these three fields. This is not to say that black and lesbian criticism have no *political* importance; on the contrary, by highlighting the different situations and often conflicting interests of specific groups of women, these critical approaches force white heterosexual feminists to re-examine their own sometimes totalitarian conception of 'woman' as a homogeneous category. These 'marginal feminisms' ought to prevent white middle-class First-World feminists from defining their own preoccupations as *universal* female (or feminist) problems. In this respect, recent work on Third-World women has much to teach us.[7] As for the complex interactions of class and gender, they too have received little attention among Anglo-American feminist critics.[8]

I have tried in this survey of Anglo-American feminist criticism to throw light on the fundamental affiliations between traditional humanist and patriarchal criticism and recent feminist scholarship. Despite

claims that Anglo-American feminist literary criticism is already generating new methods and analytical procedures, I can find little evidence
of such developments.[9] The radically new impact of feminist criticism
is to be found not at the level of theory or methodology, but at the level
of politics. Feminists have *politicized* existing critical methods and
approaches. If feminist criticism has subverted established critical
judgements it is because of its radically new emphasis on *sexual politics*. It
is on the basis of its political theory (which has already engendered
many highly divergent forms of political strategy) that feminist criticism has grown to become a new branch of literary studies. Feminists
therefore find themselves in a position roughly similar to that of other
radical critics: speaking from their marginalized positions on the out-
skirts of the academic establishments, they strive to make *explicit* the
politics of the so-called 'neutral' or 'objective' works of their col-
leagues, as well as to act as cultural *critics* in the widest sense of the
word. Like socialists, feminists can in a sense afford to be tolerantly
pluralistic in their choice of literary methods and theories, precisely
because any approach that can be successfully appropriated to their
political ends must be welcome.

The key word here is 'successfully': a political evaluation of critical
methods and theories is an essential part of the feminist critical enterprise. My reservations about much Anglo-American feminist criticism
are thus not primarily that it has remained within the lineage of male-
centred humanism but that it has done so without sufficient awareness
of the high political costs this entails. The central paradox of Anglo-
American feminist criticism is thus that despite its often strong, explicit
political engagement, it is *in the end* not quite political enough; not in
the sense that it fails to go *far* enough along the political spectrum, but
in the sense that its radical analysis of sexual politics still remains
entangled with depoliticizing theoretical paradigms. There is nothing
surprising in this: all forms of radical thought inevitably remain mort-
gaged to the very historical categories they seek to transcend. But our
understanding of this historically necessary paradox should not lead us
complacently to perpetuate patriarchal practices.

Part II

French Feminist Theory

5

FROM SIMONE DE BEAUVOIR TO JACQUES LACAN

SIMONE DE BEAUVOIR AND MARXIST FEMINISM

Simone de Beauvoir is surely the greatest feminist theorist of our time. Yet in 1949, when she published *The Second Sex*, she was convinced that the advent of socialism alone would put an end to the oppression of women and consequently considered herself a socialist, not a feminist. Today her position is somewhat different. In 1972 she joined the MLF (Women's Liberation Movement) and publicly declared herself a feminist for the first time. She explained this belated recognition of feminism by pointing to the new radicalism of the women's movement: 'The women's groups which existed in France before the MLF was founded in 1970 were generally reformist and legalistic. I had no desire to associate myself with them. The new feminism is radical, by contrast' (*Simone de Beauvoir Today*, 29). This change of emphasis has not however led her to repudiate socialism:

> At the end of *The Second Sex* I said that I was not a feminist because I believed that the problems of women would resolve themselves automatically in the context of socialist development. By feminist, I meant fighting on specifically feminine issues independently of the

class struggle. I still hold the same view today. In my definition, feminists are women – or even men, too – who are fighting to change women's condition, in association with the class struggle, but independently of it as well, without making the changes they strive for totally dependent on changing society as a whole. I would say that, in that sense, I am a feminist today, because I realised that we must fight for the situation of women, here and now, before our dreams of socialism come true.

(Simone de Beauvoir Today, 32)

In spite of its commitment to socialism, *The Second Sex* is based not on traditional Marxist theory, but on Sartre's existentialist philosophy. Beauvoir's main thesis in this epochal work is simple: throughout history, women have been reduced to objects for men: 'woman' has been constructed as man's Other, denied the right to her own subjectivity and to responsibility for her own actions. Or, in more existentialist terms: patriarchal ideology presents woman as immanence, man as transcendence. Beauvoir shows how these fundamental assumptions dominate all aspects of social, political and cultural life and, equally important, how women themselves internalize this objectified vision, thus living in a constant state of 'inauthenticity' or 'bad faith', as Sartre might have put it. The fact that women often enact the roles patriarchy has prescribed for them does not prove that the patriarchal analysis is right: Beauvoir's uncompromising refusal of any notion of a female nature or essence is succinctly summed up in her famous statement 'One is not born a woman; one becomes one'.[1]

Though most feminist theorists and critics of the 1980s acknowledge their debt to Simone de Beauvoir, relatively few of them seem to approve of her espousal of socialism as the necessary context for feminism. In this respect it would seem that her most faithful followers are to be found in Scandinavia and in Britain. In the Scandinavian social democracies the debate within the women's movement has never explicitly pitted non-socialist against socialist feminists, whereas considerable energy has been spent arguing over the kind of socialism feminists ought to adopt. Thus in the early 1970s in Norway there was a considerable degree of hostility between the centralized Maoist 'Women's Front' and the more anti-hierarchical 'Neo-feminists'

whose adherents represented everything from right-wing social dem-
ocracy to more radical, left-wing forms of socialism and Marxism.[2]
Scandinavian feminist criticism reflects this emphasis on socialism, particularly in its tendency to situate the textual analysis within a thoroughly researched account of class structures and class struggle at the
time of the literary text's production.[3] The recent rise to power of
conservative political parties in many of the Scandinavian countries has
only superficially modified this picture: in spite of the emergence of
some 'light-blue' Establishment feminists, the overwhelming majority
of Scandinavian feminists still feel at home somewhere on the political
Left.

Traditionally, British feminism has been more open to socialist ideas
than has its American counterpart. Most Marxist-feminist work in Britain, however, is not carried out within the specific field of literary
theory and criticism. In the 1980s it is women working within the
recently developed areas of cultural studies, film studies and media
studies, or in sociology or history, who are producing the most interesting political and theoretical analyses. Though Marxist or socialist
feminists like Rosalind Coward, Annette Kuhn, Juliet Mitchell, Terry
Lovell, Janet Wolff and Michèle Barrett have all written on literary
topics, their most important and challenging work nevertheless falls
outside the scope of this book.[4] My project has been to develop a
critical presentation of the current debates within feminist literary
criticism and theory. It is a sad fact that Marxist-feminist concerns have
not been central in this debate, and it is also, perhaps, an indictment of
this book that its basic structure does not represent a more radical
challenge to the current dominance of the Anglo-American and the
French critical perspectives.

In the specific field of literary studies, the Marxist-Feminist Litera-
ture Collective's pioneering article 'Women's writing: *Jane Eyre, Shirley,
Villette, Aurora Leigh*' draws on the theories of the French Marxists Louis
Althusser and Pierre Macherey in order to develop an analysis of the
marginalization of the woman writer and her work in terms of both
class and gender. This approach has been followed up and developed by
Penny Boumelha in her excellent analysis of sexual ideology in Thomas
Hardy's work (*Thomas Hardy and Women*), which also finds its basic theory
of ideology in Althusser. Cora Kaplan, an erstwhile member of the

Collective, continued its approach in her introduction to *Aurora Leigh and Other Poems*. In America, Judith Lowder Newton's *Women, Power, and Subversion* focuses on the conjuncture of class and gender in British nineteenth-century literature.

The Machereyan approach adopted by Penny Boumelha and The Marxist-Feminist Literature Collective in particular seems to open up a productive field of enquiry for feminist critics. For Macherey, the literary work is neither a unified whole, nor the unchallengeable 'message' of the Great Author/Creator. Indeed, for Macherey, the silences, gaps and contradictions of the text are more revealing of its ideological determinations than are its explicit statements. Terry Eagleton has given a succinct summary of Macherey's arguments on this point:

> It is in the significant *silences* of a text, in its gaps and absences that the presence of ideology can be most positively felt. It is these silences which the critic must make 'speak'. The text is, as it were, ideologically forbidden to say certain things; in trying to tell the truth in his own way, for example, the author finds himself forced to reveal the limits of the ideology within which he writes. He is forced to reveal its gaps and silences, what it is unable to articulate. Because a text contains these gaps and silences, it is always *incomplete*. Far from constituting a rounded, coherent whole, it displays a conflict and contradiction of meanings; and the significance of the work lies in the difference rather than unity between these meanings. . . . The work for Macherey is always '*de-centred*'; there is no central essence to it, just a continuous conflict and disparity of meanings.
>
> (*Marxism and Literary Criticism*, 34–5)

The study of the silences and contradictions of the literary work will enable the critic to link it to a specific historical context in which a whole set of different structures (ideological, economic, social, political) intersect to produce precisely those textual structures. Thus the author's personal situation and intentions can become no more than one of the many conflicting strands that make up the contradictory construct we call the text. This kind of Marxist-feminist criticism has thus been particularly interested in studying the historical construction of the categories of gender and in analysing the importance of culture in the representation and transformation of those categories. In this perspective, Marxist-feminist criticism offers an alternative both to the homogenizing author-centred readings of the Anglo-American critics and to the often ahistorical and idealist categories of the French feminist theorists.

It is, however, only fair to say that much Marxist-feminist criticism, whether British, American or Scandinavian, simply adds 'class' as another theme to be discussed within the general framework established by Anglo-American feminist criticism. And it is unfortunately equally true that, so far, few feminist critics have attempted to examine the work of Marxist theorists such as Antonio Gramsci, Walter Benjamin or Theodor Adorno in order to see whether their insights into the problems of representing the tradition of the oppressed can be appropriated for feminism.

FRENCH FEMINISM AFTER 1968

The new French feminism is the child of the student revolt of May 1968 in Paris, which almost toppled one of the more repressive of the so-called Western democracies. For a while, the realization that 'May '68' had almost managed the apparently impossible inspired an exuberant political optimism among left-wing intellectuals in France. 'Les événements' enabled them to believe both that change was at hand and that intellectuals had a real political role to play within it. At the end of the 1960s and in the early 1970s, political activism and intervention thus seemed meaningful and relevant to students and intellectuals on the Left Bank.

It was in this politicized intellectual climate, dominated by various shades of Marxism, particularly Maoism, that the first French feminist groups were formed. In many ways, the direct experience that led to the formation of the first French women's groups in the summer of 1968 was strikingly similar to that of the American women's movement.[5] In May, women had fought alongside men on the barricades only to find that they were still expected to furnish their male comrades with sexual, secretarial and culinary services as well. Predictably enough, they took their cue from American women and started to form their own women-only groups. One of the very first of these groups chose to call itself 'Psychanalyse et Politique'. Later, when the politics of feminism had reached a more advanced stage, this group, which in the meantime had founded the influential publishing house *des femmes* ('women'), renamed itself 'politique et psychanalyse', reversing the priorities of politics and psychoanalysis and dropping the hierarchical capitals once and for all. The concern with psychoanalysis signals a central preoccupation in the Parisian intellectual *milieux*. Whereas the American feminists of the 1960s had started by vigorously denouncing Freud, the French took it for granted that psychoanalysis could provide an emancipatory theory of the personal and a path to the exploration of the unconscious, both of vital importance to the analysis of the oppression of women in patriarchal society. In the English-speaking world, the feminist arguments in favour of Freud were not heard until Juliet Mitchell published her influential book *Psychoanalysis and Feminism* in 1974, which was translated and published in France by *des femmes*.

Though French feminist theory was already flourishing by 1974, it has taken a considerable period to reach women outside France. One of the reasons for the relatively limited influence of French theory on Anglo-American feminists is the 'heavy' intellectual profile of the former. Steeped as they are in European philosophy (particularly Marx, Nietzsche and Heidegger), Derridean deconstruction and Lacanian psychoanalysis, French feminist theorists apparently take for granted an audience as Parisian as they are. Though rarely wilfully obscure, the fact that few pedagogical concessions are made to the reader without the 'correct' intellectual co-ordinates smacks of elitism to the outsider. This holds for Hélène Cixous's intricate puns and Luce Irigaray's infuriating passion for the Greek alphabet, as well as for Julia Kristeva's unsettling habit of referring to everyone from St Bernard to Fichte or Artaud in the same sentence. That the exasperated reader sometimes feels alienated by such uncompromising intellectualism is hardly surprising. Once the Anglo-American reader has overcome the effects of this initial culture-shock, however, it doesn't take long to discover that French theory has contributed powerfully to the feminist debate about the nature of women's oppression, the construction of sexual difference and the specificity of women's relations to language and writing.

One problem for the English-speaking reader, however, is caused by the French word 'féminin'. In French there is only one adjective to 'femme', and that is 'féminin',[6] whereas English has two adjectives to 'woman': 'female' and 'feminine'. It has long been recognized usage among many English-speaking feminists to use 'feminine' (and 'masculine') to represent social constructs (gender) and to reserve 'female' (and 'male') for purely biological aspects (sex). The problem is that this fundamental political distinction is lost in French. Does écriture féminine, for instance, mean 'female' or 'feminine' writing? How can we know whether this or any other such expression refers to sex or to gender? There is of course no standard answer: in the following presentations my readings of the French 'féminin' are interpretations based on the context and on my overall understanding of the works in question.

For the Anglo-American feminist critic, the fact that there is very little feminist literary criticism in France may be disconcerting. With a few exceptions, such as Claudine Herrmann and Anne-Marie Dardigna,[7] French feminist critics have preferred to work on problems of textual, linguistic, semiotic or psychoanalytic theory, or to produce texts where poetry and theory intermingle in a challenge to established demarcations of genre. Despite their political commitment, such theorists have been curiously willing to accept the established patriarchal canon of 'great' literature, particularly the exclusively male pantheon of French modernism from Lautréamont to Artaud or Bataille. There can be no doubt that the Anglo-American feminist tradition has been much more successful in its challenge to the oppressive social and political strategies of the literary institution.

In the following presentation of French feminist theory I have chosen to focus on the figures of Hélène Cixous, Luce Irigaray and Julia Kristeva. They have been chosen partly because their work is the most representative of the main trends in French feminist theory, and partly because they are more closely concerned with the specific problems raised by women's relation to writing and language than many other feminist theorists in France. Thus I have decided not to discuss the work of women like Annie Leclerc, Michèle Montrelay, Eugénie Lemoine-Luccioni, Sarah Kofman and Marcelle Marini. Many American feminist critics have also found their richest source of inspiration in the theories of Jacques Lacan and Jacques Derrida, but lack of space prevents me from doing justice to the suggestive work of women such as Jane Gallop, Shoshana Felman and Gayatri Spivak.[8]

It has often been claimed that the new generation of French feminist theorists have rejected Simone de Beauvoir's existentialist feminism entirely. Turning away from Beauvoir's liberal desire for equality with men, the argument goes, these feminists have emphasized difference. Extolling women's right to cherish their specifically female values, they reject 'equality' as a covert attempt to force women to become like men.[9] The picture, however, is somewhat more complex than this. For all her existentialism, Simone de Beauvoir remains the great mother-figure for French feminists, and the symbolic value of her public support for the new women's movement was enormous. Nor is it true to say that her brand of socialist feminism remains without followers in France. In 1977 Beauvoir and other women founded the journal *Questions féministes*, which aims to provide a forum precisely for various socialist and anti-essentialist forms of feminism.[10] The Marxist-feminist sociologist Christine Delphy, who holds that women constitute a class, was, for example, one of its founding members.

In spite of her very different theoretical orientation, many of Julia Kristeva's central preoccupations (her desire to theorize a social revolution based on class as well as gender, her emphasis on the construction of femininity) have much more in common with Beauvoir's views than with Hélène Cixous's romanticized vision of the female body as the site of women's writing. Similarly, Luce Irigaray's impressive critique of the repression of woman in patriarchal discourse reads at times like a post-structuralist rewriting of Beauvoir's analysis of woman as man's Other. (Given that Heidegger seems to be the common source of both Lacan's psychoanalytic 'Other', which influenced Irigaray's study, and Beauvoir's existentialist 'Other', this is hardly surprising.) Though existentialism in general was marginalized by the shift to structuralism and post-structuralism in the 1960s, it would seem that nothing dates *The Second Sex* more, in relation to the new women's movement in France, than Beauvoir's rejection of psychoanalysis. Cixous, Irigaray and Kristeva are all heavily indebted to Lacan's (post-) structuralist reading of Freud, and any further investigation of their work therefore requires some knowledge of the most central Lacanian ideas.[11]

JACQUES LACAN

The Imaginary and the Symbolic Order constitute one of the most fundamental sets of related terms in Lacanian theory and are best explained in relation to each other. The Imaginary corresponds to the pre-Oedipal period when the child believes itself to be a part of the mother, and perceives no separation between itself and the world. In the Imaginary there is no difference and no absence, only identity and presence. The Oedipal crisis represents the entry into the Symbolic Order. This entry is also linked to the acquisition of language. In the Oedipal crisis the father splits up the dyadic unity between mother and child and forbids the child further access to the mother and the mother's body. The phallus, representing the Law of the Father (or the threat of castration), thus comes to signify separation and loss to the child. The loss or lack suffered is the loss of the maternal body, and from now on the desire for the mother or the imaginary unity with her must be repressed. This first repression is what Lacan calls the primary repression and it is this primary repression that opens up the unconscious. In the Imaginary there is no unconscious since there is no lack.

The function of this primary repression becomes particularly evident in the child's use of the newly acquired language. When the child learns to say 'I am' and to distinguish this from 'you are' or 'he is', this is equivalent to admitting that it has taken up its allotted place in the Symbolic Order and given up the claim to imaginary identity with all other possible positions. The speaking subject that says 'I am' is in fact saying 'I am he (she) who has lost something' – and the loss suffered is the loss of the imaginary identity with the mother and with the world. The sentence 'I am' could therefore best be translated as 'I am that which I am not', according to Lacan. This re-writing emphasizes the fact that the speaking subject only comes into existence because of the repression of the desire for the lost mother. To speak as a subject is therefore the same as to represent the existence of repressed desire: the speaking subject is lack, and this is how Lacan can say that the subject is that which it is not.

To enter into the Symbolic Order means to accept the phallus as the representation of the Law of the Father. All human culture and all life in society is dominated by the Symbolic Order, and thus by the phallus as the sign of lack. The subject may or may not like this order of things, but it has no choice: to remain in the Imaginary is equivalent to becoming psychotic and incapable of living in human society. In some ways it may be useful to see the Imaginary as linked to Freud's pleasure principle and the Symbolic Order to his reality principle.

This exposition of the transition from the Imaginary to the Symbolic Order requires some further comments. The Imaginary is, for Lacan, inaugurated by the child's entry into the Mirror Stage. Lacan seems to follow Melanie Klein's views of child development in so far as he postulates that the child's earliest experience of itself is one of fragmentation. One might have said that at first the baby feels that its body is in pieces, if this wouldn't give the mistaken impression that the baby *has* a sense of 'its' body at this early stage. Between the ages of 6 to 8 months the baby enters the Mirror Stage. The principal function of the Mirror Stage is to endow the baby with a unitary body image. This 'body ego', however, is a profoundly alienated entity. The child, when looking at itself in the mirror – or at itself on its mother's arm, or simply at another child – only perceives another human being with whom it merges and identifies. In the Imaginary there is, then, no sense of a separate self, since the 'self' is always alienated in the Other. The Mirror Stage thus only allows for *dual* relationships. It is only through the triangulation of this structure, which, as we have seen, occurs when the father intervenes to break up the dyadic unity between mother and child, that the child can take up its place in the Symbolic Order, and thus come to define itself as separate from the other.

Lacan distinguishes between the Other (Autre) with a capital 'O' and the other with a small 'o'. For our purposes it is useful to look at a few of the many different significations these concepts take on in Lacan's texts. The most important usages of the Other are those in which the Other represents language, the site of the signifier, the Symbolic Order or any third party in a triangular structure. Another, slightly different way of putting this is to say that the Other is the locus of the constitution of the subject or the structure that produces the subject. In yet another formulation, the Other is the differential structure of language and of social relations that constitute the subject in the first place and in which it (the subject) must take up its place.

If, for Lacan, it is the entry into the Symbolic Order that opens up the unconscious, this means that it is the primary repression of the desire for symbiotic unity with the mother that *creates* the unconscious. In other words: the unconscious emerges as the result of the repression of desire. In one sense the unconscious *is* desire. Lacan's famous statement 'The unconscious is structured like a language' contains an important insight into the nature of desire: for Lacan, desire 'behaves' in precisely the same way as language: it moves ceaselessly on from object to object or from signifier to signifier, and will never find full and present satisfaction just as meaning can never be seized as full presence. Lacan calls the various objects we invest with our desire (in the symbolic order) *objet a* ('objet petit a' – 'a' here standing for the other (autre) with a small 'a'). There can be no final satisfaction of our desire since there is no final signifier or object that can *be* that which has been lost forever (the imaginary harmony with the mother and the world). If we accept that the end of desire is the logical consequence of satisfaction (if we are satisfied, we are in a position where we desire no more), we can see why Freud, in *Beyond the Pleasure Principle*, posits death as the ultimate object of desire – as Nirvana or the recapturing of the lost unity, the final healing of the split subject.

6

HÉLÈNE CIXOUS

An imaginary utopia

Do I contradict myself?
Very well then . . . I contradict myself;
I am large . . . I contain multitudes.
(Walt Whitman)

It is largely due to the efforts of Hélène Cixous that the question of an *écriture féminine* came to occupy a central position in the political and cultural debate in France in the 1970s. Between 1975 and 1977 she produced a whole series of theoretical (or semi-theoretical) writings, all of which set out to explore the relations between women, femininity, feminism and the production of texts: *La Jeune Née* (in collaboration with Catherine Clément, 1975), 'Le Rire de la Méduse' (1975), translated as 'The laugh of the Medusa' (1976), 'Le Sexe ou la tête?' (1976), translated as 'Castration or decapitation?' (1981) and *La Venue à l'écriture* (1977). These texts are closely interrelated: thus 'Sorties', Cixous's main contribution to *La Jeune Née*, contains long passages of the separately published 'The laugh of the Medusa'. The fact that many central ideas and images are constantly repeated, tends to present her work as a continuum that encourages non-linear forms of reading.[1] Her style is often intensely metaphorical, poetic and explicitly anti-theoretical, and her central images create a dense web of signifiers that offers no obvious edge to seize hold of for the analytically minded critic. It is not easy to operate cuts into, open vistas in or draw maps of Cixous's textual jungle; moreover, the texts themselves make it abundantly clear that this resistance to analysis is entirely intentional. Cixous believes neither in theory nor analysis (though she does practise both – as for instance in her doctoral thesis *L'Exil de James Joyce ou l'art du remplacement* (1968), translated in 1972 as *The Exile of James Joyce or the Art of Replacement*, or in her *Prénoms de personne* from 1974); nor, indeed, does she approve of feminist analytical discourses: she is, after all, the woman who first flatly declared that 'I am not a feminist' (RSH, 482) and later went on to say that 'I do not have to produce theory' (Conley, 152). Accusing feminist researchers in the humanities of turning away from the present towards the past, she rejects their efforts as pure 'thematics'. According to Cixous, such feminist critics will inevitably find themselves caught up in the oppressive network of hierarchical binary oppositions propagated by patriarchal ideology (RSH, 482–3). Hopeful feminist analysts of Cixous's 'literary theory' might just as well not apply.

And yet this is not a wholly accurate picture of Cixous's position. The statements quoted, taken out of their contemporary French context, tend to fix her views in an altogether too rigid mould. Her refusal of the label 'feminism' is first and foremost based on a definition of 'feminism' as a bourgeois, egalitarian demand for women to obtain power in the present patriarchal system; for Cixous, 'feminists' are women who want power, 'a place in the system, respect, social legitimation' (RSH, 482).[2] Cixous does not reject what she prefers to call the women's *movement* (as opposed to the static rigidity of so-called 'feminism'); on the contrary, she is strongly in favour of it, and between 1976 and 1982 published all her works with *des femmes* to demonstrate her political commitment to the anti-patriarchal struggle. To many French feminists, as well as to most feminists outside France, however, this kind of scholastic wrangling over the word 'feminist' would seem to be politically damaging to the women's movement as a whole. In France it caused members of the collective 'politique et psychanalyse' to march in the streets on International Women's Day carrying placards reading 'Down with feminism!', thus generating a considerable amount of hostility and acrimony within the women's movement, much of which was displayed in public. The main effect of the 'anti-feminist' initiative of the 'politique et psychanalyse' group seems to have been the production of a general impression of rancour and disarray within French feminism. I have therefore no intention of following Cixous's lead on this point: according to accepted English usage, her indubitable commitment to the struggle for women's liberation in France, as well as her strong critique of patriarchal modes of thought, make her a feminist. Having said this, it is of course both relevant and necessary to go on to explore the kind of feminist theory and politics she represents.

PATRIARCHAL BINARY THOUGHT

One of Cixous's most accessible ideas is her analysis of what one might call 'patriarchal binary thought'. Under the heading 'Where is she?', Cixous lines up the following list of binary oppositions:

Activity/Passivity
Sun/Moon
Culture/Nature
Day/Night
Father/Mother
Head/Emotions
Intelligible/Sensitive
Logos/Pathos

(JN, 115)

Corresponding as they do to the underlying opposition man/woman, these binary oppositions are heavily imbricated in the patriarchal value system: each opposition can be analyzed as a hierarchy where the 'feminine' side is always seen as the negative, powerless instance. For Cixous, who at this point is heavily indebted to Jacques Derrida's work, Western philosophy and literary thought are and have always been caught up in this endless series of hierarchical binary oppositions that

always in the end come back to the fundamental 'couple' of male/
female.

> Nature/History
> Nature/Art
> Nature/Mind
> Passion/Action

(JN, 116)

These examples show that it doesn't much matter which 'couple' one
chooses to highlight: the hidden male/female opposition with its
inevitable positive/negative evaluation can always be traced as the
underlying paradigm.[3]

In a typical move, Cixous then goes on to locate *death* at work in this
kind of thought. For one of the terms to acquire meaning, she claims, it
must destroy the other. The 'couple' cannot be left intact: it becomes a
general battlefield where the struggle for signifying supremacy is forever re-enacted. In the end, victory is equated with activity and defeat
with passivity; under patriarchy, the male is always the victor. Cixous
passionately denounces such an equation of femininity with passivity
and death as leaving no positive space for woman: 'Either woman is
passive or she doesn't exist' (JN, 118). Her whole theoretical project
can in one sense be summed up as the effort to undo this logocentric[4]
ideology: to proclaim woman as the source of life, power and energy
and to hail the advent of a new, feminine language that ceaselessly
subverts these patriarchal binary schemes where logocentrism colludes
with phallocentrism[5] in an effort to oppress and silence women.

DIFFERENCE

Against any binary scheme of thought, Cixous sets multiple, heterogeneous *difference*. In order to understand her arguments at this point,
however, it is necessary first to examine Jacques Derrida's concept of
difference (or, rather *différance*). Many early structuralists, as for instance
A. J. Greimas in his *Sémantique structurale*, held that meaning is produced
precisely through binary oppositions. Thus in the opposition
masculine/feminine, each term only achieves significance through its

structural relationship to the other: 'masculine' would be meaningless without its direct opposite 'feminine' and vice versa. All meaning would be produced in this way. An obvious counter-argument to this theory is the many examples of adjectives or adverbs of degree (much – more – most, little – less – least), which seem to produce their meaning in relation to the other items in the same series, not in relation to their binary opposites.

Derrida's critique of binary logic, however, is more far-reaching in its implications. For Derrida, meaning (signification) is not produced in the static closure of the binary opposition. Rather it is achieved through the 'free play of the signifier'. One way of illustrating Derrida's arguments at this point is to use Saussure's concept of the *phoneme*, defined as the smallest differential – and therefore signifying – unit in language. The phoneme can in no way be said to achieve signification through binary opposition alone. In itself the phoneme /b/ does not signify anything at all. If we had only one phoneme, there would be no meaning and no language. /b/ only signifies in so far as it is perceived to be *different* from say /k/ or /h/. Thus /bat/:/kat/: /hat/ are all perceived to be different words with different meanings in English. The argument is that /b/ signifies only through a process that effectively *defers* its meaning on to other differential elements in language. In a sense it is the *other* phonemes that enable us to determine the meaning of /b/. For Derrida, signification is produced precisely through this kind of open-ended play between the presence of one signifier and the absence of others.[6]

This, then, is the basic significance of the Derridean term *différance*. Spelt with an 'a' to distinguish it – in writing, not in speech – from the normal French word for difference (*différence*), it acquires the more active sense of the ending '-ance' in French, and can therefore be translated both as 'difference' and as 'deferral' in English. As we have seen, the interplay between presence and absence that produces meaning is posited as one of *deferral*: meaning is never truly present, but is only constructed through the potentially endless process of referring to other, absent signifiers. The 'next' signifier can in a sense be said to give meaning to the 'previous' one, and so on *ad infinitum*. There can thus be no 'transcendental signified' where the process of deferral somehow would come to an end. Such a transcendental signified would have to be meaningful in itself, fully present to itself, requiring no origin and no end other than itself. An obvious example of such a 'transcendental signified' would be the Christian concept of God as Alpha and Omega, the origin of meaning and final end of the world. Similarly, the traditional view of the author as the source and meaning of his or her own text casts the author in the role of transcendental signified.

Derrida's analysis of the production of meaning thus implies a fundamental critique of the whole of Western philosophical tradition, based as it is on a 'metaphysics of presence', which discerns meaning as fully present in the Word (or Logos). Western metaphysics comes to favour speech over writing precisely because speech presupposes the presence of the speaking subject, who thus can be cast as the unitary origin of his or her discourse. The idea that a text is somehow only fully authentic when it expresses the presence of a human subject would be one example of the implicit privileging of voice or speech over writing. Christopher Norris provides an excellent summary of Derrida's views on this point:

> Voice becomes a metaphor of truth and authenticity, a source of self-present 'living' speech as opposed to the secondary lifeless emanations of writing. In speaking one is able to experience (supposedly) an intimate link between sound and sense, an inward and immediate realization of meaning which yields itself up without reserve to perfect, transparent understanding. Writing, on the contrary, destroys this ideal of pure self-presence. It obtrudes an alien, depersonalized medium, a deceiving shadow which falls between intent and meaning, between utterance and understanding. It occupies a promiscuous public realm where authority is sacrificed to the vagaries and whims of textual 'dissemination'. Writing, in short, is a threat to the deeply traditional view that associates truth with self-presence and the 'natural' language wherein it finds expression.
>
> (28)

In order to grasp Derrida's distinction between writing and speech, it is important to realize that writing as a concept is closely related to différance; thus Norris defines writing as the 'endless displacement of meaning which both governs language and places it for ever beyond the reach of a stable, self-authenticating knowledge' (29). Derrida's analysis undermines and subverts the comforting closure of the binary opposition. Throwing the field of signification wide open, writing – textuality – acknowledges the free play of the signifier and breaks open what Cixous perceives as the prison-house of patriarchal language.

ECRITURE FÉMININE 1) MASCULINITY, FEMININITY, BISEXUALITY

Cixous's concept of feminine writing is crucially related to Derrida's analysis of writing as différance. For Cixous, feminine texts are texts that 'work on the difference', as she once put it (RSH, 480), strive in the direction of difference, struggle to undermine the dominant phallogocentric logic, split open the closure of the binary opposition and revel in the pleasures of open-ended textuality.

However, Cixous is adamant that even the term écriture féminine or 'feminine writing' is abhorrent to her, since terms like 'masculine' and 'feminine' themselves imprison us within a binary logic, within the 'classical vision of sexual opposition between men and women' (Conley, 129). She has therefore chosen to speak either of a 'writing said to be feminine' (or masculine) or, more recently, of a 'decipherable libidinal femininity which can be read in writing produced by a male or a female' (Conley, 129). It is not, apparently, the empirical sex of the author that matters, but the kind of writing at stake. She thus warns against the dangers of confusing the sex of the author with the 'sex' of the writing he or she produces:

> Most women are like this: they do someone else's – man's – writing, and in their innocence sustain it and give it voice, and end up producing writing that's in effect masculine. Great care must be taken in working on feminine writing not to get trapped by names: to be signed with a woman's name doesn't necessarily make a piece of writing feminine. It could quite well be masculine writing, and conversely, the fact that a piece of writing is signed with a man's name does not in itself exclude femininity. It's rare, but you can sometimes find femininity in writings signed by men: it does happen.
>
> ('Castration', 52)

Indeed one of the reasons why Cixous is so keen to get rid of the old opposition between masculine and feminine, and even of terms like male or female, is her strong belief in the inherently *bisexual* nature of all human beings. In 'The laugh of the Medusa' (and also in *La Jeune Née* – some of the passages dealing with these themes are reproduced in both texts) she first attacks the 'classic conception of bisexuality', which is 'squashed under the emblem of castration fear and along with the fantasy of a "total" being (though composed of two halves), would do away with the difference' ('Medusa', 254/46, JN, 155). This homogeneous conception of bisexuality is designed to cater for the male fear of the Other (woman) in so far as it allows him to fantasize away the ineluctable signs of sexual difference. Opposing this view, Cixous produces what she calls the *other bisexuality*, which is multiple, variable and ever-changing, consisting as it does of the 'non-exclusion either of the difference or of one sex'. Among its characteristics is the 'multiplication of the effects of the inscription of desire, over all parts of my body and the other body, indeed, this *other bisexuality* doesn't annul differences, but stirs them up, pursues them, increases them' ('Medusa', 254/46, JN, 155).

Today, according to Cixous, it is 'for historico-cultural reasons . . . *women* who are opening up to and benefiting from this vatic bisexuality', or as she puts it: 'In a certain way, "woman" is bisexual; man – it's a secret to no one – being poised to keep glorious phallic monosexuality in view' ('Medusa', 254/46, JN, 156–7). She denies the possibility of ever *defining* a feminist practice of writing:

> For this practice can never be theorized, enclosed, coded – which doesn't mean that it doesn't exist. But it will always surpass the discourse that regulates the phallocentric system; it does and will take place in areas other than those subordinated to philosophico-theoretical domination.
>
> ('Medusa', 253/45)

She does, however, supply a definition that not only echoes Derrida's concept of *écriture*, but also seems to be identical with her own concept of the 'other bisexuality':

> To admit that writing is precisely working (in) the in-between, inspect-
> ing the process of the same and of the other without which nothing
> can live, undoing the work of death – to admit this is first to want the
> two, as well as both, the ensemble of one and the other, not fixed in
> sequence of struggle and expulsion or some other form of death but
> infinitely dynamized by an incessant process of exchange from one
> subject to another.

('Medusa', 254/46)

Here it would seem that for Cixous writing *as such* is bisexual. However,
she also argues that, at least at present, *women* (which clearly indicates
biological females as opposed to males) are much more likely to be
bisexual in this sense than men. *Bisexual* writing is therefore overwhelmingly likely to be *women's* writing, though some exceptional men
may in certain cases manage to break with their 'glorious monosexuality'
and achieve bisexuality as well. This position is clearly logical enough.
In keeping with this anti-essentialist vein, Cixous, in 'The laugh of the
Medusa', argues that in France only Colette, Marguerite Duras and Jean
Genet really qualify as feminine (or bisexual) writers. In *La Jeune Née* she
also points to Shakespeare's Cleopatra and Kleist's Penthesilea as
powerful representations of the feminine libidinal economy.

So far, then, Cixous's position would seem to constitute a forceful
feminist appropriation of Derridean theory. Anti-essentialist and anti-
biologistic, her work in this field seems to displace the whole feminist
debate around the problem of women and writing away from an
empiricist emphasis on the sex of the author towards an analysis of the
articulations of sexuality and desire within the literary text itself.
Unfortunately, this is not the whole story. As we shall see, Cixous's
theory is riddled with contradictions: every time a Derridean idea is
evoked, it is opposed and undercut by a vision of woman's writing
steeped in the very metaphysics of presence she claims she is out to
unmask.

THE GIFT AND THE PROPER

Cixous's distinction between the gift and the proper provides the first
signs of a slippage away from Derridean anti-essentialism. Though she

refuses to accept the binary opposition of femininity and masculinity, Cixous repeatedly insists on her own distinction between a 'masculine' and a 'feminine' libidinal economy. These are marked, respectively, by the Realm of the Proper and the Realm of the Gift. Masculinity or masculine value systems are structured according to an 'economy of the proper'. Proper – property – appropriate: signalling an emphasis on self-identity, self-aggrandizement and arrogative dominance, these words aptly characterize the logic of the proper according to Cixous. The insistence on the proper, on a proper return, leads to the masculine obsession with classification, systematization and hierarchization. Her attack on class has little to do with the proletariat:

> There's work to be done against *class*, against categorization, against classification – classes. 'Doing classes' in France means doing military service. There's work to be done against military service, against all schools, against the pervasive masculine urge to judge, diagnose, digest, name . . . not so much in the sense of the loving precision of poetic naming as in that of the repressive censorship of philosophical nomination/conceptualization.
>
> ('Castration', 51)

Theoretical discourse is in other words inherently oppressive, a result of masculine libidinal investment. Even the question 'What is it?' is denounced as a sign of the masculine impulse to imprison reality in rigid hierarchical structures:

> As soon as the question 'What is it?' is posed, from the moment a question is put, as soon as a reply is sought, *we are already caught up in masculine interrogation*. I say 'masculine interrogation': as we say so-and-so was interrogated by the police.
>
> ('Castration', 45)

Linking the Realm of the Proper to a 'masculine libidinal economy' is of course impeccably anti-biologistic. Defining it essentially as the male fear of castration (here labelled the 'masculine fear of the loss of the attribute'), however, is not:

One realizes that the Realm of the Proper is erected on the basis of a fear which as a matter of fact is typically masculine: a fear of expropriation, of separation, of the loss of the attribute. In other words: the impact of the threat of castration.

(JN, 147)

In her article 'Castration or decapitation?' Cixous elaborates on this idea of the proper as proper to the *male*:

Etymologically, the 'proper' is 'property', that which is not separable from me. Property is proximity, nearness: we must love our neighbors, those close to us as ourselves: we must draw close to the other so that we may love him/her, because we love ourselves most of all. The Realm of the Proper, culture, functions by the appropriation articulated, set in to play, by man's classic fear of seeing himself expropriated, seeing himself deprived ... by his refusal to be deprived, in a state of separation, by his fear of losing the prerogative, fear whose response is all of History. Everything must return to the masculine. 'Return': the economy is founded on a system of returns. If a man spends and is spent, it's on condition that his power returns.

('Castration', 50)

The now male Realm of the Proper seems a textbook illustration of Derrida's 'metaphysics of presence' (see also JN, 146–7). One might therefore expect its opponent, the Realm of the Gift, to illustrate a more deconstructive approach. Cixous distinguishes between two different kinds of gifts. First there is the gift as it is perceived by men. For the male psyche, to receive a gift is a dangerous thing:

For the moment you receive something you are effectively 'open' to the other, and if you are a man you have only one wish, and that is hastily to return the gift, to break the circuit of an exchange that could have no end ... to be nobody's child, to owe no one a thing.

('Castration', 48)

In the Realm of the Proper, the gift is perceived as establishing an inequality – a difference – that is threatening in that it seems to open up an imbalance of *power*. Thus the act of giving becomes a subtle means of aggression, of exposing the other to the threat of one's own superiority. The woman, however, gives without a thought of return. *Generosity* is one of the most positive words in Cixous's vocabulary:

> If there is a 'propriety of woman', it is paradoxically her capacity to depropriate unselfishly, body without end, without appendage, without principal 'parts'. . . . This doesn't mean that she's an undifferentiated magma, but that she doesn't lord it over her body or her desire. . . . Her libido is cosmic, just as her unconscious is worldwide. Her writing can only keep going, without ever inscribing or discerning contours, daring to make these vertiginous crossings of the other(s) ephemeral and passionate sojourns in him, her, them, whom she inhabits long enough to look at from the point closest to their unconscious from the moment they awaken, to love them at the point closest to their drives; and then further, impregnated through and through with these brief, identificatory embraces, she goes and passes into infinity. She alone dares and wishes to know from within, where she, the outcast, has never ceased to hear the resonance of fore-language. She lets the other language speak – the language of 1,000 tongues which knows neither enclosure nor death.
>
> ('Medusa', 259–60/50, JN, 161–2)

The slippage from 'feminine' to 'female' (or 'woman') can here clearly be seen. Elaborating on her theme, Cixous adds that woman gives because she doesn't suffer from castration anxiety (fear of expropriation, as she often puts it) in the way men do. In spite of its clear biologism, the Realm of the Gift does seem to correspond fairly closely to a Derridean definition of writing: the feminine/female libidinal economy is open to difference, willing to be 'traversed by the other', characterized by spontaneous generosity; the Realm of the Gift isn't really a realm at all, but a deconstructive space of pleasure and orgasmic interchange with the other. There is no doubt that Cixous explicitly tries to give her exposition of the two 'libidinal economies' a Derridean profile. She warns, for instance, that 'one must beware of blindly or complaisantly falling into essentialist ideological interpretations' (JN, 148), and refuses to accept any theory that posits a thematic origin of power and sexual difference. This effort is, however, not only partly undercut by her biologism: in her evocations of a specifically female writing she seems actively intent on promoting an utterly metaphysical case.

ECRITURE FÉMININE   2) THE SOURCE AND THE VOICE

In *La Jeune Née* Cixous first reiterates her refusal to theorize about writing and femininity, only to indicate that she is, after all, willing to open up a discussion on the matter. What she describes as some tentative comments turn out to be no less than a lyrical, euphoric evocation of the essential bond between feminine writing and the mother as source and origin of the voice to be heard in all female texts. Femininity in writing can be discerned in a privileging of the *voice*: 'writing and voice . . . are woven together' (JN, 170). The speaking woman is entirely her voice: 'She physically materializes what she's thinking; she signifies it with her body' ('Medusa', 251/44, JN, 170). Woman, in other words, is wholly and physically present in her voice – and writing is no more than the extension of this self-identical prolongation of the speech act. The voice in each woman, moreover, is not only her own, but springs from the deepest layers of her psyche: her own speech becomes the echo of the primeval *song* she once heard, the voice the incarnation of the 'first voice of love which all women preserve alive . . . in each woman sings the first nameless love' (JN, 172). It is, in short, the Voice of the Mother, that omnipotent figure that dominates the fantasies of the pre-Oedipal baby: 'The Voice, a song before the Law, before the breath [le souffle] was split by the symbolic, reappropriated into language under the authority that separates. The deepest, most ancient and adorable of visitations' (JN, 172).

Finding its source in a time before the Law came into being, the voice is nameless: it is placed firmly in the pre-Oedipal stage before the child acquires language, and thereby the capacity to name itself and its objects. The voice is the mother and the mother's body: 'Voice: inexhaustible milk. She has been found again. The lost mother. Eternity: it is the voice mixed with milk' (JN, 173). The speaking/writing woman is in a space outside time (eternity), a space that allows no naming and no syntax. In her article 'Women's Time', Julia Kristeva has argued that syntax is constitutive of our sense of chronological time by the very fact that the order of words in a sentence marks a temporal sequence: since subject, verb, object cannot be spoken simultaneously, their utterance necessarily cuts up the temporal continuum of 'eternity'. Cixous, then, presents this nameless pre-Oedipal space filled with mother's milk and honey as the source of the song that resonates through all female writing.

The fact that women have this 'privileged relationship to the voice' is due to their relative lack of defence-mechanisms: 'No woman ever heaps up as many defences against their libidinal drives as a man does' (JN, 173). Whereas man represses the mother, woman doesn't (or hardly does): she is always close to the mother as the source of good. Cixous's mother-figure is clearly what Melanie Klein would call the Good Mother: the omnipotent and generous dispenser of love, nourishment and plenitude. The writing woman is thus immensely powerful: hers is a *puissance féminine* derived directly from the mother, whose giving is always suffused with strength: 'The more you have, the more you give the more you are, the more you give the more you have' (JN, 230).

The most explicit description of an actual example of female writing produced under the Sign of the Voice, Cixous's article on the Brazilian writer Clarice Lispector, stresses both her openness and generosity ('L'approche', 410, n. 7), and, in a deeply un-Derridean passage, her capacity to endow words with their essential meaning:

> There is almost nothing left of the sea but a word without water: for we have also translated the words, we have emptied them of their speech, dried, reduced and embalmed them, and they cannot any longer remind us of the way they used to rise up from the things as the peal of their essential laughter . . . But a clarice voice only has to say: the sea, the sea, for my keel to split open, the sea is calling me, sea! calling me, waters!
>
> ('L'approche', 412)

In her article on Marguerite Duras and Hélène Cixous, Christiane Makward distinguishes between twelve different kinds of style in Cixous's novel LA: seven poetic and five narrative levels. Five of the seven poetic levels of style can be characterized as in some way biblical, liturgical or mythological. These high poetic inflections find their way into Cixous's more theoretical writings as well. *La Venue à l'écriture* opens on the biblical note of 'In the beginning I adored' (VE, 9). In this text, as in many others, Cixous casts herself, if not as a goddess, at least as a prophetess – the desolate mother out to save her people, a feminine Moses as well as the Pharaoh's daughter:

> The tears I shed at night! The waters of the world flow from my eyes, I wash my people in my despair, I bathe them, I lick them with my love, I go to the banks of the Nile to gather the peoples abandoned in wicker baskets; for the fate of the living I have the tireless love of a mother, that is why I am everywhere, my cosmic belly, I work on my world-wide unconscious, I throw death out, it comes back, we begin again, I am pregnant with beginnings.
>
> (VE, 53)

Laying claim to all possible subject positions, the speaking subject can indeed proudly proclaim herself as a 'feminine plural' (VE, 53), who through reading and writing partakes of divine eternity:

> The book – I could reread it with the help of memory and forgetting. Start over again. From another perspective, from another and yet another. Reading, I discovered that writing is endless. Everlasting. Eternal.
>   Writing or God. God the writing. The writing God.
>
> (VE, 30)

Cixous's predilection for the Old Testament is obvious, but her taste for classical antiquity is no less marked. Her capacity for identification seems endless: Medusa, Electra, Antigone, Dido, Cleopatra – in her imagination she has been them all. In fact, she declares that 'I am myself the earth, everything that happens on it, all the lives that live me there in my different forms' (VE, 52–3). This constant return to biblical and mythological imagery signals her investment in the world of myth: a world that, like the distant country of fairy tales is perceived as pervasively meaningful, as closure and unity. The mythical or religious discourse presents a universe where all difference, struggle and discord can in the end be satisfactorily resolved. Her mythical and biblical allusions are often accompanied by – or interspersed with – 'oceanic' water imagery, evoking the endless pleasures of the polymorphously perverse child:

> We are ourselves sea, sand, coral, sea-weed, beaches, tides, swimmers, children, waves. . . . Heterogeneous, yes. For her joyous benefits she is erogeneous; she is the erotogeneity of the heterogeneous: airborne swimmer, in flight, she does not cling to herself: she is dispersible, prodigious, stunning, desirous and capable of others, of the other woman that she will be, of the other woman she isn't, of him, of you.
>
> ('Medusa', 260/51)

For Cixous, as for countless mythologies, water is the feminine element *par excellence*: the closure of the mythical world contains and reflects the comforting security of the mother's womb. It is within this space that Cixous's speaking subject is free to move from one subject position to another, or to merge oceanically with the world. Her vision of female writing is in this sense firmly located within the closure of the Lacanian Imaginary: a space in which all difference has been abolished.

Such an emphasis on the Imaginary can explain why the writing woman enjoys such extraordinary freedom in Cixous's universe. In the Imaginary mother and child are part of a fundamental unity: they are *one*. Protected by the all-powerful Good Mother, the writing woman can always and everywhere feel deeply secure and shielded from danger: nothing will ever harm her, distance and separation will never disable her. Shakespeare's Cleopatra becomes an example of such triumphant femininity:

> The intelligence, the strength of Cleopatra appear particularly in the work she accomplishes – a work of love – on the distance, the gap, the separation: she only evokes the gap in order to fill it to overflowing, never tolerating a separation that could harm the lover's body.
>
> (JN, 235)

Antony and Cleopatra can risk anything since they will always save each other from harm: the self can be abandoned precisely in so far as it can always be recuperated. If Cixous's poetic discourse often acquires a haunting beauty in its evocations of the paradise of childhood, it does so not least through its refusal to accept the loss of that privileged realm. The mother's voice, her breasts, milk, honey and female waters are all invoked as part of an eternally present space surrounding her and her readers.

This Imaginary world, however, is not flawlessly homogeneous. We have already seen that the female Realm of the Gift is one of a deconstructive openness to difference, and though Cixous describes female writing largely in terms of the abiding presence of the Mother's Voice, she *also* presents the voice as an operation of detachment, splitting and fragmentation (JN, 174–5). In *La Venue à l'écriture*, the desire to write is first of all presented as a *force* that she cannot consciously control: her body contains 'another limitless space' (VE, 17) that demands she give it a written form. Fighting against it – no blackmail will make her yield – she nevertheless feels a secret fascination for this overpowering *souffle*:

> Because it [il] was so strong and so furious, I loved and feared this breath. To be lifted up one morning, snatched off the ground, swung in the air. To be surprised. To find in myself the possibility of the unexpected. To fall asleep as a mouse and wake up as an eagle! What delight! What terror. And I had nothing to do with it, I couldn't help it.
> (VE, 18)

This passage, particularly with its French use of the masculine pronoun *il* for *souffle* throughout, reads somewhat like a transposition of a well-known feminine rape fantasy: *il* sweeps the woman off her feet; terrified and delighted she submits to the attack. Afterwards she feels stronger and more powerful (like an *eagle*), as if she had integrated the power of the phallus during the scene. And as in all rape fantasies, the delight and *jouissance* spring from the fact that the woman is blameless: she didn't want it, so cannot be guilty of any illicit desires. (Needless to say, this description only concerns rape *fantasies* and has nothing whatsoever to do with the reality of rape.) This is a brilliant evocation of women's relationship to language in the phallocentric symbolic order:

if a woman is to write, she will feel guilty about her desire to obtain mastery over language unless she can fantasize away her own responsibility for such an unspeakable wish. But Cixous's account of the text as rape also constitutes the background for her vision of the text as the Good Mother: 'I was eating the texts, I was sucking, licking, kissing them, I am the innumerable child of their multitudes' (VE, 19). A Kleinian analysis of the mother's nipple as a pre-Oedipal penis image might illuminate this striking oral relationship to the text she reads – which, after all, also must be the text she guiltily hopes some day to write: 'Write? I was dying to do it for love, to give the writing what it [elle] had given to me. What an ambition! What impossible happiness. Feed my own mother. Give her, in her turn, my milk? Mad imprudence' (VE, 20). The text as mother becomes the text as rape, in a sequence of rapid transformations:

> I said 'write French'. One writes *in*. Penetration. Door. Knock before you enter. Absolutely forbidden. . . . How could I not have wanted to write? When books took me, transported me, pierced me to the depths of my soul, let me feel their disinterested potency? . . . When my being was being populated, my body traversed and fertilized, how could I have closed myself up in silence?
>
> (VE, 20–1)

Mother-text, rape-text; submission to the phallic rule of language as differential, as a structure of gaps and absences; celebration of writing as the realm of the omnipotent mother: Cixous will always incorporate differences, juxtapose contradictions, work to undo gaps and distinctions, fill the gap to overflowing, and happily integrate both penis and nipple.

IMAGINARY CONTRADICTIONS

Fundamentally contradictory, Cixous's theory of writing and femininity shifts back and forth from a Derridean emphasis on textuality as difference to a full-blown metaphysical account of writing as voice, presence and origin. In a 1984 interview, Cixous shows herself to be perfectly aware of these contradictions:

> If I were a philosopher, I could never allow myself to speak in terms of presence, essence, etc., or of the meaning of something. I would be capable of carrying on a philosophical discourse, but I do not. I let myself be carried off by the poetic word.
>
> (Conley, 151–2)

In a reference to Derrida's *Of Grammatology* she explains the relationship (or lack of it) between Derrida's concept and her own:

> In *Grammatology*, he treats of writing in general, of the text in general. When I talk about writing, that is not what I am talking about. One must displace at the moment; I do not speak about the concept of writing the way Derrida analyzes it. I speak in a more idealistic fashion. I allow this to myself; I disenfranchise myself from the philosophical obligations and corrections, which does not mean that I disregard them.
>
> (Conley, 150–1)

Though her own theoretico-poetic style apparently strives to undo the opposition, Cixous's work bases itself on a conscious distinction between 'poetry' and 'philosophy' (a distinction Derrida himself might well want to deconstruct). How then can we best illuminate Cixous's seeming passion for contradiction? Some might claim it as a cunning strategy intended to prove her own point: by refusing to accept the Aristotelian logic that excludes A from also being not A, Cixous deftly enacts her own deconstruction of patriarchal logic. But this argument assumes that Cixous's point really *is* a deconstructive one, and thus overlooks the many passages that present a thoroughly metaphysical position. From a psychoanalytic perspective, it would seem that her textual manoeuvres are designed to create a space in which the *différance* of the Symbolic Order can co-exist peacefully with the closure and identity of the Imaginary. Such co-existence, however, covers only *one* aspect of Cixous's vision: the level on which the female essence is described in deconstructive terms, as for instance in the Realm of the Gift, or in those passages relating to the heterogeneous multiplicity of the 'new bisexuality'. But we have seen that even the openness of the Giving Woman or the plurality of bisexual writing are characterized by biblical, mythological or elemental imagery that returns us to a preoccupation with the Imaginary. The difference and diversity in question thus seems more akin to the polymorphous perversity of the pre-Oedipal child than to the metonymic displacements of desire in the symbolic order. The 'new bisexuality' in particular seems ultimately an imaginary closure that enables the subject effortlessly to shift from masculine to feminine subject positions. In the end, then, the contradictions of Cixous's discourse can be shown to be contained and resolved within the secure haven of the Imaginary. Her supreme disregard for 'patriarchal' logic is not after all an indication of her Barthesian concern for the liberation of the reader, though at first glance Barthes's description of readerly *jouissance* might seem strikingly appropriate to our experience of Cixous's texts:

> Imagine someone (a kind of monsieur Teste in reverse) who abolishes within himself all barriers, all classes, all exclusions, not by syncretism but by simple discard of that old spectre: *logical contradiction*; who mixes every language, even those said to be incompatible; who silently accepts every charge of illogicality, of incongruity; who remains passive in the face of Socratic irony (leading the interlocutor to the supreme disgrace: *self-contradiction*) and legal terrorism (how much penal evidence is based on a psychology of consistency!) . . . Now this anti-hero exists: he is the reader of the text at the moment he takes his pleasure.
>
> (*The Pleasure of the Text*, 3)

The difference between the *jouissance* of the Barthesian reader and Cixous's text is that whereas the former signals absolute loss, a space in which the subject fades to nothing, the latter will always finally gather up its contradictions within the plenitude of the Imaginary.

POWER, IDEOLOGY, POLITICS

Cixous's vision of feminine/female writing as a way of re-establishing a spontaneous relationship to the physical *jouissance* of the female body may be read positively, as a utopian vision of female creativity in a truly non-oppressive and non-sexist society. Indeed a marked emphasis on the Imaginary is common in utopian writing. In 1972, for example, Christiane Rochefort published a powerful feminist utopian novel, *Archaos ou le jardin étincelant*, which in its narrative mode exhibits striking parallels to Cixous's preoccupation with the Imaginary as a utopian solution to the problem of desire.

Utopian thought has always been a source of political inspiration for feminists and socialists alike.[7] Confidently assuming that change is both possible and desirable, the utopian vision takes off from a negative analysis of its own society in order to create images and ideas that have the power to inspire to revolt against oppression and exploitation. Influenced by Frankfurt School theorists such as Ernst Bloch and Herbert Marcuse, Arnhelm Neusüss has shown that anti-utopian arguments tend to be advanced from the right as part of a strategy aiming at the neutralization or recuperation of the revolutionary contents of the utopian dream. The most pernicious and widespread of the various anti-utopian arguments described by Neusüss is the one we might call the 'realist' approach. While tending towards rationalism in its underestimation of the possible political impact of human desire, the 'realist' position also objects to the contradictory nature of many utopias: there is no point in taking them seriously, the argument goes, since they are so illogical that anybody could tell that they would never work in real life anyway.

Rejecting this position, Neusüss sees the contradictions embodied by so many utopias as a justification of their social critique: signalling the repressive effects of the social structures that gave rise to the utopia in the first place, its gaps and inconsistencies indicate the pervasive nature of the authoritarian ideology the utopian thinker is trying to undermine. If Neusüss is right, the utopian project will always be marked by conflict and contradiction. Thus, if we choose to read Cixous as a utopian feminist, at least some of the contradictory aspects of her texts may be analysed as structured by the conflict between an already contradictory patriarchal ideology and the utopian thought that struggles to free itself from that patriarchal stranglehold. But if it is true that her contradictions are finally gathered up into the homogenizing space of the Imaginary, then they are more likely also to constitute a flight from the dominant social reality.

In a critique of Norman O. Brown, Herbert Marcuse, himself a vigorous defender of utopianism, describes Brown's utopian ideal as an effort towards the 'restoration of original and total unity: unity of male and female, father and mother, subject and object, body and soul – abolition of the self, of mine and thine, abolition of the reality principle, of all boundaries' (234). While a positive effort towards abolishing existing repressive structures, Brown's Cixous-like cultivation of the pleasure principle is for Marcuse unsatisfactory precisely because it is located exclusively within the Imaginary:

> The roots of repression are and remain real roots; consequently, their eradication remains a real and rational job. What is to be abolished is not the reality principle; not everything, but such particular things as business, politics, exploitation, poverty. Short of this recapture of reality and reason Brown's purpose is defeated.
>
> (235)

It is just this absence of any specific analysis of the material factors preventing women from writing that constitutes a major weakness of Cixous's utopia. Within her poetic mythology, writing is posited as an absolute activity of which all women qua women automatically partake. Stirring and seductive though such a vision is, it can say nothing of the actual inequities, deprivations and violations that women, as social beings rather than as mythological archetypes, must constantly suffer.

Marcuse's insistence on the need to recapture reason and reality for the utopian project is a timely one. In her eagerness to appropriate imagination and the pleasure principle for women, Cixous seems in danger of playing directly into the hands of the very patriarchal ideology she denounces. It is, after all, patriarchy, not feminism, that insists on labelling women as emotional, intuitive and imaginative, while jealously converting reason and rationality into an exclusively male preserve. Utopias, then, challenge us both on the poetic and the political level. It is therefore understandable that, while acknowledging the rhetorical power of Cixous's vision, feminists should nevertheless want to examine its specific political implications in order to discover exactly what it is we are being inspired to do.

But is it justifiable to force Cixous's writing into a political straitjacket, particularly when, as she argues, she is concerned less with politics than with poetry?

I would lie if I said that I am a political woman, not at all. In fact, I have to assemble the two words, political and poetic. Not to lie to you, I must confess that I put the accent on the poetic. I do it so that the political does not repress, because the political is something cruel and hard and so rigorously real that sometimes I feel like consoling myself by crying and shedding poetic tears.

(Conley, 139–40)

The distance posited here between the political and the poetic is surely one that feminist criticism has consistently sought to undo. And though Cixous seems to be claiming 'poetic' status for her own texts, this does not prevent her from writing directly about power and ideology in relation to feminist politics. According to Cixous, ideology is a 'kind of immense membrane that envelops everything. A skin that we must know is there even if it covers us like a net or a closed eyelid' (JN, 266–7). This view of ideology as total closure parallels Kate Millett's vision of it as a monolithic unity, and suffers from exactly the same defects.[8] How could we ever discover the nature of the ideology that surrounds us if it were entirely consistent, without the slightest contradiction, gap or fissure that might allow us to perceive it in the first place? Cixous's image of ideology recreates the closure of the mythological universe in which she constantly seeks refuge from the contradictions of the material world. When Catherine Clément accuses Cixous of speaking at a non-political level, she pinpoints precisely this problem in Cixous's work:

C[atherine Clément]. I must admit that your sentences are devoid of reality for me, except if I take what you say in a poetic sense. Give me an example. . . . Your level of description is one where I don't recognize any of the things I think in political terms. It's not that it's 'false', of course not. But it's described in terms which seem to me to belong to the level of myth or poetry; it all indicates a kind of desiring, fictive, collective subject, a huge entity which alternately is free and revolutionary or enslaved, asleep or awake. . . . Those are not subjects existing in reality.

(JN, 292–3)

Equally disturbing is Cixous's discourse on power. In an interview in *La Revue des sciences humaines*, she distinguishes between one 'bad' and one 'good' kind of power:

> I would indeed make a clear distinction when it comes to the kind of power that is the will to supremacy, the thirst for individual and narcissistic satisfaction. That power is always a power over others. It is something that relates back to government, control, and beyond that, to despotism. Whereas if I say 'woman's powers', first it isn't *one* power any longer, it is multiplied, *there is more than one* (therefore it is not a question of centralization – that destroys the relation with the unique, that levels everything out) and it is a *question of power over oneself*, in other words of a relation not based on mastery but on availability [disponibilité].
>
> (RSH, 483–4)

Both kinds of power are entirely personal and individual: the struggle against oppression seems to consist in a lame effort to affirm a certain heterogeneity of woman's powers (a heterogeneity belied by the singular of 'woman'), which in any case seems to come down to claiming that a strong woman can do what she likes. In French, the term *disponibilité* carries a heavy bourgeois-liberal heritage, partly because of its central status in the works of André Gide. To be 'available' can thus imply a certain egoistic desire to be 'ready for anything', not to be bogged down in social and interpersonal obligations. Cixous's global appeal to 'woman's powers' glosses over the real differences among women, and thus ironically represses the true heterogeneity of women's powers.

Cixous's poetic vision of writing as the very enactment of liberation, rather than the mere vehicle of it, carries the same individualist overtones. Writing as ecstatic self-expression casts the individual as supremely capable of liberating herself back into union with the primeval mother. For Cixous, women seem to relate to each other exclusively on a dualistic (I/you) pattern: as mothers and daughters, lesbian couples or in some variety of the teacher/student or prophet/disciple relationship. The paucity of references to a wider community of women or to collective forms of organization is not only conspicuous in the work of a feminist activist, but indicative of Cixous's general inability to represent the non-Imaginary, triangulated structures of desire typical of social relationships.

Given the individualist orientation of Cixous's theory, it is perhaps not surprising that some of her students should present her politics as a simple prolongation of her persona, as in Verena Andermatt Conley's account of Cixous's appearance at the University of Paris at Vincennes ('a school notorious for a certain regal squalor'):

> Cixous used to enter the complex in a dazzling ermine coat whose capital worth most probably surpassed the means of many in the classroom. Her proxemics marked a progressive use of repression. As a replica of Bataille's evocation of Aztec ceremony, she surged from the context of the cheaply reinforced concrete of classroom shelters. She then became a surplus value and a zero-degree term, the sovereign center of a decorous, eminently caressive body where her politics splintered those of an archaic scene in which the king would have his wives circulate about him.
>
> (Conley, 80)

Ermine as emancipation: it is odd that the women of the Third World have been so ludicrously slow to take up Cixous's sartorial strategy.

For a reader steeped in the Anglo-American approach to women and writing, Hélène Cixous's work represents a dramatic new departure. In spite of the vicissitudes that the concept undergoes in her texts, writing for her is always in some sense a libidinal object or act. By enabling feminist criticism to escape from a disabling author-centred empiricism, this linking of sexuality and textuality opens up a whole new field of feminist investigation of the articulations of desire in language, not only in texts written by women, but also in texts by men.

As we have seen, a closer investigation of her work has to confront its intricate webs of contradiction and conflict, where a deconstructive view of textuality is countered and undermined by an equally passionate presentation of writing as a female essence. If these contradictions in the end can be seen to be abolished within the Imaginary, this in its turn raises a series of political problems for the feminist reader of Cixous: marred as much by its lack of reference to recognizable social structures as by its biologism, her work nevertheless constitutes an invigorating utopian evocation of the imaginative powers of women.

7

PATRIARCHAL REFLECTIONS

Luce Irigaray's looking-glass

Luce Irigaray's monumental doctoral thesis *Spéculum de l'autre femme* ('Speculum of the other woman', 1974) led to her immediate expulsion from Lacan's *École freudienne* at Vincennes. It is tempting to see this dramatic enactment of patriarchal power as clear evidence of the book's intrinsic feminist value: any text that annoys the Fathers to such an extent must be deserving of feminist support and applause. But if *Spéculum* has been heavily criticized by mainstream Lacanians,[1] it has also been the object of much acrimonious feminist debate. At times it looks as if the only thing Irigaray's various critics agree on is that the book is worth all the attention they so liberally bestow on it.[2]

Irigaray's first book, *Le Langage des déments* ('The language of dementia', 1973), was a study of the patterns of linguistic disintegration in senile dementia: a field that at first glance may seem far removed from the feminist preoccupations of *Spéculum*. For readers of the latter, the conclusions of *Le Langage des déments* nevertheless take on a familiar ring: 'Spoken more than speaking, enunciated more than enunciating, the demented person is therefore no longer really an active subject of the enunciation . . . He is only a possible mouthpiece for previously pronounced enunciations' (351). This passive, imitative or mimetic relationship to the structures of language is strikingly similar to the way in which, according to *Spéculum*, women relate to phallocratic discourse.

In 1977, *Spéculum* was followed by a collection of texts entitled *Ce sexe qui n'en est pas un* ('This sex which is not one'). Though a much shorter and in many ways more accessible volume than its predecessor, *Ce sexe* alone does not provide a wholly accurate impression of Irigaray's theories. Its relationship to *Spéculum* is too close for that; consisting partly of poetic or semi-theoretical texts, partly of traditionally theoretical pieces, even containing transcripts of seminars on the previous book, *Ce sexe* develops many of the central concerns first launched in *Spéculum* in a way that often requires some knowledge of that context.

Since 1977, Irigaray has published two shorter texts that focus on the relationship between mother and daughter: *Et l'une ne bouge pas sans l'autre* ('And the one doesn't stir without the other', 1979) and *Le Corps-à-corps avec la mère* ('Clasped with the mother', 1981). Continuing the critique of the Western philosophical tradition begun in *Spéculum*, she has also, in *Amante marine de Friedrich Nietzsche* ('Friedrich Nietzsche's marine lover', 1980), published a poetico-theoretical reading of Nietzsche focused on his use of water imagery. Water was the element most alien to Nietzsche, Irigaray argues, and therefore the one with the highest 'deconstructive' potential for his particular discourse. *Passions élémentaires* ('Elementary passions', 1982) represents a return to the basic themes of *Spéculum* and *Ce sexe*, this time in the form of a poetic monologue where the speaking subject, a woman, chants her pleasure in the natural elements and her passion for her male lover. *L'Oubli de l'air chez Martin Heidegger* ('Forgetting the air: the case of Martin Heidegger', 1983) provides a critique of Heidegger based on his repression of air imagery where his discourse soon becomes the point of departure for Irigaray's own analysis of air as a female element that deconstructs the simplistic divisions of male thought. In *La Croyance même* ('Even belief'/'The same belief'/ 'The belief in the Same', 1983), a short lecture on Freud's analysis of the *fort-da* game, Irigaray argues that Freud ignores the child's crucial relationship to the air as the only element that enables it to come to terms with the loss of the placenta and the mother's body. My presentation of Irigaray's feminist theory will nevertheless centre on the two texts in which she develops the main tenets of her feminist analysis: first and foremost *Spéculum de l'autre femme*, but also *Ce sexe qui n'en est pas un*.[3]

SPECULUM

Given her background in psycholinguistics and her profession as a psychoanalyst, it may seem odd that Irigaray chose to present herself for the prestigious and highly scholarly French *doctorat d'Etat* in philosophy. For Irigaray herself, the choice of philosophy was an obvious one: in our culture, philosophy has enjoyed the status of 'master discourse', as she puts it: 'It is indeed philosophical discourse one must question and disturb because it lays down the law for all the others, because it constitutes the discourse of discourses' (S, 72). If the first part of *Spéculum* contains an abrasive critique of Freud's theory of femininity, it is precisely a critique that consists in showing how Freud's otherwise revolutionary discourse submits to the misogynist rules of Western philosophical tradition as far as femininity is concerned. Irigaray, unlike Kate Millett, has no wish to reject psychoanalysis as a useless or inherently reactionary theory:

> It is more a question of displaying its still inoperative implications. To say that although Freudian theory certainly gives us something that can shake the whole philosophical order of discourse, it paradoxically remains submissive to that order when it comes to the definition of sexual difference.
>
> (CS, 70)

Spéculum de l'autre femme is divided into three main parts: the first, 'La tache aveugle d'un vieux rêve de symétrie' ('The blindspot of an old dream of symmetry'),[4] consists of a remarkably detailed reading of Freud's statements about femininity, principally in his lecture on femininity in the *New Introductory Lectures on Psychoanalysis*, but also in other texts where he approaches the question of female psychosexual development and/or sexual difference. The second part, 'Spéculum', contains a series of readings of Western philosophers from Plato to Hegel, as well as some chapters presenting Irigaray's own theoretical positions. The third part, 'L'μστερα de Platon' (Plato's hustera [cave]) is a close reading of Plato's cave parable in the light of the preceding critique of Western philosophy. Though this part of Irigaray's book will not be a central concern in the following presentation, it should be said that it is a highly sophisticated feminist deconstruction or critique of patriarchal discourse and provides much inspiration for women in search of new models for resourceful political readings of literary or philosophical texts.

The composition of *Spéculum*, however, is more intricate than this description suggests. According to the OED, a *speculum* is, among other things:

1. (Surg.) instrument for dilating cavities of human body for inspection. 2. mirror, usu. of polished metal e.g. ~*um metal* (alloy of copper and tin), esp. in reflecting telescope.

Its original Latin meaning was mirror, from *specere*, 'to look'. As we shall see, the word itself already condenses several of the main themes of Irigaray's analysis. But the construction of her book also strives to enact a speculum-like structure. By starting with Freud and ending with Plato, Irigaray reverses the normal historical order in an action which resembles that of the concave mirror which is the speculum gynaecologists use to inspect the 'cavities' of the female body. To make this point Irigaray quotes Plato, who writes of the concave mirror: 'Turned horizontally in relation to the face, this concavity will make it seem as if it was turned upside down' (S, 183).[5] But the concave mirror is also a focal point, a lens that can concentrate light-rays so as to 'shed light on the secrets of caves' and to 'pierce the mystery of the woman's sex' (S, 182). The speculum is a male instrument for the further penetration of the woman, but it is also a hollow surface, like the one it seeks to explore. A speculum entering and illuminating the woman's vagina can only do so by virtue of its own concave shape; it is, paradoxically, through the imitation of its object that the speculum objectifies it in the first place.

Irigaray's *Spéculum de l'autre femme* is shaped like a hollow surface on the model of the speculum/vagina. At the centre, the section entitled 'Spéculum' is framed by the two massive sections on Freud and Plato respectively; it is as if the more fragmentary middle section sinks between the solid, upright volumes of the master thinkers. Within the middle section, this framing technique is both repeated and reversed: Irigaray presents her own discourse in the first and last chapters, so framing the seven middle sections dealing mainly with male philosophers from Plato to Hegel. The structure is the same, but the relation between male and female has been reversed. Within the seven middle sections, yet another framing device seems to be at work: after two highly critical chapters on Plato and Aristotle, there follows a chapter 'on' Plotinus consisting entirely of excerpts from his *Enneads*. In this context (or, more appropriately, *con-texte* – *con* in French means 'cunt'), seemingly straightforward quotation undermines Plotinus's discourse: these are, after all, no longer Plotinus's words, but Irigaray's expert (literal) imitation of them. Her perfect mimicry manages subtly to expose his narcissistic phallocentrism.

This imitative chapter is placed immediately before a more traditional analysis of Descartes, which in its turn is followed by a fascinating reading of the discourse of female mystics entitled 'La mystérique'. A chapter on Kant and one on Hegel precede the last chapter, where Irigaray's own theoretical discourse takes over again. Since the Descartes chapter is at the exact centre of the 'Spéculum' section (and of the whole book), the effect is again one of a frame. Surrounded by the chapter 'on' Plotinus, entitled 'La mère de glace' ('The ice/mirror mother/ ocean'), and the chapter on 'La mystérique' ('The mystic/hysterical/mysterious woman'), Descartes sinks into the innermost cavity of the book: in a phallic, instrumental move the speculum illuminates him while simultaneously pointing to his position within the feminine, as if to demonstrate Irigaray's contention that woman constitutes the silent ground on which the patriarchal thinker erects his discursive constructs. It is perhaps not a coincidence that it is precisely Descartes, the rationalist theoretician of the body/mind split who still exercises a profound influence on French intellectual life, that Irigaray chooses to encompass in this way.

SPECUL(ARIZ)ATION AND MIMETICISM

Irigaray's style owes much to the techniques of deconstructive criticism. Since most of her points in *Spéculum* are made through the skilful
manipulation of quotations and her own comments, it is difficult to
convey the flavour of her writing without quoting her as extensively as
she quotes Freud or Plato. In the following presentation, in order to
highlight her approach as well as to focus on some of its more problematic aspects, I have chosen to concentrate mainly on her critique of
Freud and her analysis of female mysticism.

Freud

Freud's lecture on femininity takes as its point of departure the mystery
of woman. Aiming to shed some scientific light on the dark continent
of femininity, Freud starts by posing the question 'What is woman?'
His use of light/darkness imagery, Irigaray argues, already reveals his
subservience to the oldest of 'phallocratic' philosophical traditions.
The Freudian theory of sexual difference is based on the visibility of
difference: it is the eye that decides what is clearly true and what isn't.[6]
Thus the basic fact of sexual difference for Freud is that the male has an
obvious sex organ, the penis, and the female has not; when he looks at
the woman, Freud apparently sees nothing. The female difference is
perceived as an absence or negation of the male norm.

This point is crucial for Irigaray's argument: in our culture, woman
is outside representation: 'The feminine has consequently had to be
deciphered as forbidden [*interdit*], in between signs, between the real-
ized meanings, between the lines' (S, 20). She is, Irigaray claims, the
negative required by the male subject's 'specularization'. 'Specializa-
tion' suggests not only the mirror-image that comes from the visual
penetration of the speculum inside the vagina; it also hints at a basic
assumption underlying all Western philosophical discourse: the necessity of postulating a subject that is capable of reflecting on its own being.
The philosophical meta-discourse is only made possible, Irigaray
argues, through a process whereby the speculating subject contem-
plates himself; the philosopher's *speculations* are fundamentally narcissistic. Disguised as reflections on the general condition of man's Being,

Woman is
~~Not~~
does not
allow Philosophical
reflex

the philosopher's thinking depends for its effect on its specularity (its self-reflexivity); that which exceeds this reflective circularity is that which is _unthinkable_. It is this kind of specul(ariz)ation Irigaray has in mind when she argues that Western philosophical discourse is incapable of representing femininity/woman other than as the negative of its own reflection.

This logic of the _same_, according to Irigaray, can be traced in Freud's account of the development of sexual difference. For Freud there is no sexual difference in the pre-Oedipal stage: through the oral, anal and phallic phases, the little girl is no different from the little boy. It is at the moment of Oedipal crisis that the crucial change in the little girl's orientation occurs: whereas the little boy continues to take his mother as his object, the little girl has to turn from her pre-Oedipal attachment to the mother and take her father as love-object instead. This shift is not only hard to explain; it is also difficult to accomplish: it is even dubious, as Freud freely admits, whether most women really manage wholly to relinquish their pre-Oedipal attachment and develop a fully 'mature' femininity.[7] Irigaray's argument is that Freud was forced into developing this incoherent, contradictory and misogynist theory of femininity by his unwitting subservience to the specular logic of the same. For his theory amounts to casting the little girl as fundamentally the _same_ as the little boy: she is, as Irigaray caustically puts it, not a little girl but a little man. In the phallic stage the clitoris is perceived by the little girl herself as an inferior penis, Freud argues, thus deftly suppressing the intrusion of difference into his reflections. This visual perception of deficiency on the part of the little girl is the fundamental assumption behind the controversial Freudian theory of penis envy.

To hold that the woman first sees her clitoris as a small penis and then decides that she has already been castrated, can be read, Irigaray argues, in a manner reminiscent of Kate Millett, as a projection of the _male_ fear of castration: as long as the woman is thought to envy the man his penis, he can rest secure in the knowledge that he must have it after all. The function of female penis envy, in other words is to bolster up the male psyche. 'To castrate the woman is to inscribe her in the law of the _same_ desire, of desire for the same', Irigaray comments (CS 64). The thinking man not only projects his desire for a reproduction of himself (for his own reflection) on to the woman; he is, according to Irigaray, incapable of thinking outside this specular structure. Thus the female castration complex becomes still more of the Same. Woman is not only the Other, as Simone de Beauvoir discovered, but is quite specifically man's Other: his negative or mirror-image. This is why Irigaray claims that patriarchal discourse situates woman *outside* representation: she is absence, negativity, the dark continent, or at best a lesser man. In patriarchal culture the feminine *as such* (and whatever that might be will be the subject of further discussion) is repressed; it returns only in its 'acceptable' form as man's specularized Other.

Castrated Penis

Freud's own texts, particularly 'The uncanny', theorize the *gaze* as a phallic activity linked to the anal desire for sadistic mastery of the object.[8] The specularizing philosopher is the potent master of his insight; as the example of Oedipus demonstrates, the fear of blindness is the fear of castration. As long as the master's scopophilia (i.e. 'love of looking') remains satisfied, his domination is secure. No wonder then that the little girl's *rien à voir* ('nothing to be seen') is threatening to the male sexual theorist. As Jane Gallop has reminded us, the Greek *theoria* comes from *theoros*, 'spectator', from *thea*, 'a viewing' (Gallop, 58). If our theorist were to think the feminine, he might find himself tumbling from his phallic lighthouse into the obscurity of the dark continent.

Irigaray demonstrates the importance of the look (or gaze) in Freudian theory in her characteristic style: posing as an inquisitive little girl daring to challenge the father's authority, she slowly unravels his constructions. Quoting Freud's graphic account of the little girl's desire to have a penis instead of her own inferior clitoris, she finds herself musing over its implications:

> Not a bad dramatization. And one could imagine or dream up scenes of this kind of recognition taking place in the consulting room of Freud the psychoanalyst. Although the question of their respective relations to the look, to the eye and to sexual difference ought to crop up since he tells us that one has to see in order to believe. Should one then not see [*ne pas voir*] in order to review [*revoir*] the matter? Probably. . . . But still. . . . Unless all the power and the difference (?) there has shifted into the look(s)? So that Freud can see without being seen? Without being seen seeing? Not even questioned as to

the power of his gaze? Is that where the envy of the omnipotence of this look, of this knowledge, comes from? Power over the genitals/woman/sex [*le sexe*]. Envy, jealousy of the penis-eye, the phallic look? He would see that I haven't got it, would decide as much in a twinkling of an eye. I can't see whether he's got one. Whether he's got more than I have. But he will let me know. Castration displaced? *Right away the look would be at stake.* One really ought not to forget what 'castration', or the knowledge of/about castration owes to the look, in Freud's case at any rate. The look at stake/in play [*en jeu*] as always. . . .

But the little girl, the woman, would have *nothing* to show. She would expose, exhibit the possibility of a *nothing to be seen*.

(S, 53)

The woman, for Freud as for other Western philosophers, becomes a mirror for his own masculinity. Irigaray concludes that in our society representation, and therefore also social and cultural structures, are products of what she sees as a fundamental hom(m)osexualité. The pun in French is on *homo* ('same') and *homme* ('man'): the male desire for the same. The pleasure of self-representation, of her desire for the same, is denied woman: she is cut off from any kind of pleasure that might be specific to her.

Caught in the specular logic of patriarchy, woman can choose either to remain silent, producing incomprehensible babble (any utterance that falls outside the logic of the same will by definition be incomprehensible to the male master discourse), or to enact the specular representation of herself as a lesser male. The latter option, the woman as mimic, is, according to Irigaray, a form of hysteria. The hysteric mimes her own sexuality in a masculine mode, since this is the only way in which she can rescue something of her own desire. The hysteric's dramatization (or *mise en scène*) of herself is thus a result of her exclusion from patriarchal discourse. No wonder, then, that phallocracy perceives the hysteric's symptoms as an inauthentic copy of an original drama relating to the male (her desire to seduce her own father). And no wonder, either, that Freud's treatment of little Hans exhibits a startling degree of identification between the analyst and his little clone, whereas his analysis of Dora bears all the marks of his own fear of losing control and succumbing to the terrifying castrating void (the *rien à voir*) exhibited in Dora's hysteria.[9]

Mysticism

The first chapter of the middle section of *Spéculum* starts with an examination of the concept of subjecthood: 'All theories of the subject have always been appropriated to the "masculine". When the woman submits to them, she unknowingly gives up her specific relationship to the imaginary' (S, 165). Subjectivity is denied to women, Irigaray claims, and this exclusion guarantees the constitution of relatively stable objects for the (specularizing) subject. If one imagined that the woman imagines anything at all, the object (of speculation) would lose its stability and thus unsettle the subject itself. If the woman cannot represent the ground, the earth, the inert or opaque matter to be appropriated or repressed, how can the subject be secure in its status as a subject? Without such a non-subjective foundation, Irigaray argues, the subject would not be able to construct itself at all. The blindspot of the master thinker's discourse is always woman: exiled from representation, she constitutes the ground on which the theorist erects his specular constructs, but she is therefore also always the point on which his erections subside.

If, as Irigaray argues, the mystical experience is precisely an experience of the loss of subjecthood, of the disappearance of the subject/object opposition, it would seem to hold a particular appeal for women, whose very subjectivity is anyway being denied and repressed by patriarchal discourse. Though not all mystics were women, mysticism nevertheless seems to have formed the one area of high spiritual endeavour under patriarchy where women could and did excel more frequently than men. For Irigaray, mystical discourse is the 'only place in Western history where woman speaks and acts in such a public way' (S, 238). Mystical imagery stresses the night of the soul: the obscurity and confusion of consciousness, the loss of subjecthood. Touched by the flames of the divine, the mystic's soul is transformed into a fluid stream dissolving all difference. This orgasmic experience eludes the specular rationality of patriarchal logic: the sadistic eye/I must be closed; if he is to discover the delights of the mystic, the philosopher must escape from his philosophy in a 'blind flight out of the closed chamber of philosophy, of the speculative matrix where he has enclosed himself in order clearly to consider the all' (S, 239). The ecstatic vision (from the Greek *ex*, 'outside', and *histēmi*, 'place') is one that seems to escape specularity. If women sought and obtained ecstasy (or *ex-stase* as Irigaray spells it) it was because they were already outside scopic representation; the mystic's ignorance, her utter abjection before the divine, was part and parcel of the feminine condition she was brought up in: '[In this system] the poorest in science and the most ignorant were the most eloquent and the richest in revelations. Historically therefore women. Or at least the "feminine"' (S, 239).

But what if there is a mirror/speculum hidden at the centre even of this bottomless abyss? The mystics do after all frequently use the image of the *burning mirror* (or *miroir ardent*) to describe certain aspects of their experience. Though the burning mirror does seem to be the one mirror that reflects nothing, the phrase nevertheless signals a move towards the specularization of the mystical experience. This, Irigaray argues, is due to the theologization of mysticism. Theology makes mysticism teleological by providing it with a (masculine) object: the mystic experience comes to reflect God in all his glory, and is thus reduced to yet another example of male specularization where the hom(m)osexual economy of God desiring his Son (and vice versa) becomes reflected in the nothingness (*néant*) in the mystic's heart. But, as Irigaray notes, this effort towards male recuperation of mysticism may well backfire: God, even in theology, exceeds all representation; the human incarnation of the Son is the 'most feminine of all men' (S, 249). Christ undoes specular logic, and the mystic's self-abasement re-enacts his passion: victory is to be attained precisely in the deepest of all abysses. The mystic's self-representation escapes the specular logic of non-representation imposed on her under patriarchy. Modelled on the image of the suffering Christ, the mystic's often self-inflicted abjection paradoxically opens up a space where her own pleasure can unfold. Though still circumscribed by male discourse, this is a space that nevertheless is vast enough for her to feel no longer exiled.

The inexorable logic of the Same

Irigaray's exaltation of mysticism may come as a surprise to many feminists. Her argument, after all, is that the mystic experience allows femininity to discover itself precisely through the deepest acceptance of patriarchal subjection. But mysticism is nevertheless a special case. Irigaray is perhaps not claiming that all women really are mystics at heart, simply that under patriarchy, mysticism (like hysteria a few centuries later) offers women a real if limited possibility of discovering some aspects of a pleasure that might be specific to their libidinal drives. But how can we know what 'woman's pleasure' is or might be? If specular logic dominates all Western theoretical discourse, how can Luce Irigaray's doctoral thesis escape its pernicious influence? If her study of the mystics leads her to take pleasure in the image of woman imitating the sufferings of Christ, is she not caught in a logic that requires her to produce an image of woman that is exactly the same as the specular constructions of femininity in patriarchal logic? In a perceptive passage, Shoshana Felman has raised a series of pertinent questions that pinpoint the problems Irigaray faces when she presents herself as a woman theorist or a theorist of woman:

> If 'the woman' is precisely the Other of any conceivable Western theoretical locus of speech, how can the woman as such be speaking in this book? Who is speaking here, and who is asserting the other-ness of the woman? If, as Luce Irigaray suggests, the woman's silence or the repression of her capacity to speak, are constitutive of philo-sophy and of theoretical discourse as such, from what theoretical locus is Luce Irigaray herself speaking in order to develop her own theoretical discourse about women? Is she speaking *as* a woman, or *in the place of* the (silent) woman, *for* the woman, *in the name of* the woman? Is it enough to *be* a woman in order to *speak as* a woman? Is 'speaking as a woman' a fact determined by some biological *condition* or by a strategic, theoretical *position*, by anatomy or by culture? What if 'speaking as a woman' were not a simple 'natural' fact, could not be taken for granted? (Felman, 3)

Though Irigaray never actually acknowledges the fact, her analysis of male specular logic is deeply indebted to Derrida's critique of Western philosophical tradition. If the textual analyses of *Spéculum* are inspiring examples of anti-patriarchal criticism, it is because Irigaray knows how to expose the flaws and inconsistencies of phallocentric discourse. It is Irigaray's work, not least, that Gayatri Spivak has in mind when she commends certain aspects of French feminism for its resourceful approach to the ruling forms of discourse:

> In the long run, the most useful thing that a training in French feminism can give us is politicized and critical examples of 'Symptomatic reading' not always following the reversal-displacement technique of a deconstructive reading. The method that seemed recuperative when used to applaud the avant-garde is productively conflictual when used to expose the ruling discourse.
>
> (Spivak, 177)

But if, as Derrida has argued, we are still living under the reign of metaphysics, it is impossible to produce new *concepts* untainted by the metaphysics of presence. This is why he sees deconstruction as an activity rather than as a new 'theory'. Deconstruction is in other words self-confessedly parasitic upon the metaphysical discourses it is out to subvert. It follows that any attempt to formulate a general theory of femininity will be metaphysical. This is precisely Irigaray's dilemma: having shown that so far femininity has been produced exclusively in relation to the logic of the Same, she falls for the temptation to produce her own positive theory of femininity. But, as we have seen, to define 'woman' is necessarily to essentialize her.

Irigaray herself is aware of this problem and struggles hard to avoid falling into the essentialist trap. Thus at one point she explicitly rejects any attempt to define 'woman'. Women ought not to try to become the equals of men, she writes:

> They must not pretend to rival them by constructing a logic of the feminine that again would take as its model the onto-theological. They must rather try to disentangle this question from the economy of the logos. They must therefore not pose it in the form 'What is woman?' They must, through repetition-interpretation of the way in which the

feminine finds itself determined in discourse – as lack, default, or as mime and inverted reproduction of the subject – show that on the feminine side it is possible to *exceed* and *disturb* this logic.

(CS, 75–6)

One way of disrupting patriarchal logic in this way is through mimeticism, or the mimicry of male discourse. We have already seen how Irigaray herself uses such a mimetic strategy with considerable success in her chapter 'on' Plotinus. In reply to Shoshana Felman's questions one might well claim that Irigaray, in *Spéculum*, is speaking as a woman miming male discourse. Thus the academic apparatus of the doctoral thesis, still perceptible in *Spéculum*, may be an ironic gesture: coming from a woman arguing the case Irigaray is presenting, her impeccably theoretical discourse is displaced and relocated as a witty parody of patriarchal modes of argument. If as a woman under patriarchy, Irigaray has, according to her own analysis, no language of her own but can only (at best) imitate male discourse, her own writing must inevitably be marked by this. She cannot pretend to be writing in some pure feminist realm outside patriarchy: if her discourse is to be received as anything other than incomprehensible chatter, she must copy male discourse. The feminine can thus only be read in the blank spaces left between the signs and lines of her own mimicry.

But if this is the case, then Irigaray's mimicry in *Spéculum* becomes a conscious acting out of the hysteric (mimetic) position allocated to all women under patriarchy. Through her acceptance of what is in any case an ineluctable mimicry, Irigaray doubles it back on itself, thus raising the parasitism to the second power. Hers is a theatrical staging of the mime: miming the miming imposed on woman, Irigaray's subtle specular move (her mimicry mirrors that of all women) intends to undo the effects of phallocentric discourse simply by *overdoing* them. Hers is a fundamentally paradoxical strategy that reflects that of the mystics: if the mystic's abject surrender becomes the moment of her liberation, Irigaray's undermining of patriarchy through the overmiming of its discourses may be the one way out of the straitjacket of phallocentrism.

The question, however, is whether and under what circumstances this strategy actually works. One way of studying the effects of mimicry in Irigaray's texts is by looking at her use of analogic or comparative arguments. In *Spéculum* she sees analogic reading as a typical expression of the male passion for the Same:

> The interpreters of dreams themselves had only one desire: to find the same. Everywhere. And it was certainly insistent. But from that moment, didn't *interpretation* also get caught up in this dream of an identity, equivalence, analogy, homology, symmetry, comparison, imitation etc. which would be more or less *right*, that is to say, more or less *good*?
>
> (S, 27)

We might therefore expect Irigaray to mime this kind of thinking through equivalence and homology in order to undo its stabilizing, hierarchical effects. But this is not always what happens. In her essay 'Le marché des femmes' ('Women on the market', CS, 165–85), she claims that 'Marx's analysis of the commodity as the basic form of capitalist wealth can . . . be understood as an interpretation of the status of woman in so-called patriarchal societies' (CS, 169). According to Irigaray, woman can in the first instance be read both as use value and as exchange value: she is 'nature' (use value), which is subjected to human labour and transformed into exchange value. It is in her role as exchange value that she can be analyzed as a commodity on the market: her value resides not in her own being but in some transcendental standard of equivalence (money, the phallus). In a significant footnote Irigaray defends the case for her extensive use of analogy in this essay:

> And didn't Aristotle, a 'giant thinker' according to Marx, determine the relationship between form and matter through an analogy with the relationship between male and female? To return to the question of sexual difference is therefore rather a new passage [*retraversée*] through analogism.
>
> (CS, 170)

In other words: when she as a woman employs a particular rhetorical strategy, that strategy is immediately placed in a new (nonmale?) context with different political effects. Thus the question of the political efficacy of female mimicry comes to hinge on the power of the new context provided by the woman's miming. If the strategy proved to be highly successful in the case of Plotinus, it was due to the anti-sexist analysis provided immediately before the imitative chapter 'on' Plotinus. But in the case of Marx, it is difficult to see how Marxist discourse is undermined by her mimicry. Rather it would seem that Irigaray is using Marx's analysis in an entirely conventional way: apparently delighted at having discovered the Same, she proceeds to develop the suggestive implications of her analogy rather than to expose the flaws of what presumably is Marx's phallocentric discourse. Her essay thus reads more like a vindication of Marx's insights than as a critique of his specular logic. In another essay, 'La "mécanique" des fluides' ('The "mechanics" of fluids', CS, 103–16), the analogic mimicry seems to fail entirely as a political device. Here the analogy lies between femininity and masculinity on the one hand and fluids and solids on the other. Phallocratic science is unable to account for the movement of fluids, Irigaray claims, just as it cannot account for woman. Thus woman's language, she argues, behaves just like the fluids scorned by male physicists:

> It is continuous, compressible, dilatable, viscous, conductive, diffusible. . . . It never ends, it is powerful and powerless through its resistance to that which can be counted, it takes its pleasure and suffers through its hypersensitivity to pressure; it changes – in volume or strength, for instance – according to the degree of heat, it is in its physical reality determined by the friction between two infinitely neighbouring forces – a dynamics of proximity and not of property.
>
> (CS, 109–10)

Here her mimicry of the patriarchal equation between woman and fluids (woman as the life-giving sea, as the source of blood, milk and amniotic fluid . . .) only succeeds in reinforcing the patriarchal discourse. This failure is due to her figuring of fluidity as a positive alternative to the depreciating scopophilic constructions of the patriarchs. The mimicry fails because it ceases to be perceived as such: it is no longer merely a mockery of the absurdities of the male, but a perfect reproduction of the logic of the Same. When the quotation marks, so to speak, are no longer apparent, Irigaray falls into the very essentialist trap of defining woman that she set out to avoid.

Mimicry or impersonation clearly cannot be rejected as unsuitable for feminist purposes, but neither is it the panacea Irigaray occasionally takes it to be. Shoshana Felman's questions (Is Irigaray speaking *as* a woman? For the woman? In the place of the woman?) cannot be outflanked by a theory of female mimicry of male discourse. Felman is insistently raising the question of positionality. From which (political) position is Irigaray speaking? It is in her failure to confront this question that Irigaray's own blindspot appears. For what she seems not to see is that sometimes a woman imitating male discourse is just a woman speaking like a man: Margaret Thatcher is a case in point. It is the *political context* of such mimicry that is surely always decisive.

WOMANSPEAK: A TALE TOLD BY AN IDIOT?

We have seen how Irigaray's attempt to establish a theory of femininity that escapes patriarchal specul(ariz)ation necessarily lapses into a form of essentialism. Her efforts to provide woman with a 'gallant representation of her own sex' are likewise doomed to become another enactment of the inexorable logic of the Same (S, 130). It is interesting to note that in spite of certain divergences, Irigaray's vision of femininity and of feminine language remains almost indistinguishable from Cixous's. Irigaray's theory of 'woman' takes as its starting point a basic assumption of analogy between woman's psychology and her 'morphology' (Gr. *morphē*, 'form'), which she rather obscurely takes to be different from her anatomy. Woman's form is repressed by patriarchal phallocentrism, which systematically denies woman access to her own pleasure: female *jouissance* cannot even be thought by specular logic. Male pleasure, she claims, is seen as monolithically unified, represented as analogous with the phallus, and it is this mode that is forcibly imposed upon women. But as she argues in the article 'This sex which is not one', woman's sex is not one: her sexual organs are composed of many different elements (lips, vagina, clitoris, cervix, uterus, breasts) and her *jouissance* is therefore multiple, non-unified, endless:

A woman 'touches herself' constantly without anyone being able to forbid her to do so, for her sex is composed of two lips which embrace continually. Thus, within herself she is already two – but not divisible into ones – who stimulate each other.

(MC, 100, CS, 24)[10]

Woman therefore gives privilege not to the visual, but to the touch:

The prevalence of the gaze, discrimination of form, and individualization of form is particularly foreign to female eroticism. Woman finds pleasure more in touch than in sight and her entrance into a dominant scopic economy signifies, once again, her relegation to passivity: she will be the beautiful object. . . . In this system of representation and desire, the vagina is a flaw, a hole in the representation's scopophilic objective. It was admitted already in Greek statuary that this 'nothing to be seen' must be excluded, rejected from such a scene of representation. Woman's sexual organs are simply absent from this scene: they are masked and her 'slit' is sewn up.

(MC, 101, CS, 25–6)

Irigaray posits femininity as plural and multiple: woman's economy is not specular in the sense that it does not work on an either/or model. Her sexuality is inclusive: she doesn't after all have to choose between clitoral and vaginal pleasure, as Freud assumed, but can have it both ways. Like Cixous, Irigaray holds that woman is situated outside all 'property':

Property and propriety are undoubtedly rather foreign to all that is female. At least sexually. *Nearness*, however, is not foreign to woman, a nearness so close that any identification of one or the other, and therefore any form of property, is impossible. Woman enjoys a closeness with the other which is *so near she cannot* possess it, any more than she can possess herself.

(MC, 104–5, CS, 30)

Irigaray's analysis of femininity is closely bound up with her idea of a specific woman's language which she calls 'le parler femme', or 'womanspeak'. 'Le parler femme' emerges spontaneously when women speak together, but disappears again as soon as men are present. This is one of the reasons why Irigaray sees women-only groups as an indispensable step towards liberation, though she does warn against these groups becoming simple reversals of the existing order: 'If their goal is to reverse the existing order – even if that were possible – history would simply repeat itself and return to phallocratism, where neither women's sex, their imaginary, nor their language can exist' (MC, 106, CS, 32). Otherwise, the first thing to be said about "womanspeak" is that nothing can be said *about* it: 'I simply cannot give you an account of "womanspeak": one speaks it, it cannot be meta-spoken' (CS, 141), she once declared in a seminar. She nevertheless provides a definition of woman's *style* in terms of its intimate connection with fluidity and the sense of touch:

> This 'style' does not privilege the gaze but takes all figures back to their *tactile* birth. There she re-touches herself without ever constituting herself, or constituting herself in another kind of unity. *Simultaneity* would be her 'property'. A property that never fixes itself in the possible identity of the self to another form. Always *fluid* without forgetting the characteristics of fluids which are so difficult to idealize: this friction between two infinitely neighbouring forces that creates their dynamics. Her 'style' resists and explodes all firmly established forms, figures, ideas, concepts.
>
> (CS, 76)

The most famous – or infamous – passage in 'This sex which is not one' is one in which she returns to the question of woman and her language in order to show how woman *escapes* patriarchal logic. The question is whether the attempt backfires, showing that Irigaray's 'woman' is a product of the same patriarchal logic:

Multiple Femininity

> 'She' is indefinitely other in herself. That is undoubtedly the reason she is called temperamental, incomprehensible, perturbed, capricious – not to mention her language in which 'she' goes off in all directions and in which 'he' is unable to discern the coherence of any meaning. Contradictory words seem a little crazy to the logic of reason, and inaudible for him who listens with ready-made grids, a code prepared

in advance. In her statements – at least when she dares to speak out – woman retouches herself constantly. She just barely separates from herself some chatter, an exclamation, a half-secret, a sentence left in suspense – when she returns to it, it is only to set out again from another point of pleasure or pain. One must listen to her differently in order to hear an *'other meaning' which is constantly in the process of weaving itself, at the same time ceaselessly embracing words and yet casting them off to avoid becoming fixed, immobilized*. For when 'she' says something, it is already no longer identical to what she means. Moreover, her statements are never identical to anything. Their distinguishing feature is one of contiguity. They touch (*upon*). And when they wander too far from this nearness, she stops and begins again from 'zero': her body-sex organ.

It is therefore useless to trap women into giving an exact definition of what they mean, to make them repeat (themselves) so that the meaning will be clear. They are already elsewhere than in the discursive machinery where you claim to take them by surprise. They have turned back within themselves, which does not mean the same thing as 'within yourself'. They do not experience the same interiority that you do and which perhaps you mistakenly presume they share. 'Within themselves' means *in the privacy of this silent, multiple, diffuse tact*. If you ask them insistently what they are thinking about, they can only reply: nothing. Everything.

(MC, 103, CS, 28–9)

Again, Shoshana Felman's question about the positionality of Irigaray's discourse springs to mind. For who is speaking here? Who is this speaking subject who addresses herself to a masculine (?) 'you', reducing 'women' to the anonymous objects of her discourse? ('They do not experience the same interiority that you do'.) Is the speaking subject a woman? And if so, how can she presume to speak anything but 'contradictory words [which] seem a little crazy to the logic of reason'? For Monique Plaza at least, the answer is clear: Irigaray is a patriarchal wolf in sheep's clothing:

Luce Irigaray pursues her construction, cheerfully prescribing woman's social and intellectual existence from her 'morphology' . . . .

Her method remains fundamentally naturalist and completely under the influence of patriarchal ideology. For one cannot describe morphology as though it presented itself to perception, without ideological mediation. The positivism of the Irigarayan construction is here matched by a flagrant empiricism. . . . Every mode of existence which ideology imputes to women as part of the Eternal Feminine and which for a moment Luce Irigaray seemed to be posing as the result of oppression, is from now on woman's essence, woman's being. All that 'is' woman comes to her in the last instances from her anatomical sex, which touches itself all the time. Poor woman.

(Plaza, 31–2)

IDEALISM AND AHISTORICISM

Writing in *Questions féministes*, the journal founded by Simone de Beauvoir, Monique Plaza criticizes Irigaray from a materialist perspective. Reading *Spéculum*, it is easy to believe that power is a question of philosophy alone. But, as Plaza argues, women's oppression is by no means purely ideological or discursive:

The notion of 'Woman' is imbricated in the materiality of existence: women are *enclosed* in the family circle and work *for free*. The patriarchal order is not only ideological, it is not in the simple domain of 'value'; it constitutes a specific, material oppression. To reveal its existence and lay bare its mechanisms, it is necessary to bring down the idea of 'woman', that is, to denounce the fact that the category of sex has invaded gigantic territories for oppressive ends.

(Plaza, 26)

Domestic economy does not figure alongside the specular and photologic economies Irigaray studies in *Spéculum*: the material conditions of women's oppression are spectacularly absent from her work.[11] But without specific material analysis, a feminist account of power cannot transcend the simplistic and defeatist vision of male power pitted against female helplessness that underpins Irigaray's theoretical investigations. The paradox of her position is that while she strongly defends the idea of 'woman' as multiple, decentred and undefinable, her unsophisticated approach to patriarchal power forces her to analyze 'woman' (in the singular) throughout as if 'she' were indeed a simple, unchanging unity, always confronting the same kind of monolithic patriarchal oppression. For Irigaray, patriarchy would seem a univocal, non-contradictory force that prevents women from expressing their real nature. And one of the reasons why she fails in practice to carry through her theoretical programme of recognizing the multiplicity of women (rather than of 'woman') is her refusal to consider power as anything but a male obsession. For her, power is something women are *against*: 'I for my part refuse to shut myself up in one single "group" within the women's liberation movement. Particularly if it falls into the trap of wanting to exercise power' (CS, 161). But women's relationship to power is not exclusively one of victimization. Feminism is not simply about rejecting power, but about transforming the existing power structures – and, in the process, transforming the very *concept* of power itself. To be 'against' power is not to abolish it in a fine, post-1968 libertarian gesture, but to hand it over to somebody else.

Linked to the absence of a materialist analysis of power is the lack of historical orientation displayed in *Spéculum*. It is not that the book is unhistorical – on the contrary, it shows how some patriarchal discursive strategies have remained constant from Plato to Freud. Also, there is a good case for arguing that *some aspects* of women's oppression in the Western world may well have remained relatively unchanged over the centuries, and Irigaray does an important job in trying to expose certain recurrent patriarchal strategies. *Spéculum* is ahistorical, rather, in that it implies that this is *all* there is to say about patriarchal logic. Irigaray signally fails to study the historically changing impact of patriarchal discourses on women. Thus *Spéculum* cannot really address the question of historical specificity: what makes women's lives in the post-Freudian era different from the lives of Plato's mother and sisters? If the dominant discourses have barely changed, why aren't we still living in the gynaeceum?

Irigaray's failure to consider the historical and economic specificity of patriarchal power, along with its ideological and material contradictions, forces her into providing exactly the kind of metaphysical definition of woman she declaredly wants to avoid. She thus comes to analyze 'woman' in idealist categories, just like the male philosophers she is denouncing. Her superb critique of patriarchal thought is partly undercut by her attempt to name the feminine. If, as I have previously argued, all efforts towards a definition of 'woman' are destined to be essentialist, it looks as if feminist theory might thrive better if it abandoned the minefield of femininity and femaleness for a while and approached the questions of oppression and emancipation from a different direction. This, to a great extent, is what Julia Kristeva has tried to do. But it is also paradoxically one of the reasons why Kristeva, as opposed to Cixous and Irigaray, cannot strictly speaking be considered a purely feminist theorist.

8

MARGINALITY AND SUBVERSION

Julia Kristeva

L'ETRANGÈRE

When Roland Barthes in 1970 sat down to write an enthusiastic review of one of Kristeva's early works, he chose to call it 'L'étrangère', which translates approximately as 'the strange, or foreign, woman'. Though an obvious allusion to Kristeva's Bulgarian nationality (she first arrived in Paris in 1966), this title captures what Barthes saw as the unsettling impact of Kristeva's work. 'Julia Kristeva changes the place of things', Barthes wrote, 'she always destroys the latest preconception, the one we thought we could be comforted by, the one of which we could be proud . . . she subverts authority, the authority of monologic science' (19).[1] Barthes's implication is that Kristeva's alien discourse under-mines our most cherished convictions precisely because it situates itself outside our space, knowingly inserting itself along the borderlines of our own discourse. No wonder, then, that Kristeva defiantly assumes her disturbing position in the very first sentence of Séméiotiké: 'To work on language, to labour in the materiality of that which society regards as a means of contact and understanding, isn't that at one stroke to declare oneself a stranger (*étranger*) to language?'[2] And no wonder either that I, as an alien to this country and this language, have found precisely in Kristeva, another *étrangère*, the most challenging point of departure for my own feminist enquiry.

If the introductory chapter of this book drew on some of her ideas in order to stage a confrontation with several currents in Anglo-American feminist criticism, I would like to repeat that manoeuvre here and examine Anglo-American feminist linguistics from a position informed by Kristevan semiotics. This approach has the added advantage of presenting the *étrangère* in terms of more familiar theories, but it also runs the risk of unwittingly domesticating the alien. It is therefore important to realize that Kristevan theory is only partly and fragmentarily commensurate with what, in spite of the strong Australian influence in this particular field, I have chosen to call Anglo-American feminist linguistics. I should also make it clear that Kristeva herself, to my knowledge, has never published any comments on this kind of linguistics. What follows is, therefore, my own attempt to examine some of the issues raised by feminist linguistics from a 'Kristevan' perspective.[3]

KRISTEVA AND ANGLO-AMERICAN FEMINIST LINGUISTICS

According to Cheris Kramer, Barrie Thorne and Nancy Henley, the main areas of concern to Anglo-American feminist linguistics are:

> (1) Sex differences and similarities in language use, in speech and nonverbal communication; (2) sexism in language, with emphasis on language structure and content; (3) relations between language structure and language use (two topics usually treated separately); (4) efforts and prospects for change.
>
> (639)

The worrying aspect of this enumeration is the lack of any discussion of what 'language' might mean: it is as if the field or object of study ('language') is unproblematical for these researchers. Kristeva, on the other hand, spends much time discussing precisely the problem of 'language'. From the start she is acutely aware that 'language' is whatever linguists choose to define as their object of study. In an essay entitled 'The ethics of linguistics', she confronts modern linguistics with the ethical and political implications of its conception of 'language'. Accusing a 'prominent modern grammarian' of behaving in a 'Janus-like fashion', she points out that 'in his linguistic theories he sets forth a logical, normative basis for the speaking subject, while in politics, he claims to be an anarchist' (23). For her, contemporary linguistics is still

> bathed in the aura of *systematics* that prevailed at the time of its inception. It is discovering the rules governing the coherence of our fundamental social code: language, either system of signs or strategy for the transformation of logical sequences.
>
> (24)

Kristeva sees the ideological and philosophical basis for modern linguistics as fundamentally authoritarian and oppressive:

> As wardens of repression and rationalizers of the social contract in its most solid substratum (discourse), linguists carry the Stoic tradition to its conclusion. The epistemology underlying linguistics and the ensuing cognitive processes (structuralism, for example), even though constituting a bulwark against irrational destruction and sociologizing dogmatism, seem helplessly anachronistic when faced with the contemporary mutations of subject and society.
>
> (24)

The way out of this impasse, she argues, lies in a shift away from the Saussurian concept of *langue* towards a re-establishment of the *speaking subject* as an object for linguistics. This would move linguistics away from its fascination with language as a monolithic, homogeneous structure and towards an interest in language as a heterogeneous process. This will only happen, however, if one avoids defining the 'speaking subject' as any kind of transcendental or Cartesian ego. The speaking subject must instead be constructed in the field of thought developed after Marx, Freud and Nietzsche. Without the divided, decentred, overdetermined and differential notion of the subject proposed by these thinkers, Kristevan semiotics is unthinkable.[4] For Kristeva, the speaking subject is posited as the 'place, not only of structure and its repeated transformation, but especially, of its loss, its outlay' (24). Language then, for her, is a complex signifying *process* rather than a monolithic *system*. If linguists studied poetry, she writes, they would change their view of language and come away 'suspecting that the signifying process is not limited to the language system, but that there is also speech, discourse, and within them, a causality other than linguistic: a heterogeneous destructive causality' (27).

Sex differences in language use

Turning back to the aims of Anglo-American feminist linguistics quoted above, we can start by focusing on 'sex differences and similarities in language use, in speech and nonverbal communication'. One needs little recourse to theory to see that this kind of research may quickly lead to a dead end. Kramer, Thorne and Henley, for instance, glumly state that 'What is notable is how few expected sex differences have been firmly substantiated by empirical studies of actual speech' (640). The research is further confused, they say, by the fact that 'similar speech by females and by males has been shown to be perceived differentially (e.g. boys' "anger" vs. girls' "fear") and evaluated in different ways' (640–1). Thorne and Henley put this point more forcefully in another context, when they write that: 'In short, the significance of gestures changes when they are used by men or women; no matter what women do, their behavior may be taken to symbolize inferiority' (28). Kramer, Thorne and Henley also conclude that: 'A cluster of findings about who interrupts whom in conversations suggests that differences of power and status are more salient than those of gender alone' (641). If we add to these difficulties Helen Petrie's observation that in her research it seemed that *topic* was more important than *sex* in producing differences in speech,[5] we are in a position to question the basic assumption of difference underlying this kind of project.

It would seem that the pursuit of sex difference in language is not only a theoretical impossibility, but a political error. The concept of difference is theoretically tricky in that it denotes an absence or a gap more than any signifying presence. Difference, Jacques Derrida has argued, is not a *concept*.[6] Differences always take us *elsewhere*, we might say, involve us in an ever proliferating network of displacement and deferral of meaning. To see difference principally as the gap between the two parts of a binary opposition (as for instance between masculinity and femininity) is therefore to impose an arbitrary closure on the differential field of meaning.

This is precisely what much research on sex differences in language does, and the effect is theoretically predictable: masculinity and femininity are posited as stable, unchanging essences, as meaningful presences between which the elusive difference is supposed to be located. This is not to say that the researchers believe in *biological* essences; on the contrary, they often work with the anthropological theory of women as a 'muted group',[7] which suggests that in a social power relationship it is the subordinate group's different *social* experience that constitutes their different relationship to language. This does not, however, prevent the theory from becoming oppressive in nature: once 'women' are constituted as always and unchangingly subordinate and 'men' as unqualifiedly powerful, the language structures of these groups are perceived as rigid and unchanging. The researchers in this field therefore find themselves obliged to search ceaselessly for ways in which language *hampers* women's linguistic projects. Nothing could testify more to their scientific integrity than the candour with which they bleakly report the *absence* of such confirmation of their hypothesis. Politically, this projection of male and female as unquestioned essences is surely always dangerous for feminists: if any sex difference were ever to be found, it could always (and always would) be used against us, largely to prove that some particularly unpleasant activity is 'natural' for women and alien to men. The binary model of difference as enclosed or captured between the two opposite poles of masculinity and femininity blinds us to that which escapes this rigid structuration.

Kristeva's theory of language as a heterogeneous signifying process located in and between speaking subjects suggests an alternative approach: the study of specific linguistic strategies in specific situations. But this kind of study will not allow us to generalize our findings. In fact, it will take us towards a study of language as specific *discourse* rather than as universal *langue*. If we follow Kristeva's example and turn to the Soviet linguist V. N. Vološinov and his book *Marxism and the Philosophy of Language*, first published in 1929,[8] we may find some indication of what this would entail. In order to focus on discourse, linguistics must transcend the hitherto sacrosanct sentence barrier. More than fifty years ago, Vološinov launched a sustained assault on structuralist or system-oriented linguistics, which he labelled 'abstract objectivism':

> Linguistic thought goes no further than the elements that make up the monologic utterance. The structure of a complex sentence (a period) — that is the furthest limit of linguistic reach. The structure of a whole utterance is something linguistics leaves to the competence of other disciplines — to rhetoric and poetics. Linguistics lacks any approach to the compositional forms of the whole. Therefore, there is no direct transition between the linguistic forms of the elements of an utterance and the forms of its whole, indeed, no connection at all! Only by making a jump from syntax can we arrive at problems of composition.
>
> (78–9)

Vološinov and Kristeva are in other words out to undo — to deconstruct — the old disciplinary barriers between linguistics, rhetoric and poetics in order to construct a new kind of field: *semiotics* or *textual theory*.

If, as Vološinov suggests, *all* meaning is contextual, it becomes vital to study the context of each and every utterance. It does not follow, however, that 'context' should be understood as a unitary phenomenon, to be isolated and determined once and for all. In his meditation *Eperons* (*Spurs*), Jacques Derrida has shown how a text can be taken to have any number of contexts. Inscribing a specific context for a text does not *close* or *fix* the meaning of that text once and for all: there is always the possibility of reinscribing it within other contexts,[9] a possibility that is indeed in principle boundless, and that is *structural* to any piece of language. As far as the study of sex differences in language goes, any analysis of isolated fragments (sentences) in literature, as for instance in the much-quoted case of Virginia Woolf's theory of the 'woman's sentence', will warrant no specific conclusions whatever, since the very same structures can be found in male writers (Proust, for example, or other modernists). The only way of producing interesting results from such texts is to take the whole of the utterance (the whole text) as one's object, which means studying its ideological, political and psychoanalytical articulations, its relations with society, with the psyche and – not least – with other texts. Indeed, Kristeva has coined the concept of intertextuality to indicate how one or more systems of signs are transposed into others. Léon Roudiez writes that 'Any signifying practice is a field (in the sense of space traversed by lines of force) in which various signifying systems undergo such a transposition' (15). This, among other things, is what Kristeva has in mind when she stresses the necessity of 'establishing poetic language as the object of linguistics' attention' ('The ethics of linguistics', 25), and then goes on to specify that:

> What is implied is that language, and thus sociability, are defined by boundaries admitting of upheaval, dissolution and transformation. Situating our discourse near such boundaries might enable us to endow it with a current ethical impact. In short, the ethics of a linguistic discovery may be gauged in proportion to the poetry that it presupposes.
>
> (25)

Sexism in language

If we turn now to the second main category of Anglo-American feminist linguistic research, the study of sexism in language, it becomes evident that we run up against many of the same assumptions as in the study of sex differences. Cheris Kramarae defines sexism in language ('language' here seems to refer to the English language) as the way in which the 'English lexicon is a structure organized to glorify maleness and ignore, trivialize or derogate femaleness' (42). In Man Made Language Dale Spender asserts that:

> The English language has been literally man made and . . . it is still primarily under male control. . . . This monopoly over language is one of the means by which males have ensured their own primacy, and consequently have ensured the invisibility or 'other' nature of females,

and this primacy is perpetuated while women continue to use, unchanged, the language which we have inherited.

(12)

This kind of project is clearly interested in language as a system or structure, and thus falls under Kristeva's strictures on a potentially authoritarian linguistics. This is not 'merely' a theoretical point: even if we grant the viability of the project of locating sexism in language (and after all, as we shall see, even Kristeva concedes that language is *also* in some way structured), we immediately run into problems. For if we hold with Vološinov and Kristeva that *all* meaning is contextual, it follows that isolated words or general syntactical structures have no meaning until we provide a context for them. How then can they be defined as either sexist or non-sexist *per se*? (A *dictionary* of course constitutes one such specific, ideologically significant context.) If it is the case, as Thorne and Henley argue, that similar speech by men and by women tends to be interpreted quite differently, then there is surely nothing inherent in any given word or phrase that can always and forever be constructed as sexist. The crudely conspiratorial theory of language as 'man-made', or as a male plot against women, posits an *origin* (men's plotting) to language, a kind of non-linguistic transcendental signifier for which it is impossible to find any kind of theoretical support. I will therefore try to supply an alternative explanation of the well-documented instances of sexism in language.

The question of sexism is a question of the power relationship between the sexes, and this power struggle will of course be part of the *context* of all utterances under patriarchy. It does not follow, however, that in each and every individual case the feminine interlocutor will emerge as the underdog. As Michèle Barrett has written: 'An analysis of gender ideology in which women are always innocent, always passive victims of patriarchal power, is patently not satisfactory' (*Women's Oppression Today*, 110). If we now follow Vološinov's analysis of the relationship of the class struggle to language, we will see how this analysis might be appropriated for feminist use. 'Class', Vološinov writes,

does not coincide with the sign community, i.e. with the community, which is the totality of users of the same set of signs for ideological communication. Thus various different classes will use one and the same language. As a result, differently oriented accents intersect in every ideological sign. Sign becomes an arena of the class struggle.

(23)

This point is crucial to a non-essentialist feminist analysis of language. It posits that we all use the same language but that we have different *interests* – and interests must here be taken to mean political and power-related interests which intersect in the sign. The *meaning* of the sign is thrown open – the sign becomes 'polysemic' rather than 'univocal' – and though it is true to say that the dominant power group at any given time will dominate the intertextual production of meaning, this is not to suggest that the opposition has been reduced to total silence. The power struggle *intersects* in the sign.

Kristeva's view of the *productivity* of the sign accounts for feminist discourse itself, which on a strict reading of Dale Spender's model would be an impossibility. If language is *productive* (as opposed to a mere *reflection* of social relations), then this explains how it is that we can get more out of it than we put in. In more practical terms this means that one can wholeheartedly accept all the empirical studies that show how sexism dominates the English language (and probably all other languages as well). It is just that this fact does not necessarily have to do with the inherent structure of the language, let alone with any conscious plot. It is an effect of the dominant power relationship between the sexes. The fact that feminists have managed to fight back, have already made many people feel uncomfortable in using the generic 'he' or 'man', have questioned the use of words like 'chairman' and 'spokesman' and vindicated 'witch' and 'shrew' as positive terms surely proves the point: there is no inherent sexist essence in the English language, since it shows itself appropriable, through struggle, for feminist purposes. If we won the struggle against patriarchy and sexism the sign would *still* be an arena of this and other struggles, but this time the power balance would have shifted and the context of our utterances would therefore be dramatically different. What the studies of sexism in language reveal is the past and present social-power balance between the sexes.

One specific argument within the study of sexism in language is the question of naming. Feminists have consistently argued that 'those who have the power to name the world are in a position to influence reality' (Kramarae, 165). It is argued that women lack this power and that, as a consequence, many female experiences lack a name. Cheris Kramarae discusses one such case in detail:

> The women attending discussed shared experiences for which there are no labels, and lists were drawn up of the things, relationships, and experiences for which there are no labels. For example, one woman talked about a common occurrence in her life which needed a label. She and her husband, both working full-time outside the home, usually arrive home at about the same time. She would like him to share the dinner-making responsibilities but the job always falls upon her. Occasionally he says, 'I would be glad to make dinner. But you do it so much better than I.' She was pleased to receive this compliment but as she found herself in the kitchen each time she realized that he was using a verbal strategy for which she had no word and thus had more difficulty identifying and bringing to his awareness. She told people at the seminar, 'I had to tell you the whole story to explain to you how he was using flattery to keep me in my female place.' She said she needed a word to define the strategy, or a word to define the person who uses the strategy, a word which would be commonly understood by both women and men. Then, when he tried that strategy, she could explain her feelings by turning to him and saying, 'You are . . .,' or 'What you are doing is called . . .' (7–8)

It seems to me that this woman managed perfectly well to convey what was going on in her marriage even without a 'label', and that her desire for a 'label' was based on a wish to fix meaning and use that closure as a means of aggression: as an authoritative statement to which there could be no reply. There is obviously everything right and nothing wrong in hitting back at the oppressor, though one might question how far one should use his own weapons. Definitions can certainly be constructive. But – and this is the point overlooked by such arguments – they can also be constraining. As we have seen, many French feminists reject labels and names, and 'isms' in particular – even 'feminism' and 'sexism' – because they see such labelling activity as betraying a phallo-gocentric drive to stabilize, organize and rationalize our conceptual universe. They argue that it is masculine rationality that has always privileged reason, order, unity and lucidity, and that it has done so by silencing and excluding the irrationality, chaos and fragmentation that has come to represent femininity. My own view is that such conceptual terms are at once politically crucial and ultimately metaphysical; it is necessary at once to deconstruct the opposition between traditionally 'masculine' and traditionally 'feminine' values and to confront the full political force and reality of such categories. We must aim for a society in which we have ceased to categorize logic, conceptualization and rationality as 'masculine', not for one from which these virtues have been expelled altogether as 'unfeminine'.

To impose names is, then, not only an act of power, an enactment of Nietzsche's 'will-to-knowledge'; it also reveals a desire to regulate and organize reality according to well-defined categories. If this is some-times a valuable counter-strategy for feminists, we must nevertheless be wary of an obsession with nouns. Contrary to what St Augustine believed, language is not primarily constructed as a series of names or nouns, and we do not actually learn to speak in the way he suggested: 'When they (my elders) named some object, and accordingly moved towards something, I saw this and grasped that the thing was called by the sound they uttered when they meant to point it out'.[10] As Wittgen-stein ripostes: 'An ostensive definition can be variously interpreted in *every* case' (§28). The attempt to fix meaning is always in part doomed to failure, for it is of the nature of meaning to be always already else-where. As Bertolt Brecht puts it in *Mann ist Mann*: 'When you name yourself, you always name another'. This is not to say that we could or should avoid naming – simply that it is a more slippery business than it seems, and we should be alive to the dangers of fetishization. Even the much-praised term 'sexism' is showing signs of being shaken by the power struggle between the sexes, as Vološinov well might have pre-dicted: some men now nod benignly at the word and agree that we all hate and despise sexism, only to say later 'I'm not being sexist, I'm just being rational'. Sexism has become something that other, less-enlightened, men do. Labels, in other words, are no safe haven for anxious feminists; as Gayatri Spivak has enquired, how are we to choose between the average macho guerilla fighter in the jungle of El Salvador, and the Vice-President of Standard Oil who has learnt to say 'he or she'?

LANGUAGE, FEMININITY, REVOLUTION

The acquisition of language

We have seen how Kristevan semiotics emphasizes the marginal and the heterogeneous as that which can subvert the central structures of traditional linguistics. In order to show how Kristeva can posit language as being at once structured and heterogeneous, and why this view presupposes an emphasis on language as discourse uttered by a speaking subject, it is necessary to study her theory of the acquisition of language as it appears in her monumental doctoral thesis *La Révolution du langage poétique*, published in Paris in 1974. Philip E. Lewis has pointed out that all of Kristeva's work up to 1974 constitutes an extensive attempt to define or apprehend what she calls the *procès de signifiance* or the 'signifying process' (Lewis, 30). In order to approach this problem, she displaces Lacan's distinction between the Imaginary and the Symbolic Order into a distinction between the *semiotic* and the *symbolic*.[11] The interaction between these two terms then constitutes the signifying process.

The semiotic is linked to the pre-Oedipal primary processes, the basic pulsions of which Kristeva sees as predominantly anal and oral; and as simultaneously dichotomous (life v. death, expulsion v. introjection) and heterogeneous. The endless flow of pulsions is gathered up in the *chora* (from the Greek word for enclosed space, womb), which Plato in the *Timaeus* defines as 'an invisible and formless being which receives all things and in some mysterious way partakes of the intelligible, and is most incomprehensible' (Roudiez, 6). Kristeva appropriates and redefines Plato's concept and concludes that the *chora* is neither a sign nor a position, but 'a wholly provisional articulation that is essentially mobile and constituted of movements and their ephemeral stases. . . . Neither model nor copy, it is anterior to and underlies figuration and therefore also specularization, and only admits analogy with vocal or kinetic rhythm' (*Révolution*, 24).[12]

For Kristeva, *signifiance* is a question of positioning. The semiotic continuum must be split if signification is to be produced. This splitting (*coupure*) of the semiotic *chora* is the *thetic* phase (from *thesis*) and it enables the subject to attribute differences and thus signification to what was the ceaseless heterogeneity of the *chora*. Kristeva follows Lacan in positing the mirror phase as the first step that 'opens the way for the constitution of all objects which from now on will be detached from the semiotic *chora*' (*Révolution*, 44), and the Oedipal phase with its threat of castration as the moment in which the process of separation or splitting is fully achieved. Once the subject has entered into the Symbolic Order, the *chora* will be more or less successfully repressed and can be perceived only as pulsional *pressure* on symbolic language: as contradictions, meaninglessness, disruption, silences and absences in the symbolic language. The *chora* is a rhythmic pulsion rather than a new language. It constitutes, in other words, the heterogeneous, disruptive dimension of language, that which can never be caught up in the closure of traditional linguistic theory.

Kristeva is acutely aware of the contradictions involved in trying to theorize the untheorizable *chora*, a contradiction located at the centre of the semiotic enterprise. She writes:

> Being, because of its explanatory metalinguistic force, an agent of social cohesion, semiotics contributes to the formation of that reassuring image which every society offers itself when it understands everything, down to and including the practices which voluntarily expend it.
>
> ('System', 53)

If Kristeva nevertheless argues that semiotics should replace linguistics, it is in the belief that although this new science is always already caught up in the multiple networks of conflicting ideologies, it can still *unsettle* these frameworks:

> *Semanalysis* carries on the semiotic discovery . . . it places itself at the service of the social law which requires systematization, communication, exchange. But if it is to do this, it must inevitably respect a further, more recent requirement – and one which neutralizes the

phantom of 'pure science': the subject of the semiotic metalanguage must, however briefly, call himself in question, must emerge from the protective shell of a transcendental ego within a logical system, and so restore his condition with that negativity – drive-governed, but also social, political and historical – which rends and renews the social code.

('System', 54–5)

It is already possible to distinguish here the theme of revolution within Kristeva's linguistic theory. Before we approach this question, however, we must take a closer look at her views of the relationship between language and femininity.

Femininity as marginality

Kristeva flatly refuses to define 'woman': 'To believe that one "is a woman" is almost as absurd and obscurantist as to believe that one "is a man" ', she states in an interview with women from the 'psychanalyse et politique' group published in 1974 ('La femme', 20). Though political reality (the fact that patriarchy defines women and oppresses them accordingly) still makes it necessary to campaign in the name of women, it is important to recognize that in this struggle a woman cannot *be*: she can only exist negatively, as it were, through her refusal of that which is given: 'I therefore understand by "woman" ', she continues, 'that which cannot be represented, that which is not spoken, that which remains outside naming and ideologies' ('La femme', 21). Though this is reminiscent of Irigaray's image of woman, Kristeva, unlike Irigaray, sees her proposed 'definition' as entirely relational and strategic. It is an attempt to locate the negativity and refusal pertaining to the marginal in 'woman', in order to undermine the phallocentric order that defines woman as marginal in the first place. Thus the ethics of subversion that dominate Kristeva's linguistic theory here feed into her feminism as well. Her deep suspicion of identity ('What can "identity", even "sexual identity", mean in a new theoretical and scientific space where the very notion of identity is challenged?' [Woman's time, 34])[13] leads her to reject any idea of an *écriture féminine* or a *parler femme* that would be inherently feminine or female: 'Nothing in women's past or present publications seems to allow us to affirm that there is a feminine writing (*écriture féminine*)', she claims in an interview published in 1977 ('A partir de', 496). It is possible, Kristeva admits, to distinguish various recurrent stylistic and thematic peculiarities in writing by women; but it is not possible to say whether these characteristics should be ascribed to a 'truly feminine specificity, socio-cultural marginality or more simply to a certain structure (for instance hysteric) which the present market favours and selects among the totality of feminine potentiality' ('A partir de', 496).

In a sense, then, Kristeva does not have a theory of 'femininity', and even less of 'femaleness'. What she does have is a theory of marginality, subversion and dissidence.[14] In so far as women are defined as marginal by patriarchy, their struggle can be theorized in the same way as any other struggle against a centralized power structure. Thus Kristeva uses exactly the same terms to describe dissident intellectuals, certain *avant-garde* writers and the working class:

> As long as it has not analysed their relation to the instances of power, and has not given up the belief in its own identity, any libertarian movement (including feminism) can be recuperated by that power and by a spirituality that may be laicized or openly religious. The solution? . . . Who knows? It will in any case pass through that which is repressed in discourse and in the relations of production. Call it 'woman' or 'oppressed classes of society', it is the same struggle, and never the one without the other.
>
> ('La femme', 24)

The strength of this approach is its uncompromising anti-essentialism; its principal weakness the somewhat glib homologization of quite distinct and specific struggles, a problem that will be further discussed in the last section of this chapter.

The anti-essentialist approach is carried over into her theorization of sexual difference. So far, we have seen that her theory of the constitution of the subject and the signifying process is mostly concerned with developments in the pre-Oedipal phase where sexual difference does not exist (the *chora* is a pre-Oedipal phenomenon). The question of difference only becomes relevant at the point of entry into the symbolic order, and Kristeva discusses the situation for little girls at this point in her book *Des Chinoises* (translated as *About Chinese Women*), published in France in the same year as *La Révolution du langage poétique*. She points out that since the semiotic *chora* is pre-Oedipal, it is linked to the mother, whereas the symbolic, as we know, is dominated by the Law of the Father. Faced with this situation, the little girl has to make a choice: 'either she identifies with her mother, or she raises herself to the symbolic stature of her father. In the first case, the pre-Oedipal phases (oral and anal eroticism) are intensified' (*Chinese*, 28). If on the other hand the little girl identifies with her father, 'the access she gains to the symbolic dominance [will] censor the pre-Oedipal phase and wipe out the last traces of dependence on the body of the mother' (29).

Kristeva thus delineates two different options for women: mother-identification, which will intensify the pre-Oedipal components of the woman's psyche and render her marginal to the symbolic order, or father-identification, which will create a woman who will derive her identity from the same symbolic order. It should be clear from these passages that Kristeva does not define femininity as a pre-Oedipal and revolutionary essence. Far from it, femininity for Kristeva comes about as the result of a series of options that are also presented to the little boy. This is surely why at the beginning of *About Chinese Women* she repeats her contention that '*woman as such* does not exist' (16).

The claim advanced by the Marxist-Feminist Literature Collective (30) and by Beverly Brown and Parveen Adams that Kristeva associates the semiotic with the feminine is thus based on a misreading. The fluid motility of the semiotic is indeed associated with the pre-Oedipal phase, and therefore with the pre-Oedipal mother, but Kristeva makes it quite clear that like Freud and Klein she sees the pre-Oedipal mother as a figure that encompasses both masculinity and femininity. This fantasmatic figure, which looms as large for baby boys as for baby girls, cannot, as Brown and Adams are well aware (40), be reduced to an example of 'femininity', for the simple reason that the opposition between feminine and masculine does not exist in pre-Oedipality. And Kristeva knows this as well as anybody. Any strengthening of the semiotic, which knows no sexual difference, must therefore lead to a weakening of traditional gender divisions, and not at all to a reinforcement of traditional notions of 'femininity'. This is why Kristeva insists so strongly on the necessary refusal of any theory or politics based on the belief in any absolute form of identity. Femininity and the semiotic do, however, have one thing in common: their marginality. As the feminine is defined as marginal under patriarchy, so the semiotic is marginal to language. This is why the two categories, along with other forms of 'dissidence', can be theorized in roughly the same way in Kristeva's work.

It is difficult, then, to maintain that Kristeva holds an essentialist or even biologistic notion of femininity.[15] It is certainly true that she believes with Freud that the body forms the material basis for the constitution of the subject. But this in no way entails a simplistic equation of desire with physical needs, as Jean Laplanche has shown. For Laplanche 'oral' and 'anal' drives are 'oral' and 'anal' because they are first produced as a spin-off to (as 'anaclitic' to) the satisfaction of the purely physical needs linked to the mouth and anus, although they in no way are reducible to or identical with those needs.

If 'femininity' has a definition at all in Kristevan terms, it is simply, as we have seen, as 'that which is marginalized by the patriarchal symbolic order'. This relational 'definition' is as shifting as the various forms of patriarchy itself, and allows her to argue that men can also be constructed as marginal by the symbolic order, as her analyses of male avant-garde artists (Joyce, Céline, Artaud, Mallarmé, Lautréamont) have shown. In *La Révolution du langage poétique*, for instance, she claims that Artaud, among others, strongly stresses the fluidity of sexual identification for the artist when he states that 'the "author" becomes at once his "father", "mother" and "himself"' (606).

Kristeva's emphasis on femininity as a patriarchal construct enables feminists to counter all forms of biologistic attacks from the defenders of phallocentrism. To posit all women as necessarily feminine and all men as necessarily masculine is precisely the move that enables the patriarchal powers to define, not femininity, but all *women* as marginal to the symbolic order and to society. If, as Cixous and Irigaray have shown, femininity is defined as lack, negativity, absence of meaning, irrationality, chaos, darkness – in short, as non-Being – Kristeva's emphasis on marginality allows us to view this repression of the feminine in terms of *positionality* rather than of essences. What is perceived as marginal at any given time depends on the position one occupies. A

brief example will illustrate this shift from essence to position: if patriarchy sees women as occupying a marginal position within the symbolic order, then it can construe them as the limit or borderline of that
order. From a phallocentric point of view, women will then come to
represent the necessary frontier between man and chaos; but because
of their very marginality they will also always seem to recede into and
merge with the chaos of the outside. Women seen as the limit of the
symbolic order will in other words share in the disconcerting proper-
ties of all frontiers: they will be neither inside nor outside, neither
known nor unknown. It is this position that has enabled male culture
sometimes to vilify women as representing darkness and chaos, to view
them as Lilith or the Whore of Babylon, and sometimes to elevate them
as the representatives of a higher and purer nature, to venerate them as
Virgins and Mothers of God. In the first instance the borderline is seen
as part of the chaotic wilderness outside, and in the second it is seen as
an inherent part of the inside: the part that protects and shields the
symbolic order from the imaginary chaos. Needless to say, neither
position corresponds to any essential truth of woman, much as the
patriarchal powers would like us to believe that they did.

Feminism, Marxism, anarchism

Kristeva's work can in no way be characterized as primarily feminist: it is
not even consistently political in its approach. Having started out as a
linguist in the late 1960s, she first wrote about topics related to women
and feminism in 1974, roughly at the time she was beginning her training as a psychoanalyst. From the late 1970s onwards her work has been
marked by an increasing interest in psychoanalytic issues, often focusing
on problems of sexuality, femininity and love. Feminists will find much
of value in, for example, her approach to the question of motherhood.
Already in *La Révolution du langage poétique* she has claimed that it is not *woman*
as such who is repressed in patriarchal society, but *motherhood* (453). The
problem is not women's *jouissance* alone, as Lacan has it in *Encore*, but the
necessary relationship between reproduction and *jouissance*:

> If the position of women in the social code is a problem today, it does
> not at all rest in a mysterious question of feminine *jouissance* . . . but

deeply, socially and symbolically in the question of reproduction and the *jouissance* that is articulated therein.

(*Révolution*, 462)

This perspective opens an interesting field of investigation for feminists, and Kristeva has herself contributed several intriguing analyses of the representation of motherhood in Western culture, particularly as embodied in the figure of the Madonna ('Héréthique de l'amour') and in Western pictorial art ('Motherhood according to Giovanni Bellini'). Her preoccupation with the figure of the Madonna constitutes a significant development of her work in *La Révolution du langage poétique* in that it questions the role of women in the symbolic order through an ideological and psychoanalytical analysis of what is also the material basis for women's oppression: motherhood. Similarly, much of her more recent work, like *Pouvoirs de l'horreur* (1980, translated as *Powers of Horror*, 1982) and particularly *Histoires d'amour* ('Love stories', 1983), could be valuably appropriated for feminism.

It is no secret that Kristeva's early commitment to Marxism, mixed with various Maoist and anarchist influences, has given way to a new scepticism towards political engagement. Rejecting in the late 1970s her early idealization of Mao's China, she suddenly revealed an alarming fascination with the libertarian possibilities of American-style late capitalism.[16] Her cavalier disregard for the unpalatable side of American capitalism rightly disconcerted the great majority of her readers on the political Left. Their dismay was compounded by her wholesale dismissal of politics as a new orthodoxy that it is time to outflank: 'I am not interested in groups. I am interested in individuals', she declared in a recent debate in London. Faithful to her own theory, she explains this development away from politics in terms of her own specific circumstances: 'It's a point of personal history. I suppose from different people here in this room, having different histories, the appreciation of political actuality would be different' (ICA, 24–5). This development away from Marxism and feminism is not as surprising as it may seem at first glance. Kristeva's early Marxist or feminist work, with its emphasis on the marginal, already reveals strong anarchist tendencies, and the gap between libertarianism and straightforward liberal individualism has never been difficult to bridge. In the following brief examination of her positions I will try to show how many of Kristeva's most valuable insights draw at times on highly contentious forms of subjectivist politics.

Even in her early, more feminist work, Kristeva does not try to speak from or for the 'feminine'. For her, to 'speak as a woman' would in any case be meaningless, since, as we know, she argues that 'woman as such does not exist'. Instead of an exclusive emphasis on the gender of the speaker, she recommends an analysis of the many discourses (including sexuality and gender) that together construct the individual:

> It is there, in the analysis of her difficult relation to her mother and to her own difference from everybody else, men and women, that a woman encounters the enigma of the 'feminine'. I favour an understanding of femininity that would have as many 'feminines' as there are women.
>
> ('A partir de', 499)

Thus the specificity of the individual subject is foregrounded at the expense of a general theory of femininity and even of political engagement *tout court*. Her later individualism (the rejection of 'groups') is clearly implicit in such statements.

Many women have objected to Kristeva's highly intellectual style of discourse on the grounds that as a woman and a feminist committed to the critique of all systems of power, she ought not to present herself as yet another 'master thinker'.[17] From one viewpoint, this accusation would seem to be somewhat unfair: what seems marginal from one perspective may seem depressingly central from another (*absolute* marginality cannot be had), and one cannot logically set out to subvert dominant intellectual discourses (as Kristeva does) without simultaneously laying oneself open to the accusation of being intellectualist. However, from another perspective, Kristeva, with her university chair in linguistics and her psychoanalytic practice, would certainly seem to have positioned herself at the very centre of the traditional intellectual power structures of the Left Bank.

If the Kristevan subject is always already inserted in the symbolic order, how can such an implacably authoritarian, phallocentric structure be broken up? It obviously cannot happen through a straightforward *rejection* of the symbolic order, since such a total failure to enter into human relations would, in Lacanian terms, make us psychotic. We have to accept our position as already inserted into an order that precedes us and from which there is no escape. There is no *other space* from which we can speak: if we are able to speak at all, it will have to be within the framework of symbolic language.

The revolutionary subject, whether masculine or feminine, is a subject that is able to allow the *jouissance* of semiotic motility to disrupt the strict symbolic order. The example *par excellence* of this kind of 'revolutionary' activity is to be found in the writings of late-nineteenth century *avant-garde* poets like Lautréamont and Mallarmé or modernist writers such as Joyce. Since the semiotic can never take over the symbolic, one may ask how it can make itself felt at all. Kristeva's answer to this point is that the only possible way of releasing some of the semiotic pulsions into the symbolic is through the predominantly anal (but also oral) activity of *expulsion* or *rejection*. In textual terms this translates itself as a *negativity* masking the death-drive, which Kristeva sees as perhaps the most fundamental semiotic pulsion. The poet's negativity is then analysable as a series of ruptures, absences and breaks in the symbolic language, but it can also be traced in his or her thematic preoccupations. One of the problems with this account of the 'revolutionary' subject is that it slides over the question of revolutionary agency. Who or what is acting in Kristeva's subversive schemes? In a political context her emphasis on the semiotic as an unconscious force precludes any analysis of the conscious decision-making processes that must be part of any *collective* revolutionary project. The stress on negativity and disruption, rather than on questions of organization and solidarity, leads Kristeva in effect to an anarchist and subjectivist political position. And on this point I would agree with the Marxist-Feminist Literature Collective who arraign her poetics as 'politically unsatisfactory' (30). Allon White also accuses Kristeva of political ineffectiveness, claiming that her politics 'remain purified anarchism in a perpetual state of self-dispersal' (16–17).

In the end, Kristeva is unable to account for the relations between the subject and society. Though she discusses in exemplary fashion the social and political context of the poets she studies in *La Révolution du langage poétique*, it is still not clear why it is so important to show that certain literary practices break up the structures of language when they seem to break up little else. She seems essentially to argue that the disruption of the subject, the *sujet en procès* displayed in these texts, prefigures or parallels revolutionary disruptions of society. But her only argument in support of this contention is the rather lame one of comparison or homology. Nowhere are we given a specific analysis of the actual social or political structures that would produce such a homologous relationship between the subjective and the social.

Equally noticeable is the lack of materialist analysis of social relations in Kristeva's concept of 'marginality', which lumps together all kinds of marginal and oppositional groups as potentially subversive of the social order. When in her article 'Un nouveau type d'intellectuel: le dissident' ('A new kind of intellectual: the dissident', 1977) she paraphrases Marx and exclaims that 'A spectre is haunting Europe: the spectre of the dissidents' (4), she conveniently chooses to overlook the differences between the 'dissident' groups she enumerates: the rebel (who attacks political power), the psychoanalyst, the *avant-garde* writer and women. Elsewhere, as we have seen, she equates the struggle of women with that of the working class. But in Marxist terms these groups are fundamentally disparate because of their different location in relation to the mode of production. The working class is potentially revolutionary because it is indispensable to the capitalist economy, not because it is marginal to it. In the same way women are central – not marginal – to the process of reproduction. It is precisely because the ruling order cannot maintain the *status quo* without the continued exploitation and oppression of these groups that it seeks to mask their central economic role by marginalizing them on the cultural, ideological and political levels. The paradox of the position of women and the working class is that they are at one and the same time central and marginal(ized). In the case of the intelligentsia, whether *avant-garde* artists or psychoanalysts, it may well be the case that their role under late capitalism is truly peripheral in the sense that they have no crucial function in the economic order, much like the *Lumpenproletariat* Brecht idealized in his *Threepenny Opera*. Thus Kristeva's grossly exaggerated confidence in the

political importance of the *avant-garde* is based precisely on her misrec-
ognition of the differences between its political and economic position
and that of women or the working class. Like the early Brecht,
Kristeva's romanticizing of the marginal is an anti-*bourgeois*, but not
necessarily anti-*capitalist*, form of libertarianism.

The criticisms levelled here against Kristeva's politics should not be
allowed to overshadow the positive aspects of her work. Her commitment to thorough theoretical investigation of the problems of marginality and subversion, her radical deconstruction of the identity of the
subject, her often extensive consideration of the material and historical
contexts of the works of art she studies, have opened up new perspectives for further feminist enquiry. Her theory of language and its dis-
rupted subject (*sujet en procès*) allows us to examine both women's and
men's writing from an anti-humanist, anti-essentialist perspective.
Kristeva's vision is not exclusively or essentially feminist, but it is one
in which the hierarchical closure imposed on meaning and language
has been opened up to the free play of the signifier. Applied to the field
of sexual identity and difference, this becomes a feminist vision of a
society in which the sexual signifier would be free to move; where the
fact of being born male or female no longer would determine the
subject's position in relation to power, and where, therefore, the very
nature of power itself would be transformed.

Jacques Derrida once put the question: 'What if we were to
approach . . . the area of a relationship to the other where the code of
sexual marks would no longer be discriminating?' ('Choreographies',
76). I would like to end with his response, which, like many utopian
utterances, is at once sibylline and suggestive:

> The relationship [to the other] would not be a-sexual, far from it, but
> would be sexual otherwise: beyond the binary difference that governs
> the decorum of all codes, beyond the opposition feminine/masculine,
> beyond homosexuality and heterosexuality which come to the same
> thing. As I dream of saving the chance that this question offers, I
> would like to believe in the multiplicity of sexually marked voices.
> I would like to believe in the masses, this indeterminable number of
> blended voices, this mobile of non-identified sexual marks whose

choreography can carry, divide, multiply the body of each 'individual', whether he be classified as 'man' or 'woman' according to the criteria of usage.

(76)

AFTERWORD

Politics and theory, then and now

FROM 'LITERARY THEORY' to 'THEORY'

Sexual/Textual Politics was written from 1982 to 1984 and published in September 1985. The text is reprinted here without changes. In my view, there is no way to update *Sexual/Textual Politics*. It is firmly a book of its time and its moment, the moment of the 'theory revolution' of the early 1980s, such as it was experienced in Britain. In the late 1990s, I found that I had to write a very different kind of book about feminist theory, namely *What Is a Woman?* (1999).[1]

Yet readers continue to find *Sexual/Textual Politics* useful. I suppose this means that it raises questions that have remained relevant to feminist theory, either because they still preoccupy us, or because they are now considered necessary starting points for understanding later developments in feminist theory. As long as this continues to be the case, the book serves a useful purpose. Yet that purpose has changed. In the early 1980s feminist theory was still a marginal and somewhat suspect intellectual activity in the eyes of many academics in Britain and Norway, where I was living then. Today feminist theory is an established part of academia, not least in the United States where I am living now. The change in cultural context has changed the nature of *Sexual/Textual Politics*: in 1985 it was a controversial, cutting-edge intervention in a subversive field; in 2002 it has become a textbook.

I wrote *Sexual/Textual Politics* with two objectives in mind: first of all I wanted to produce a serious and lucid analysis of what I took to be the key issues in contemporary feminist theory. I was, essentially, trying to write the book for which I had been searching in vain when I was struggling to write a feminist PhD thesis in the late 1970s. But I also wanted to intervene in the feminist debates that surrounded me as an unemployed PhD living in Oxford. Intellectually, the anti-essentialist argument that runs through the book owes everything to Simone de Beauvoir's 'One is not born but rather becomes a woman'. Politically, however, it was a response to the discussions raging around me at the time. Two events were particularly important: the Falklands War and the women's peace camp at Greenham Common.

On April 2, 1982 Argentina invaded the Falkland Islands. Mrs. Thatcher immediately sent a Royal Navy task force to the South Atlantic. British nationalism and militarism erupted with a vengeance. Thus the sinking of the *Belgrano* with the loss of hundreds of lives provoked the infamous headline 'Gotcha!' in the then rabidly pro-Thatcher tabloid paper *The Sun*.[2] By mid-July 1982 the war was over, leaving 255 British and 652 Argentines dead. Mrs. Thatcher's popularity reached an all-time high. As early as the end of August 1981, the first women had pitched their tents outside Greenham Common, an air force base near Newbury, less than two hours' drive from Oxford. They were protesting against a NATO decision to deploy Cruise missiles in Britain. The protest provoked intense debate about women's nature, their relationship to war and peace, and about men's relationship to feminism. (In 1982, after much controversy, the camp became women-only.) On December 12, 1982 more than 20,000, perhaps as many as 30,000, women came to Greenham Common and joined hands to 'embrace the base'.[3]

Greenham Common proved that women were more peace-loving than men, some feminists claimed. But what about Mrs. Thatcher's evident pleasure in the Falklands War? Surely that undermined any easy claims about women and peace? No, I was told, Mrs. Thatcher didn't count because she wasn't a 'real woman', she was 'male-identified', an 'honorary man'. I felt then, and still feel, that any feminist theory that tries to define some women as 'real women' and others as 'deviant', or 'unfeminine', or 'masculine' is doomed to failure.[4] Feminism needs to acknowledge women's obvious and striking differences. These differences comprise but are not reducible to differences of race and sexual orientation. Sexual/Textual Politics is based on the idea that any theory that sets out to define women's essence or women's nature is detrimental to the goal of feminism: to obtain freedom and equality for women.

In the aftermath of Greenham Common, many feminists in Oxford felt that compared to feminist activism intellectual feminism was pointless. Sexual/Textual Politics is a passionate attempt to convince such feminists that even fairly abstract kinds of theory may have a political point. Thus the introductory chapter ('Who's Afraid of Virginia Woolf?') sets out to make the case for theory by showing that feminists who think they're not being theoretical are mistaken. They are not without a theory, I claim, they are in the grip of a theory they have failed to recognize as such. If we (feminists) could become more theoretically sophisticated, we would also become more politically astute, more aware of the implications of our own positions. There is a psychoanalytic undertone to this project: I assume that unacknowledged theoretical allegiances are far more difficult to change than those we are able to name and think about.

Sexual/Textual Politics, then, was not conceived as a survey of feminist theory and criticism, but as a sustained argument in favor of theory. Yet the book uses the word theory in two quite different ways. (This was far from evident to me at the time.) Sometimes 'theory' means 'literary theory'; sometimes it means 'feminist, poststructuralist and Marxist theory'. At the time, I took the first meaning to be quite self-evident. At the University of Bergen I had received solid training in traditional literary theory. I had taken seminars on narratology, new criticism, Russian and Czech formalism, structuralism according to Greimas and Genette, and hermeneutics according to Schleiermacher and Gadamer. In the late 1970s in Bergen, to study psychoanalytic literary theory meant worrying about psychoanalytic interpretations of texts, not about the general development of subjectivity. In the same way, our seminars on Marxist literary theory discussed realism and literary form, not ideology and modes of production. In 1980, then, literary theory to me still meant theories about the relations between text and reader, text and author, text and society.

Together with all the other books on 'theory' published in the 1980s, *Sexual/Textual Politics* helped to change the meaning of the word. As a result, *Sexual/Textual Politics* itself is somewhat torn between the old and the new conception of theory. It starts with 'literary theory', and ends with a concept of 'theory' that is starting to mean what it means today, namely something like Marxist, poststructuralist, postcolonial, psychoanalytical, queer, feminist or variously postmodern thoughts about subjectivity, meaning, ideology and culture in their widest generality. 'Literary theory' in the traditional sense is the focal point of the first part of the book. The title of that part, 'Anglo-American Feminist Criticism', was meant to indicate how much leading American feminist critics owed to the critical tradition commonly referred to as 'Anglo-American New Criticism'. That allusion, I suspect, is lost today. The only poststructuralist theory I use in the first part of the book is poststructuralist textual theory, as when I draw on Roland Barthes's famous essay 'The Death of the Author' to argue against the idea that the author's intention should be the sole determinant of literary meaning (see p. 63).

'Literary theory' in the traditional sense had usually not been considered political. I wanted to show that such theory did have political implications. My main point is that it is contradictory for anti-authoritarian feminists to go in for theories that set up the (woman) writer as a God-like authority. Feminists have to be free to question all authority, including that of women. *Sexual/Textual Politics* consistently favours the freedom of readers over the power of writers. The project of the first half of the book, then, was to trace the relationship between traditional literary theory (aesthetics) and feminist politics.

The second half of the book is entitled 'French feminist theory'. In this half the meaning of 'theory' starts to shift. In the early 1980s the shift from 'literary theory' to 'theory' was by no means easy to pin down and define. For Kristeva, Cixous and Irigaray could all be considered literary theorists in the traditional sense – they did, after all, write about female creativity, about writing, texts and language. Yet, crucially, the works that seemed most exciting and significant for feminists were not, or not exactly, works of literary criticism. Although Cixous was clearly a very 'literary' thinker, and although Kristeva was, among other things, a theorist of the novel, and a linguist, their appeal to feminists lay in their explorations of femininity, subjectivity and meaning in culture. Shifting from part I to part II, from Showalter and Gilbert and Gubar to Cixous, Irigaray and Kristeva, the book shifts from literary to philosophical and psychoanalytical questions. Although theories of texts and meaning remain a focus of interest throughout the book, by the end, the transition from 'literary theory' to 'theory' is pretty much complete.

A LOSS OF VOICE? WOMEN, SUBJECTIVITY AND PERFORMATIVITY

Sexual/Textual Politics is highly critical of homogenous, non-contradictory, non-conflictual models of subjectivity. Against Romantic theories of intentionality, the book proposes a psychoanalytic understanding of the subject. The Kristevan concept of the embodied 'speaking subject' is fundamental to the book. In my view (now as then), there is always someone who speaks, acts, thinks, writes.[5] That someone does not have to be pictured as a wholly present, non-contradictory intentionality. In *Sexual/Textual Politics* the subject is split, decentred, fragile, always threatened by disintegration. At the same time, this split and decentred subject has the capacity to act and make choices. Such choices and acts, however, are always overdetermined, that is to say deeply influenced by unconscious ideological allegiances and unconscious emotional investments and fantasies as well as by conscious motivations.

When I wrote *Sexual/Textual Politics*, then, it never occurred to me to doubt that there are women in the world, that women have agency and that they are responsible for their actions. To me, there was no contradiction between writing *Sexual/Textual Politics* and moving on to my next book project, a study of Simone de Beauvoir as an intellectual woman.[6] I did not (and still don't) take women to be the mere effects of gender discourses, or the mere victims of sexist circumstances, nor did I feel any need to cast aspersions on the very word 'woman'. To me, as to Simone de Beauvoir and most other people, a woman is a human being with the usual biological and anatomical sexual characteristics.[7] The point of arguing strongly against essentialism, is to stop sexist generalizations about this class of people, it is not to deny that such a class of people exists.

What I didn't imagine back in 1985 was that a wave of new theorists ready to criticize the very word 'woman' would shortly emerge. Already in 1989, Diana Fuss claimed that the very word 'woman,' whether used in the singular or the plural, imposed homogeneity and erased women's differences (see *Essentially Speaking*, particularly 3–4). And in 1990 Judith Butler published her immensely influential *Gender Trouble*, which provocatively claimed that sex was as constructed as gender, and that gender was 'performative'.[8] She followed up these claims in *Bodies That Matter* (1993), by claiming that matter itself (the matter of which the body is made) is nothing but the result of a 'process of materialization that stabilizes over time to produce the effect of boundary, fixity, and surface we call matter' (*Bodies*, 9). I discuss these theories at some length in *What Is a Woman* (particularly 30–59), and will not repeat that analysis here. Let me just say that in much poststructuralist gender theory, and certainly in Butler's, the word 'gender' is substituted for the word 'woman', or rather: the words 'woman' and 'gender' are taken to be synonymous. At the same time 'gender' is opposed to 'sex'. The result is that women are divorced from their bodies, and that 'woman' is turned into a discursive and performative effect. It is difficult to see what the advantage of such a convoluted view might be.

To avoid essentialism and biological determinism all we need to do is to deny that biology gives rise to social norms. We don't have to claim that there are no women, or that the category 'woman' in itself is ideologically suspect. This is not to deny that sexists try to impose all kinds of ideologies on the word 'woman'. It is, however, to deny that they always succeed. Although economic, social, political and ideological oppression exists, and although such oppression deprives women of freedom, there is no reason to draw the conclusion that women can't work towards change, that our oppression is so complete, so fully internalized by our female psyche that we can never struggle free from the sexist blindfold. Nor is there any need to presume that our only possible strategy of resistance would be mimicry or parody.[9]

The shift away from a psychoanalytic or phenomenological theory of subjectivity to agentless notions of sex, gender, 'regulatory discourses' and 'performativity' arrived as part of a general poststructuralist critique of the subject. This critique was originally directed against full-blown metaphysical Romantic theories of intentionality.[10] But most poststructuralist gender theorists soon came to sound as if they thought that *any* reference to agency, subjectivity and responsibility was proof positive of Romantic metaphysics. Needless to say, this was an overreaction. The poststructuralist hatred of agency, the wish to deny that there is a 'doer behind the deed', imagines that speakers and writers are nothing but cogs in a big discursive machinery. A specific philosophical picture of what it is to speak and write is at work here: a picture of a situation in which the speaker or writer feels that her words are not hers; that someone else is speaking through her; that she is unable to mean what she says, or to say what she means.[11] Her words are alien to her, and she to them. Such a speaker will feel isolated, lonely, and misunderstood.

In his magisterial analysis of the various forms of modern scepticism, Stanley Cavell speaks of a 'fantasy, or fear, either of inexpressiveness, one in which I am not merely unknown, but in which I am powerless to make myself known, or one in which what I express is beyond my control' (*Claim*, 351). This fantasy is present in two cultural locations that I have investigated: in poststructuralist theory and in nineteenth century melodrama. It is a fantasy well known to feminists: Madame de Staël's Corinne suffers from it too.[12] Yet the fantasy of not being able to make oneself understood, of being powerless to show others who one is, is at once bound to arise, not least in oppressed women, and deeply unhelpful to feminism. Corinne dies unhappy and alone, convinced that the world is not worthy of her. Feminist theory needs to understand why we are all driven to melodrama from time to time, but it also needs to know how to find its way back to the ordinary and the everyday, where our political battles are actually fought. The melodrama of poststructuralist theory is an inescapable part of our feminist heritage; it should not be our only heritage.

THE 'POLITICS OF THEORY': MELODRAMA
AND THE ORDINARY

As we have seen, *Sexual/Textual Politics* participated in the revolution that transformed 'literary theory' into 'theory'. It was written at a time and in a place when to be doing theory, particularly feminist theory, was perceived by all parties (theorists and antitheorists) to be subversive of the academic institution. At the time, the phrase the 'politics of theory' appeared to make obvious and automatic sense. Now that 'theory' has ensconced itself as the dominant academic doxa these things no longer go without saying. It is no longer possible to believe that theory simply is political, or to continue the search for the perfect theory, the 'theory that guarantees political radicalism and, ideally, political effectiveness', to quote Jonathan Culler (218). In 2002 it is time to take a new look at the relationship between politics and theory.

The question about the 'politics of theory' has in fact mostly been raised by poststructuralists, whose theories have to do with language, discourse and subjectivity. But to speak of the 'politics of theory' is to speak in far too general terms. There are all kinds of theories, used by all kinds of people in all kinds of contexts. A theory of truth and discourse does not have the same relationship to politics as a theory of global capitalism or women's oppression. In the same way, the word 'politics' means different things at different times, in different situations. In the 1930s a political play was likely to be about class, or fascism. Now a political play may be about AIDS, or race or gender, or sexuality.

To the question 'Is theory political?' all one can reply is 'It depends.'[13] What we cannot do is to provide a 'guarantee'. What picture of the relationship between politics and theory must one have to make it look as if a 'guarantee' of radical effects (or should this be radical intentions?) can be had? To me there is something metaphysical, something melodramatic, about the idea of a guarantee, something that reminds me of Stanley Cavell's analysis of scepticism and its 'demand for absoluteness':

> We impose a demand for absoluteness [. . .] upon a concept, and then, finding that our ordinary use of this concept does not meet our demand, we accommodate this discrepancy as nearly as possible.

> Take these familiar patterns: we do not really see material objects, but
> only see them indirectly; we cannot be certain of any empirical prop-
> osition, but only practically certain; we cannot really know what
> another person is feeling, but only infer it.
>
> ('Aesthetic Problems', 77)

In short, to ask about the 'politics of theory' is to impose a demand for
absoluteness on a human activity that will yield no such thing. To such
a question, any answer we could give would either be metaphysical or
meaningless, or both.

To ask about the 'politics of theory' is not the only way to think
about the political value of intellectual work. Nor is the demand for
absoluteness confined to contemporary literary theorists. To show what
I mean, I shall turn to two statements by Sartre and Beauvoir. 'Faced
with a dying child, *Nausea* isn't worth much', Sartre said in 1964, the
year in which he published *The Words*.[14] At roughly the same time, in
1963, Simone de Beauvoir wrote: 'I am an intellectual, I take words
and the truth to be of value' (*Force of Circumstance*, 378).[15] There are two
different attitudes towards politics and words at work in these statements. I now want to show why I think of Sartre's image as not just
metaphysical but *melodramatic*, in contrast to what I shall call Beauvoir's
ordinary view of intellectual commitment. (My choice of words is
meant to indicate my debt to Stanley Cavell, and through him, to
Wittgenstein.[16])

At the time, many took Sartre's statement to mean that he thought
there was no justification for literature in a starving world. It is unclear
whether Sartre himself thought this, or whether he just meant to raise
the question of the political effects of writing by saying something
provocative. I shall ascribe the common, extreme interpretation to
'Sartre', but it may well be that what I am describing is not Sartre, but
those who take his statement in this way, then and now.

In 1964 Sartre was 59, he was slowly going blind, and he suffered
from alarming levels of hypertension. He was also a world famous
intellectual, tirelessly campaigning for radical causes. Given his specific
circumstances, the most politically effective thing he could do, was
to continue to write. This is exactly what he did. Yet the image of
the dying child is immensely more powerful than any practical

considerations. However justified he may have been in his choices, that image makes Sartre's intellectual life appear insufficient, even callous. The image tells us that regardless of what he does as an intellectual, Sartre is painfully aware that it is not always enough.

The phrase 'not always enough' reveals what the problem is. Of *course* writing is not always enough. How could it be? What human activity is 'always enough'? Enough for what? In the vague, unspecific and generalized turn of phrase 'not always enough', metaphysics— Cavell's 'demand for absoluteness'—rears its head. For if we are faced with a dying child, we tend to her. We feed her, care for her, hold her, provide as much medicine and comfort as we possibly can. In such a case tending to the child is simply what we do. Only a cold-blooded murderer would turn her back on the child and return to her desk.

But if this is right, then Sartre's image actually tells us nothing about the political and ethical value of intellectual work. We all know that novels or theory don't feed the hungry or heal the sick. To whom was he speaking? Who would feel illuminated by the thought that *Nausea* will not save a dying child? The answer is clear: only someone who once fervently hoped that it would. Sartre's youthful faith in salvation through literature, which happens to be a major preoccupation of *The Words*, instantly comes to mind. But the same attitude can be found in those present-day intellectuals who have excessive faith in the power of theory to put everything politically right, as if every kind of oppression would vanish if only we could elaborate the right theory of subjectivity, or discourse, or truth.

In Sartre's example of the dying child there is an immensely seductive fantasy of being able to produce writing powerful enough to save a dying child. There is no middle ground here: either writing does it all, or it does nothing. I don't mean to overlook the fact that Sartre's statement has the form of a negation, that he is saying that *Nausea* can't do much for a dying child. On the contrary, the very form of the statement carries out psychic work, for its task is to *negate* the fantasy of the omnipotence of writing, a fantasy Sartre himself so masterly explored in *The Words*. 'Negation is a way of taking cognizance of what is repressed. [. . .] A negative judgment is the intellectual substitute for repression', Freud writes (235–6). By saying that his writing is *not* justified, Sartre keeps the dream of justification by literature alive, but the affect has shifted, from exuberant jubilation at the omnipotence of writing to abject disappointment and guilt at the failure of writing.

The very intensity of the image reinforces and expresses the contrasting affects contained in the negated fantasy. Juxtaposing a dying child and an aging male intellectual, Sartre pits wronged innocence against guilt and decay. Pressing the question of intellectual responsibility to the extreme, he trades in the stark absolutes, the all-or-nothing logic of melodrama.[17] In this way he invites us to believe that politics is the only possible *raison d'être* of writing, and that if writing doesn't save a dying child, it is of no use at all.

Among intellectuals today the tell-tale symptoms of Sartre's anxiety-inducing fantasy are excessive feelings of anguish and guilt about the political failure or impotence of intellectuals. The inevitable flip side of this is excessive optimism about the power of theory. Once we lose faith in that, we are ripe for Sartre's melodrama. Unless we can find an alternative to see-sawing between these equally intense and affect-laden positions, we will become embittered and lose all faith in the value of intellectual work. The irony is that the more intensity we invest in our quest for political justification, the more we court ultimate political disaffection.

How do we get off the see-saw? Beauvoir's 'I take words and the truth to be of value', rings truer to me than Sartre's melodrama of the intellectual and the dying child. It is significant, for example, that she simply says 'of value', and not 'of absolute value', or 'always of *political* value'. To my ears, Beauvoir invites us to consider what value words and the truth have in a given situation, no more, but also no less. Beauvoir's approach enables us to discuss the relationship between theory and politics in ordinary, everyday terms, and not in the empty terms of metaphysics.

For her, then, the question of where, when and how the intellectual should commit herself becomes a concrete, individual and practical (as opposed to an abstract, general and metaphysical) one: Can I justify doing what I do? How good am I at it? Do I have the talents and skill required to do something else? Could I acquire them fairly effectively? Is the cause I believe in better served by a mediocre guerrilla fighter or a first rate writer? Let us say that I really want to know what intellectuals can do to save dying children. I read in the paper that: 'The

United Nations calculates that the world population's basic needs for food, drinking water, education and medical care could be covered by a levy of less than 4% on the accumulated wealth of the 225 largest fortunes [in the world]' (Ramonet 1). It would seem that the people who can do the most to help dying children are not intellectuals, but the owners of those 225 fortunes.

As intellectuals we can work to spread this knowledge. But we also need to acknowledge that unless we are economists or doctors, our daily work is not going to be concretely concerned with the prevention of famine and death. Thus intellectuals working in the humanities have to ask not simply what intellectuals in general can do, but what we can do that people from other disciplines can't do better, and under what circumstances we can do them. What is the point of working with ideas, with culture, with writing, in a starving world? These questions are important, and they do have answers. They just don't have *absolute* answers.

The advantage of Beauvoir's attitude is that it enables us to acknowledge the distress that fuels Sartre's stark image, without having to give up the thought that words and writing can have political significance. The only alternative to political guilt and anguish is not complaisant acquiescence in the death of children. It is part of intellectual life constantly to ask what the political, ethical and existential value of one's work is. What I am trying to say here is that there doesn't have to be one answer to that, let alone one answer to be given once and for all, on behalf of all intellectuals.

But the question of justification remains. Are we justified in speaking about theory? Or about anything at all? Even if we don't think that children are dying because we are writing, we may feel vaguely guilty about giving ourselves the right to speak and write when so many millions cannot. Isn't there an unbearable arrogance here? Since we are no better and no worse than anyone else, what justifies our 'arrogation of voice' (as Stanley Cavell calls it)?[18]

I'll be blunt: the answer is *nothing*. Our speaking – even the most passionate political call to arms – is never justified by anything but our own wish to speak: 'Who beside myself could give me the authority to speak for us?' Cavell writes (Pitch 9). To ask for *general* justification is to ask for a metaphysical ground beneath our feet. There is something arrogant and something unjust about writing anything at all. How can I write when millions of others cannot? How can I justify my arrogation of voice? How can anyone? If we do decide to write, it is pointless to consume ourselves in guilt about the 'exclusionary' effects of writing per se. The question, therefore, is not how to justify writing anything at all, but rather what one aims to do with one's writing.

Beauvoir says that to write is to appeal to the freedom of the other.[19] If we follow the implications of that, we will realize that there is no way to control the political effects of our own writing. Readers are free to meet our appeals with anything from enthusiasm to indifference, contempt and silence. To appeal to the freedom of others is to risk their rebuff. If we want to be politically committed, all we can do is to say what we have to say, and take responsibility for our words. In short, we have to mean what we say.[20]

In the light of all this, does *Sexual/Textual Politics* itself count as a political intervention? There is no doubt that I thought it did back in 1985. Although I didn't always manage to say exactly what I meant, I certainly meant what I said. My passionate advocacy for feminist anti-essentialism was at once intellectual and political, and actually did change some people's minds. The book also helped to make feminism more acceptable in academic circles. *Sexual/Textual Politics* was my first book; it taught me that it is possible for anyone – me, for example – to speak up, to have a say, to participate in the feminist project. In 2002 feminism needs new visions and new voices. I know that this book has inspired many feminist students to speak up, to express their passionate disagreement or agreement. In translation the book has mattered and continues to matter to readers all over the world. If *Sexual/Textual Politics* continues to inspire discussion for some years to come, it will still be a useful book.

Durham, North Carolina
January 2002.

NOTES

PREFACE

1   I wrote this sentence some months before the publication of Ken
    Ruthven's *Feminist Literary Studies*, which claims to be the 'first broad
    survey of both the dominant theories of feminist literary criticism and
    the critical practices which result from those theories'. Although I am
    delighted to be able to acknowledge his book as the first full-length
    survey of the field, I also feel that I do not really need to change my
    introductory sentence, not least because I never intended my own
    book as a survey of practical feminist criticism. *Feminist Literary
    Studies* discusses the field of feminist criticism as it appears to an
    academic engaged in the study of English literature. This approach
    seems to have prevented Ruthven from discussing French feminist
    theory, and his book can therefore not be said to engage fully with the
    problems of feminist *theory* today.

    My major objection to Ruthven's study is not primarily that it is
    written by a man: while sharing his view that men *in principle* can be
    feminist critics, I disagree with his far too rash dismissal of the polit-
    ical reasons why they ought not to try for a leading role in this particu-
    lar field today. I also object to the idea that men should enjoy certain
    advantages over women when it comes to engaging in rational criti-
    cism of feminist theory: 'In some respects it is easier for men than for
    women to object to the more ridiculous manifestations of feminist

criticism', Ruthven argues, 'simply because the intimidatory rhetoric of radical feminism designates any woman who is sharply critical of feminist discourse as a female equivalent of the "white arsed nigger" of separatist black rhetoric' (14). But surely feminists are perfectly capable of intervening in their own debates without having to hire male liberals to take the flak on their behalf?

The main problem with *Feminist Literary Studies*, however, is the way in which it seeks to depoliticize feminist critical discourse. For Ruthven, feminist criticism consists in 'rendering visible the hitherto invisible component of 'gender' in all discourses produced by the humanities and the social sciences' (24). This, *pace* Ruthven, is not necessarily a feminist act: it might just as well be an example of patri-archal aggression. His definition would make the sentence 'You say this because you are a woman' unambiguously feminist. My point is simply that only a political definition of feminist criticism and theory will enable us to analyze the difference between feminist and sexist uses of that and similar statements.

INTRODUCTION: WHO'S AFRAID OF VIRGINIA WOOLF?
FEMINIST READINGS OF WOOLF

1   Anna Coombes's reading of *The Waves* shows a true Lukácsian dis-taste for the fragmented and subjective web of modernism, as when she writes that 'My problem in writing this paper has been to attempt to politicize a discourse which obstinate [sic] seeks to exclude the political and the historical, and, where this is no longer possible, then tries to aestheticize glibly what it cannot "realistically" incorporate' (238).

2   For further discussion of this point, see the section on Gilbert and Gubar pp. 56–68.

3   The term 'Anglo-American' must be taken as an indication of a specific approach to literature, not as an empirical description of the critic's nationality. The British critic Gillian Beer, in her essay 'Beyond deter-minism: George Eliot and Virginia Woolf' raises the same kind of objections to Showalter's reading of Woolf as I have done in this paper. In her 1984 essay, 'Subject and object and the nature of reality: Hume and elegy in *To the Lighthouse*', Beer develops this approach in a more philosophical context.

4   For an introduction to Derrida's thought and to other forms of deconstruction see Norris.

5 My presentation of Kristeva's position here is based on her *La Révolution du langage poétique*.

6 One feminist critic, Barbara Hill Rigney, has tried to show that in *Mrs Dalloway* 'madness becomes a kind of refuge for the self rather than its loss' (52). This argument in my view finds little support in the text and seems to depend more on the critic's desire to preserve her Laingian categories than on a responsive reading of Woolf's text.

1 TWO FEMINIST CLASSICS

1 The information here is based on Robin Morgan's introduction to the anthology *Sisterhood is Powerful*.

2 Quoted in Morgan, 35–6.

3 Ultimately one might even argue that all discourse is ironic, since it rapidly becomes theoretically and practically impossible to distinguish between ironic and non-ironic discourse. See Culler for a discussion of this problem in relation to a literary text.

4 *The Female Eunuch* is not discussed in this book because it is not primarily a work of literary criticism. In the chapter called 'Romance', Greer does however try her hand at a reading of popular romantic fiction.

2 'IMAGES OF WOMEN' CRITICISM

1 I was unable to consult the 1972 original edition. My comments are therefore based on the 1973 reprint.

2 See Ascher, 107–22.

3 Robinson and Vogel's contribution.

4 Katz-Stoker's essay.

5 Register is here quoting Martin.

3 WOMEN WRITING AND WRITING ABOUT WOMEN

1 As quoted by Register, 13–14.

2 Quoted on the flyleaf of the Women's Press edition of *Literary Women*.

3 In Scandinavia, the Swedish critic Birgitta Holm has made creative use of the central ideas in *The Madwoman in the Attic* for her influential study of Fredrika Bremer, the creator of the Swedish realist novel. The first Norwegian realist novel, *Amtmandens døttre*, was also written by a woman, Camilla Collett, and Holm tries to locate the reasons why

precisely women writers were at the vanguard of Scandinavian realism. Later women also became the leading naturalist novelists in
Scandinavia: in Norway Amalie Skram (*Constance Ring, Lucie*) and in
Sweden Victoria Benedictsson (*Pengar* – 'Money') wrote gripping
feminist novels about the battle between the sexes in the 1880s and
1890s.
4 Gilbert and Gubar's italics. They are quoting Said, 162.
5 See chapter 1, pp. 28–9.
6 For a different account of Mary Shelley's attitude towards femininity
   see Jacobus, 'Is there a woman in this text?'
7 See Part Two for further discussion of French feminist theory in general, and pp. 103–6 for a presentation of some aspects of Derridean
   theory.

4 THEORETICAL REFLECTIONS

1 For further discussion of the relationship between politics and aesthetics, see the section on Jehlen, pp. 79–86.
2 Lukács, Brecht, Stalin, Trotsky, Benjamin, Gramsci and Althusser are
   all considered Marxists, and psychoanalysis comprises names as
   divergent as Freud, Adler, Jung, Reich, Horney, Fromm, Klein and
   Lacan.
3 For further discussion of Showalter's work, see the introductory
   chapter on Woolf, pp. 1–18, and chapter 3, pp. 54–6.
4 Jehlen's article can be found in Keohane, Rosaldo and Gelpi (eds) and
   in Abel and Abel (eds). I am quoting from the original publication in
   Signs.
5 In the second part of her article Jehlen puts her aesthetic theories to
   practical use in an effort to elaborate a theory of the novel with special
   emphasis on the sentimental novel.
6 For a first introduction to lesbian criticism see Zimmerman; for further
   study see Rich, 'Compulsory heterosexuality and lesbian existence'
   and *On Lies, Secrets and Silence*; also Fadermann, and Rule. For an
   introduction to black feminist criticism see Smith.
7 See for instance Spivak.
8 One early exception is Lillian S. Robinson's work, collected in her *Sex,
   Class and Culture*.
9 See Kolodny, 'Turning the lens on "The Panther Captivity"', 175.

5 FROM SIMONE DE BEAUVOIR TO JACQUES LACAN

1 The politics of *The Second Sex* has been the object of much debate. For an introduction to some of the issues raised see the articles by Felstiner, Le Doeuff, Dijkstra and Fuchs in *Feminist Studies*, 6, 2, Summer 1980.

2 For an account of this and other developments in the new women's movement in Norway see Haukaa.

3 In Denmark Jette Lundboe Levy has furnished a superbly researched study of the historical context of the great Swedish novelist Victoria Benedictsson. In Norway Irene Engelstad and Janneken Øverland have explored the representation of class and sexuality in the works of Amalie Skram and Cora Sandel respectively (see the articles in their joint collection *Frihet til å skrive*).

4 As examples of their more challenging work one could mention: Coward and Ellis, *Language and Materialism*; Coward, *Patriarchal Precedents* and *Female Desire*; Kuhn and Wolpe (eds), *Feminism and Materialism*; Lovell, *Pictures of Reality*; Wolff, *The Social Production of Art*; and Barrett, *Women's Oppression Today*.

5 See pp. 21–4.

6 The French 'femelle', denoting a female animal, is only used pejoratively about women.

7 The pioneering work was Herrmann's *Les Voleuses de langue*. Due to the fact that the author teaches in the US, it is more 'American' than 'French' in its outlook.

8 For American introductions to French feminism see Jones, 'Writing the body', and the articles by Stanton, Féral, Makward, Gallop and Burke in Eisenstein and Jardine (eds), 71–122. Several American reviews have devoted special issues or sections to French feminism: *Signs*, 7, 1; *Yale French Studies*, 62; *Feminist Studies*, 7, 2; *Diacritics*, Winter 1975 and Summer 1982. A good general history and overview of the French feminist scene can be found in the editors' introductions to Marks and Courtivron (eds).

9 This development parallels the American move towards a 'woman-centred' analysis. For a full account of the politics of woman-centred feminism see Eisenstein.

10 *Questions féministes* also runs an American edition entitled *Feminist Issues*. Their manifesto is reprinted under the title 'Variations on common themes' in Marks and Courtivron (eds), 212–30.

11 Other short introductions to Lacan are provided in Wright and in Eagleton (1983). For a fuller presentation see Lemaire.

6 HÉLÈNE CIXOUS: AN IMAGINARY UTOPIA

1 All quotations from Cixous's works are in English, principally from published English translations, but when no such has been available, I have supplied my own. In the case of a published translation, except for the article 'Castration or decapitation?', where I have been unable to consult the French original, page references refer first to the translation, then to the original French. The following abbreviations have been used: JN – *La Jeune Née*, VE – *La Venue à l'écriture* and RSH – interview in *Revue des sciences humaines*.

2 In *Eperons* (which translates as *Spurs*), Derrida would seem to be using the word 'feminist' in the same, derogatory sense.

3 In her article 'Is female to male as nature is to culture?', in Rosaldo and Lamphere (eds), Sherry Ortner's analysis of the male/female and culture/nature oppositions arrives at conclusions that are strikingly similar to some of Cixous's observations. Arguing that 'everywhere, in every known culture, women are considered in some degree inferior to men' (69), Ortner sees this 'universal devaluation of women' (71) as a result of an all-pervasive binary logic in which male/female is pictured as parallel to culture/nature, and where 'nature' always is seen as representing a 'lower order of existence' (72).

4 Cixous here follows Derrida who labels the mainstream of Western thinking *logocentric*, due to its consistent privileging of the *Logos*, the Word as a metaphysical presence.

5 *Phallocentrism* denotes a system that privileges the phallus as the symbol or source of power. The conjuncture of logocentrism and phallocentrism is often called, after Derrida, *phallogocentrism*.

6 The argument illustrated on the level of phonemes would be the same on the level of signifiers. For Saussure, the *sign* ('word') consists of two terms: *signifier* and *signified*. The signifier is the material aspect of the sign (sound or letters) whereas the signified is its 'meaning' or ideational representation. The signified is *not* the 'real thing' in the world, which Saussure labels the *referent*. For Saussure, signifier and signified are inseparable, like the two sides of a sheet of paper, whereas post-structuralism, in particular Lacanian theory, has questioned this closure of the sign and shown how the signifier can 'slide' in relation to the signified.

7 For a fascinating account of utopian thought in nineteenth-century socialism and feminism see Barbara Taylor.

8 See the discussion of Millett in chapter 1, pp. 24–31.

7 PATRIARCHAL REFLECTIONS: LUCE IRIGARAY'S LOOKING-GLASS

1 See Lemoine-Luccioni's review in *Esprit*.

2 References to *Spéculum* will be abbreviated to S. 'S, 130' means *Spéculum*, p. 130; 'CS, 76' means *Ce sexe qui n'en est pas un*, p. 76. Two articles from *Ce sexe* are translated in Marks and Courtivron (eds). Quotations from these translations will be marked MC, followed by a reference to the original French, i.e. 'MC, 100, CS, 24'. All translations except the ones marked MC are mine.

3 For other introductions to Irigaray, or some of the problems she raises, see Burke, 'Introduction to Luce Irigaray's "When our lips speak together"' and 'Irigaray through the looking glass'; also Wenzel, 'Introduction to Luce Irigaray's "And the one doesn't stir without the other"' and Brown and Adams, 'The feminine body and feminist politics'.

4 See Gallop's discussion of the implications of this title in her chapter headed 'The father's seduction' (Gallop, 56–79).

5 It is often difficult to tell exactly where Irigaray quotes from. In a postscript to *Spéculum* she states that she often has preferred not to signal quotations at all. Given that woman is excluded from theory, Irigaray argues, she doesn't need to relate to it in the way prescribed by the same theory.

6 For a further discussion of the status of visual evidence in Freudian theory see Heath.

7 For a succinct overview of theories of female sexuality from Freud until today see Janine Chasseguet-Smirgel's introduction to Chasseguet-Smirgel (ed.), or (in French) Irigaray's admirably lucid chapter entitled 'Retour sur la théorie psychanalytique', CS, 35–65. For a discussion of possible feminist appropriations of these theories see Mitchell, *Psychoanalysis and Feminism* and *Women: The Longest Revolution*, Mitchell's and Rose's introductions to Mitchell and Rose (eds) and also (in French) the whole of Kofman's fascinating re-reading of Freud, which in many ways can be read as a critical reply to Irigaray. Lemoine-Luccioni, in *Partage des femmes*, and Montrelay take the debate on to more specifically Lacanian terrain.

8 Roughly summarized, Freud's argument links the act of seeing to anal *activity*, which he sees as expressing a desire for *mastery* or for the exercise of *power* over one's (libidinal) objects, a desire that underlies later (phallic or Oedipal) fantasies about phallic (masculine) power. Thus the *gaze* enacts the voyeur's desire for sadistic power, in which

the object of the gaze is cast as its passive, masochistic, feminine victim.

9 For further analysis of Freud's anxiety in 'Dora' see Moi.

10 Translated by Claudia Reeder in Marks and Courtivron (eds), 99–106.

11 Rachel Bowlby has also criticized Irigaray (along with Montrelay and Cixous) for her 'lack of any coherent social theory' (Bowlby, 67).

8 MARGINALITY AND SUBVERSION: JULIA KRISTEVA

1 The first part of this quotation is translated by Roudiez (1), the second part by me.

2 Quoted by Barthes, 1970 (20). My translation.

3 For other English-language introductions to Kristeva see Coward and Ellis, and Féral (1978).

4 For further discussion of this notion of the decentred subject see my introduction to Lacan in chapter 5, pp. 97–9.

5 In her lecture 'Sex differences in language: a psychological approach' in the Oxford University Women's Studies Committee's lecture series on 'Women and language,' 10 May 1983.

6 See the brief presentation of Derrida's use of the word *différance*, pp. 103–6.

7 See Ardener. For an exposition of feminist linguistics in relation to the 'muted group' theory see Kramarae, chapter 1, 1–32.

8 The name Vološinov is now generally considered to be a cover for the leading Soviet literary theorist Mikhail Bakhtin.

9 In the chapter entitled 'J'ai oublié mon parapluie' in *Eperons*, 103–13.

10 As quoted by Wittgenstein, §1.

11 For an introduction to these concepts in Lacan see chapter 5, pp. 97–9.

12 Throughout this chapter, when no English translation is listed in the bibliography, all quotations from Kristeva's work are translated by me.

13 For further discussion of the political implications of Kristeva's theory at this point, see my introductory chapter pp. 12–13.

14 See her article on dissidence, 'Un nouveau type d'intellectuel'.

15 For a discussion of this problem from a somewhat different angle see Pajaczkowska.

16 For Kristeva's discovery of America see 'Pourquoi les Etats-Unis?'

17 For an example of a disappointed and resentful feminist response to Kristeva see Stone.

NOTES TO THE AFTERWORD

1　Anyone interested in my recent analysis of questions in feminist theory should look at *What Is a Woman?*, particularly chapters 1, 2 and 9. The preface to *What Is a Woman?* also contains some reflections on *Sexual/Textual Politics*.

2　*The Sun*, 4 May 1982, front page.

3　I want to thank Abigail Salerno, my research assistant, for finding and checking dates and figures concerning the Falklands War and Greenham Common.

4　For further discussion of the problems with generalizations about femininity, see *What Is a Woman?*, particularly the section of the title essay called 'Against Femininity' (99–112).

5　Today I would add that the Kristeva-inspired psychoanalytic understanding of subjectivity that dominates the book is broadly compatible with the phenomenological approach of Simone de Beauvoir and Maurice Merleau-Ponty. I try to show the affinities between Freud, Beauvoir and Merleau-Ponty in my essay 'Is anatomy destiny?' (*What is a Woman?* 369–93). This essay should be read in conjunction with 'What is a woman?', particularly the section entitled 'The body as a situation' (59–83). In *Sexual/Textual Politics* the main source for my understanding of Kristeva is *Revolution in Poetic Language* (first published in French in 1974; an excellent, but incomplete translation appeared in English in 1984). I don't mean to say that all of Kristeva's writings after 1984 are compatible with my own feminism, or indeed with her own early writings. Many of the Kristeva texts referred to in *Sexual/Textual Politics* are included in my edition of *The Kristeva Reader*.

6　See Moi, *Simone de Beauvoir: The Making of an Intellectual Woman* (1994).

7　One should not conclude that I think that there are no ambiguous or difficult cases, no transsexuals, no intersexed people, no transvestites and so on. My point is simply that the existence of intermediate categories does not invalidate the usual definition of the word 'woman'. (I discuss this claim, as well as the status of transsexuals and other transgendered people at some length in the title essay of *What Is a Woman?*)

8　See Butler, *Gender Trouble* 25, 141.

9　In keeping with these views I criticize Cixous for thinking of ideology as an entirely self-consistent, non-contradictory membrane, which leaves no space for women to come to critical consciousness of that ideology (see 122), and I permit myself to doubt that Irigaray's 'mimicry' is *always* the best oppositional strategy for women (see 139–42).

10   An excellent example of such a critique can be found in Derrida's essay on J. L. Austin, entitled 'Signature event context', which happens to be the very essay that furnishes Butler with her concept of 'citationality' or 'iteration'. In my view Derrida entirely fails to encounter Austin's thought. A truly outstanding analysis of Derrida's reading of Austin is Stanley Cavell's 'Counter-philosophy and the pawn of voice,' in Cavell, *A Pitch of Philosophy* 53–127.

11   The reference to a 'philosophical picture' is a reference to Wittgenstein's 'A *picture* held us captive. And we could not get outside it, for it lay in our language and language seemed to repeat it to us inexorably' (*Philosophical Investigations*, §115).

12   For my reading of this fantasy in a melodramatic text, see my essay on *Corinne*, 'A woman's desire to be known', particularly 166–71.

13   Cora Diamond puts the phrase 'it depends' to good philosophical use in her brilliant essay on feminist epistemology or 'women's ways of knowing' entitled 'Knowing tornadoes and other things'. See also my discussion of Diamond's essay in Moi, *What Is a Woman?* 156–60.

14   'En face d'un enfant qui meurt, *La Nausée* ne fait pas le poids'. Sartre made this statement in an interview with Jacqueline Piatier entitled 'Jean Paul Sartre s'explique sur *Les Mots*', published in *Le Monde* 18 April 1964. I am quoting from Contat and Rybalka 398.

15   'Je suis une intellectuelle, j'accorde du prix aux mots et à la vérité' (*La Force des choses* 2: 120).

16   That there is a strong relationship between melodramatic form and the kind of metaphysics called scepticism is a point Cavell explores in *Contesting Tears*, and that I make use of for feminist purposes in an essay on Mme de Staël's *Corinne* ('A woman's desire to be known'). My most sustained attempt to explore the ways in which Beauvoir's existentialism and Cavell's ordinary language philosophy illuminate each other can be found in *What Is a Woman?* particularly 169–250.

17   In his influential study *The Melodramatic Imagination*, Peter Brooks writes: 'The connotations of the word [melodrama] include: the indulgence of strong emotionalism; moral polarization and schematization; extreme states of being, situations, actions; overt villainy, persecution of the good [. . .]' (11).

18   The term 'arrogation of voice' stresses the unfounded moment of arrogation contained in any theoretical or philosophical speech act, as well as the inevitable arrogance of the act of claiming for oneself the

right to appeal to the judgment of others. See Cavell, *A Pitch of Philosophy* 1–51, and Moi, *What Is a Woman?* 233–5 and 249–50.

19 'Language is an appeal to the freedom of the other, because the sign only becomes sign when it is grasped by a consciousness,' Beauvoir writes in *Pyrrhus et Cinéas* (104). 'I can only appeal to the other's freedom, not constrain it', she adds (112). (My translation in both cases.) For further discussion of the idea of the appeal to the other, see Moi *What Is a Woman?* 226–37.

20 I develop the ideas outlined here in an essay called 'Meaning what we say: The "politics of theory" and the responsibility of intellectuals', written for a collection of essays edited by Emily Grosholz.

REFERENCES

Abel, Elizabeth and Abel, Emily (eds) (1983) *The 'Signs' Reader: Women, Gender, and Scholarship*. Chicago: University of Chicago Press.

Ardener, Edwin (1975) 'The "problem" revisited', in Ardener, Shirley (ed.), *Perceiving Women*. London: Malaby Press.

Ascher, Carol (1981) *Simone de Beauvoir: A Life of Freedom*. Brighton: Harvester.

Auerbach, Nina (1978) *Communities of Women: An Idea in Fiction*. Cambridge, Mass.: Harvard University Press.

Bakhtin, Mikhail (1968) *Rabelais and His World*. Cambridge, Mass.: MIT Press.

Barrett, Michèle (ed.) (1979) *Virginia Woolf: Women and Writing*. London: The Women's Press.

—— (1980) *Women's Oppression Today*. London: Verso.

Barthes, Roland (1970) 'L'étrangère', *La quinzaine littéraire*, 94, 1–15 mai, 19–20.

—— (1976) *The Pleasure of the Text*, trans. Miller, Richard. London: Jonathan Cape.

—— (1977) 'The death of the Author', in Heath, Stephen (ed.) *Image Music Text*. London: Fontana.

Bazin, Nancy Topping (1973) *Virginia Woolf and the Androgynous Vision*. New Brunswick, N.J.: Rutgers University Press.

Beauvoir, Simone de (1944) *Pyrrhus et Cinéas*. Paris: Gallimard.

—— (1949) *Le deuxième sexe*. Paris: Gallimard. Trans. Parshley, H.M. (1972) *The Second Sex*. Harmondsworth: Penguin.

—— (1963) *La force des choses*. Paris: Gallimard (Coll. Folio), 2 vols.

—— (1984) *Simone de Beauvoir Today. Conversations with Alice Schwartzer 1972–1982*. London: Chatto.

—— (1987) *Force of Circumstance*. Trans. Richard Howard. Harmondsworth: Penguin.

Beer, Gillian (1979) 'Beyond determinism: George Eliot and Virginia Woolf', in Jacobus, Mary (ed.), *Women Writing and Writing About Women*. London: Croom Helm, 80–99.

—— (1984) 'Hume, Stephen and elegy in *To the Lighthouse*', *Essays in Criticism*, 34, 33–55.

Beer, Patricia (1974) *Reader, I Married Him: A Study of the Women Characters of Jane Austen, Charlotte Brontë, Elizabeth Gaskell and George Eliot*. London: Macmillan.

Belsey, Catherine (1980) *Critical Practice*. London: Methuen.

Boumelha, Penny (1982) *Thomas Hardy and Women: Sexual Ideology and Narrative Form*. Brighton: Harvester.

Bowlby, Rachel (1983) 'The feminine female', *Social Text*, 7, Spring and Summer, 54–68.

Brooks, Peter (1985) *The Melodramatic Imagination: Balzac, Henry James, Melodrama, and the Mode of Excess (1976)*. New York: Columbia University Press.

Brown, Beverly and Adams, Parveen (1979) 'The feminine body and feminist politics', *m/f*, 3, 35–50.

Brown, Cheryl L. and Olson, Karen (eds) (1978) *Feminist Criticism: Essays on Theory, Poetry and Prose*. Metuchen: Scarecrow Press.

Burke, Carolyn (1980) 'Introduction to Luce Irigaray's "When our lips speak together"', *Signs*, 6, 1, Autumn, 66–8.

—— (1981) 'Irigaray through the looking glass', *Feminist Studies*, 7, 2 Summer, 288–306.

Butler, Judith (1990) *Gender Trouble: Feminism and the Subversion of Identity*. New York: Routledge.

—— (1993) *Bodies That Matter: On the Discursive Limits of 'Sex'*. New York: Routledge.

Cavell, Stanley (1969) 'Aesthetic problems of modern philosophy', *Must We Mean What We Say?* Cambridge: Cambridge University Press, 73–96.

—— (1994) *A Pitch of Philosophy: Autobiographical Exercises*. Cambridge, Mass.: Harvard University Press.

—— (1996) *Contesting Tears: The Hollywood Melodrama of the Unknown Woman*. Chicago: University of Chicago Press.

—— (1999) *The Claim of Reason: Wittgenstein, Skepticism, Morality, and Tragedy*. New York: Oxford University Press. With a new preface.

Chasseguet-Smirgel, Janine (ed.) (1970) *Female Sexuality*. Ann Arbor: University of Michigan Press.

Chodorow, Nancy (1978) *The Reproduction of Mothering. Psychoanalysis and the Sociology of Gender*. Berkeley: University of California Press.

Cixous, Hélène (1968) *L'Exil de James Joyce ou l'art du remplacement*. Paris: Grasset. Trans. Purcell, Sally (1972) *The Exile of James Joyce or the Art of Replacement*. New York: David Lewis.

—— (1974) *Prénoms de personne*. Paris: Seuil.

—— (1975) *La Jeune Née* (en collaboration avec Catherine Clément). Paris: UGE, 10/18. An excerpt from 'Sorties' is trans. by Liddle, Ann, in Marks, Elaine and Courtivron, Isabelle de (eds) (1980) *New French Feminisms*. Brighton: Harvester, 90–8.

—— (1975) 'Le Rire de la Méduse', *L'Arc*, 61, 39–54. Trans. Cohen, Keith and Cohen, Paula (1976) 'The laugh of the Medusa', *Signs*, 1, Summer, 875–99. Here quoted from the reprint in Marks, Elaine and Courtivron, Isabelle de (eds) (1980) *New French Feminisms*. Brighton: Harvester, 245–64.

—— (1976) *LA*. Paris: Gallimard.

—— (1976) 'La Missexualité, où jouis-je?', *Poétique*, 26, 240–9.

—— (1976) 'Le Sexe ou la tête?' *Les Cahiers du GRIF*, 13, 5–15. Trans. Kuhn, Annette (1981) 'Castration or decapitation?', *Signs*, 7, 1, 41–55.

—— (1976) *Portrait de Dora*. Paris: des femmes. Trans. Burd, Sarah (1983) *Portrait of Dora, Diacritics*, 13, 1, Spring, 2–32.

—— (1977) 'Entretien avec Françoise van Rossum-Guyon', *Revue des sciences humaines*, 168, octobre-décembre, 479–93.

—— (1977) *La Venue à l'écriture* (en collaboration avec Annie Leclerc et Madeleine Gagnon). Paris: UGE, 10/18.

—— (1979) 'L'Approche de Clarice Lispector', *Poétique*, 40, 408–19.

Conley, Verena Andermatt (1984) *Hélène Cixous: Writing the Feminine*. Lincoln and London: University of Nebraska Press. Includes the appendix 'An exchange with Hélène Cixous', 129–61.

Contat, Michel, and Rybalka, Michel (1970) *Les écrits de Sartre*. Paris: Gallimard.

Coombes, Anna (1979) 'Virginia Woolf's *The Waves*: a materialist reading of an almost disembodied voice', in Barker, Francis *et al.* (eds), *Proceedings of the Essex Conference on the Sociology of Literature, July*

1978. Vol. 1: 1936: The Politics of Modernism. Colchester: University of Essex, 228–51.

Cornillon, Susan Koppelman (ed.) (1972) *Images of Women in Fiction: Feminist Perspectives.* Bowling Green, Ohio: Bowling Green University Popular Press.

Coward, Rosalind (1983) *Patriarchal Precedents. Sexuality and Social Relations.* London: Routledge & Kegan Paul.

—— (1984) *Female Desire. Women's Sexuality Today.* London: Paladin.

—— and Ellis, John (1977) *Language and Materialism.* London: Routledge & Kegan Paul.

Culler, Jonathan (1974) *Flaubert. The Uses of Uncertainty.* London: Paul Elek.

—— (1992) 'Literary Theory', in Gibaldi, Joseph (ed.) *Introduction to Scholarship in Modern Languages and Literatures.* 2nd ed. New York: MLA, 201–35.

Dahlerup, Pil (1972) 'Omedvetna attityder hos en recensent', in Berg, Karin Westman (ed.), *Könsdiskriminering förr och nu.* Stockholm: Prisma, 37–45.

Dardigna, Anne-Marie (1981) *Les Châteaux d'Eros ou les infortunes du sexe des femmes.* Paris: Maspéro.

Delphy, Christine (1984) *Close to Home. A Materialist Analysis of Women's Oppression,* trans. and ed. Leonard, Diana. London: Hutchinson.

Derrida, Jacques (1967) *De la grammatologie.* Paris: Minuit. Trans. Spivak, Gayatri (1976) *Of Grammatology.* Baltimore: Johns Hopkins University Press.

—— (1967) *L'Ecriture et la différence.* Paris: Seuil, Trans. Bass, Alan (1978) *Writing and Difference.* Chicago: University of Chicago Press.

—— (1975) 'The purveyor of truth', *Yale French Studies,* 52, 31–114.

—— (1978) *Eperons. Les styles de Nietzsche.* Paris: Flammarion.

—— (1982) 'Choreographies'. Interview with Christie V. McDonald, *Diacritics,* 12, 2, 66–76.

—— (1988) 'Signature event context', *Limited Inc.* Evanston, Ill.: Northwestern University Press, 1–23.

Diacritics (1975) Winter.

—— (1982) Summer.

Diamond, Cora (1991) 'Knowing tornadoes and other things', *New Literary History* 22: 1001–15.

Dijkstra, Sandra (1980) 'Simone de Beauvoir and Betty Friedan: the politics of omission', *Feminist Studies,* 6, 2, Summer, 290–303.

Doederlein, Sue Warrick (1982) 'Comment on Jehlen', *Signs*, 8, 1, 164–6.

Donovan, Josephine (1972) 'Feminist style criticism', in Cornillon, Susan Koppelman (ed.), *Images of Women in Fiction: Feminist Perspectives*. Bowling Green, Ohio: Bowling Green University Popular Press, 341–54.

—— (ed.) (1975) *Feminist Literary Criticism: Explorations in Theory*. Lexington: The University Press of Kentucky.

Eagleton, Terry (1976) *Marxism and Literary Criticism*. Berkeley: University of California Press.

—— (1983) *Literary Theory. An Introduction*. Oxford: Blackwell.

Eisenstein, Hester (1984) *Contemporary Feminist Thought*. London: Allen & Unwin.

—— and Jardine, Alice (eds) (1980) *The Future of Difference*. Boston, Mass.: G. K. Hall.

Ellmann, Mary (1968) *Thinking About Women*. New York: Harcourt.

Engelstad, Irene and Øverland, Janneken (1981) *Frihet til å skrive. Artikler om kvinnelitteratur fra Amalie Skram til Cecilie Løveid*. Oslo: Pax.

Faderman, Lillian (1981) *Surpassing the Love of Men: Romantic Friendship and Love Between Women From the Renaissance to the Present*. New York: William Morrow.

Felman, Shoshana (1975) 'The critical phallacy', *Diacritics*, Winter, 2–10.

Felstiner, Mary Lowenthal (1980) 'Seeing *The Second Sex* through the second wave', *Feminist Studies*, 6, 2, Summer, 247–76.

Feminist Studies (1981) 7, 2, Summer.

Féral, Josette (1978) 'Antigone or the irony of the tribe', *Diacritics*, Fall, 2–14.

—— (1980) 'The powers of difference', in Eisenstein, Hester and Jardine, Alice (eds), *The Future of Difference*. Boston, Mass.: G. K. Hall, 88–94.

Freud, Sigmund (1905) 'Dora', in *Case Histories I*. Pelican Freud Library. Vol. 8. Harmondsworth: Penguin (1977).

—— (1919) 'The uncanny', in *Standard Edition*. Vol. 17, 219–52.

—— (1923) 'Negation' in Strachey, James (trans. and ed.) *The Standard Edition of the Complete Psychological Works*, 24 vols. London: The Hogarth Press, 1953–74. Vol. 19, 233–9.

—— (1933) 'On femininity', in *New Introductory Lectures on Psychoanalysis*, Lecture 33. Pelican Freud Library. Vol. 2. Harmondsworth: Penguin (1971).

Friedan, Betty (1963) *The Feminine Mystique*. New York: Dell.

Fuchs, Jo-Ann P. (1980) 'Female eroticism in *The Second Sex*', *Feminist Studies*, 6, 2, Summer, 304–13.

Fuss, Diana (1989) *Essentially Speaking: Feminism, Nature and Difference*. New York: Routledge.

Gallop, Jane (1982) *Feminism and Psychoanalysis: The Daughter's Seduction*. London: Macmillan.

—— and Burke, Carolyn G. (1980) 'Psychoanalysis and feminism in France', in Eisenstein, Hester and Jardine, Alice (eds), *The Future of Difference*. Boston, Mass.: G. K. Hall, 106–22.

Gilbert, Sandra M. and Gubar, Susan (1979) *The Madwoman in the Attic: The Woman Writer and the Nineteenth-Century Literary Imagination*. New Haven: Yale University Press.

Greer, Germaine (1970) *The Female Eunuch*. London: MacGibbon & Kee.

Greimas, Algirdas Julien (1966) *Sémantique structurale. Recherche de méthode*. Paris: Larousse.

Haukaa, Runa (1982) *Bak Slagordene. Den nye kvinnebevegelsen i Norge*. Oslo: Pax.

Heath, Stephen (1978) 'Difference', *Screen*, 19, 3, Autumn, 51–112.

Heilbrun, Carolyn G. (1973) *Toward Androgyny. Aspects of Male and Female in Literature*. London: Victor Gollancz.

Herrmann, Claudine (1976) *Les Voleuses de langue*. Paris: des femmes.

Holly, Marcia (1975) 'Consciousness and authenticity: towards a feminist aesthetic', in Donovan, Josephine (ed.), *Feminist Literary Criticism. Explorations in Theory*. Lexington: The University Press of Kentucky, 38–47.

Holm, Birgitta (1981) *Fredrika Bremer och den borgerliga romanens födelse. Romanens mödrar I*. Stockholm: Norstedt.

Irigaray, Luce (1973) *Le Langage des déments*. Paris: Mouton.

—— (1974) *Spéculum de l'autre femme*. Paris: Minuit.

—— (1976) 'Women's Exile'. Interview in *Ideology and Consciousness* (1977) 1, May, 62–76. First published as 'Kvinner i eksil', in Haugsgjerd, Svein and Engelstad, Fredrik (eds) (1976) *Seks samtaler om psykiatri*. Oslo: Pax.

—— (1977) *Ce sexe qui n'en est pas un*. Paris: Minuit. Three articles from *Ce sexe* have been translated into English: 'Ce sexe qui n'en est pas un', as 'This sex which is not one', and 'Des marchandises entre elles', as 'When the goods get together', both trans. Reeder, Claudia (1980), in Marks, Elaine and Courtivron, Isabelle de (eds), *New French Feminisms*, Brighton: Harvester, 99–106 and 107–10 respectively; and 'Quand nos lèvres se parlent', trans. Burke,

Carolyn (1980) 'When our lips speak together', *Signs* 6, 1, Autumn, 69–79.

—— (1977) 'Misère de la psychanalyse', *Critique*, 30, 365, octobre, 879–903.

—— (1979) *Et l'une ne bouge pas sans l'autre*. Paris: Minuit. Trans. Wenzel, Hélène Vivienne (1981) 'And the one doesn't stir without the other', *Signs*, 7, 1, Autumn, 60–7.

—— (1980) *Amante marine de Friedrich Nietzsche*. Paris: Minuit.

—— (1981) *Le Corps-à-corps avec la mère*. Montréal: les éditions de la pleine lune.

—— (1982) *Passions élémentaires*. Paris: Minuit.

—— (1983) *La Croyance même*. Paris: Galilée.

—— (1983) *L'Oubli de l'air chez Martin Heidegger*. Paris: Minuit.

Jacobus, Mary (1979) 'The buried letter: feminism and romanticism in *Villette*', in Jacobus, Mary (ed.), *Women Writing and Writing About Women*. London, Croom Helm, 42–60.

—— (ed.) (1979) *Women Writing and Writing About Women*. London: Croom Helm.

—— (1981) 'Review of *The Madwoman in the Attic*', *Signs*, 6, 3, 517–23.

—— (1982) 'Is there a woman in this text?', *New Literary History*, XIV, 1, 117–41.

Jehlen, Myra (1981) 'Archimedes and the paradox of feminist criticism', *Signs*, 6, 4, 575–601.

Jones, Ann Rosalind (1981) 'Writing the body: toward an understanding of l'écriture féminine', *Feminist Studies*, 7, 2, Summer, 247–63.

Kaplan, Cora (1978) 'Introduction' to Elizabeth Barrett Browning, *Aurora Leigh and Other Poems*. London: The Women's Press.

—— (1979) 'Radical feminism and literature: rethinking Millett's *Sexual Politics*', *Red Letters*, 9, 4–16.

Katz-Stoker, Fraya (1972) 'The other criticism: feminism vs. formalism', in Cornillon, Susan Koppelman (ed.), *Images of Women in Fiction: Feminist Perspectives*. Bowling Green, Ohio: Bowling Green University Popular Press, 315–27.

Keohane, Nannerl O., Rosaldo, Michelle Z. and Gelpi, Barbara C. (eds) (1982) *Feminist Theory: A Critique of Ideology*. Chicago: The University of Chicago Press.

Kofman, Sarah (1980) *L'Énigme de la femme: la femme dans les textes de Freud*. Paris: Galilée.

Kolodny, Annette (1975) 'Some notes on defining a "feminist literary criticism"', *Critical Inquiry*, 2, 1, 75–92. Reprinted in Brown, Cheryl L. and

Olson, Karen (eds) (1978) *Feminist Criticism: Essays on Theory, Poetry and Prose*. Metuchen: Scarecrow Press, 37–58.

—— (1980) 'Dancing through the minefield: some observations on the theory, practice and politics of a feminist literary criticism', *Feminist Studies*, 6, 1, 1–25.

—— (1981) 'Turning the lens on "The Panther Captivity": a feminist exercise in practical criticism', *Critical Inquiry*, 8, 2, 329–45. I quote from the reprint in Abel, Elizabeth (ed.) (1982) *Writing and Sexual Difference*. Chicago: The University of Chicago Press, 159–75.

Kramarae, Cheris (1981) *Women and Men Speaking. Frameworks for Analysis*. Rowley, Mass.: Newbury House.

Kramer, Cheris, Thorne, Barrie and Henley, Nancy (1978) 'Perspectives on language and communication', *Signs*, 3, 3, 638–51.

Kristeva, Julia (1969) *Séméiotiké. Recherches pour une sémanalyse*. Paris: Seuil.

—— (1974) *Des Chinoises*. Paris: des femmes. Trans. Barrows, Anita (1977) *About Chinese Women*. London: Boyars.

—— (1974) 'La femme, ce n'est jamais ça', *Tel Quel*, 59, Automne, 19–24.

—— (1974) *La Révolution du langage poétique*. Paris: Seuil.

—— (1975) 'The system and the speaking subject', in Sebeok, Thomas A. (ed.), *The Tell-Tale Sign. A Survey of Semiotics*. Lisse, Netherlands: The Peter de Ridder Press, 47–55.

—— (1977) 'A partir de *Polylogue*'. Interview with Françoise van Rossum-Guyon in *Revue des sciences humaines*, 168, décembre, 495–501.

—— (1977) 'Héréthique de l'amour', *Tel Quel*, 74, Hiver, 30–49. Reprinted as 'Stabat mater', in Kristeva, Julia (1983) *Histoires d'amour*. Paris: Denoël, 225–47.

—— (1977) *Polylogue*. Paris: Seuil.

—— (1977) 'Pourquoi les Etats-Unis?' (avec Marcelin Pleynet, Philippe Sollers), *Tel Quel*, 71/73, Automne, 3–19. (1978) 'The U.S. now: a conversation', *October*, 6, Fall, 3–17.

—— (1977) 'Un nouveau type d'intellectuel: le dissident', *Tel Quel*, 74, Hiver, 3–8.

—— (1980) *Desire in Language: A Semiotic Approach to Literature and Art*. Ed. Roudiez, Léon S., trans. Jardine, Alice, Gora, Thomas and Roudiez, Léon. Oxford: Blackwell.

—— (1980) 'Motherhood according to Giovanni Bellini', in Kristeva, Julia, *Desire in Language: A Semiotic Approach to Literature*. Oxford: Blackwell, 237–70. The first part of this essay is also translated under the title 'The maternal body', trans. Pajaczkowska, Claire (1981), *m/f*, 5 and 6, 158–63.

—— (1980) *Pouvoirs de l'horreur*. Paris: Seuil. Trans. Léon Roudiez (1982) *Powers of Horror*. New York: Columbia University Press.

—— (1980) 'The ethics of linguistics', in Kristeva, Julia, *Desire in Language: A Semiotic Approach to Literature*. Oxford: Blackwell, 23–35.

—— (1981) 'Women's time', Trans. Jardine, Alice and Blake, Harry, *Signs*, 7, 1, 13–35.

—— (1983) *Histoires d'amour*. Paris: Denoël.

—— (1984) 'Julia Kristeva in Conversation with Rosalind Coward', in Appignanesi, Lisa (ed.) *Desire*. London: ICA Documents, 22–7.

—— (1984) *Revolution in Poetic Language*, trans. Waller, Margaret. New York: Columbia University Press.

—— (1986) *The Kristeva Reader*. Moi, Toril (ed.). Oxford: Blackwell.

Kuhn, Annette and Wolpe, Ann Marie (eds) (1978) *Feminism and Materialism: Women and Modes of Production*. London: Routledge & Kegan Paul.

Lacan, Jacques (1966) *Ecrits*. Paris: Seuil. A selection trans. Sheridan, Alan (1977) *Ecrits*. London: Tavistock.

—— (1975) *Encore. Le séminaire livre XX*. Paris: Seuil.

Laplanche, Jean (1976) *Life and Death in Psychoanalysis*, trans. Mehlman, Jeffrey. Baltimore: Johns Hopkins University Press.

Leclerc, Annie (1974) *Parole de femme*. Paris: Grasset.

Le Doeuff, Michèle (1980) 'Simone de Beauvoir and existentialism', *Feminist Studies*, 6, 2, Summer, 277–89.

Lemaire, Anika (1977) *Jacques Lacan*. London: Routledge & Kegan Paul.

Lemoine-Luccioni, Eugénie (1975) 'Review of *Spéculum*', *Esprit*, 43, 3, 466–9.

—— (1976) *Partage des femmes*. Paris: Seuil.

Levy, Jette Lundboe (1980) *Dobbeltblikke. Om at beskrive kvinder. Ideologi og aestetik i Victoria Benedictssons forfatterskab*. København: Tiderne Skifter.

Lewis, Philip E. (1974) 'Revolutionary semiotics', *Diacritics*, 4, 3, Fall, 28–32.

Lovell, Terry (1982) *Pictures of Reality. Aesthetics, Politics and Pleasure*. London: British Film Institute.

Lukács, Georg (1972) 'Preface', in *Studies in European Realism. A Sociological Survey of the Writings of Balzac, Stendhal, Zola. Tolstoy, Gorki and others*. London: Merlin Press, 1–19.

Macherey, Pierre (1966) *Pour une théorie de la production littéraire*. Paris:

Maspéro. Trans. Wall, Geoffrey (1978) *A Theory of Literary Production*. London: Routledge & Kegan Paul.

Makward, Christiane (1978) 'Structures du silence/du délire: Marguerite Duras, Hélène Cixous', *Poétique*, 35, septembre, 314–24.

—— (1984) 'To be or not to be. . . . a feminist speaker', in Eisenstein, Hester and Jardine, Alice (eds), *The Future of Difference*. Boston, Mass.: G. K. Hall, 95–105.

Marcus, Jane (1981) 'Thinking back through our mothers', in Marcus, Jane (ed.), *New Feminist Essays on Virginia Woolf*. London: Macmillan, 1–30.

Marcuse, Herbert (1968) 'A critique of Norman O. Brown', in *Negations: Essays in Critical Theory*. With translations from the German by Jeremy J. Shapiro, London, Allen Lane, 227–47.

Marder, Herbert (1968) *Feminism and Art. A Study of Virginia Woolf*. Chicago: The University of Chicago Press.

Marini, Marcelle (1977) *Territoires du féminin avec Marguerite Duras*. Paris: Minuit.

Marks, Elaine and Courtivron, Isabelle de (eds) (1980) *New French Feminisms*. Brighton: Harvester.

Martin, Wendy (1970) 'The feminine mystique in American fiction', in Howe, Florence (ed.) *Female Studies II*. Pittsburgh: KNOW.

Marxist-Feminist Literature Collective (1978) 'Women's writing: *Jane Eyre, Shirley, Villette, Aurora Leigh*', *Ideology and Consciousness*, 1, 3, Spring, 27–48.

Meisel, Perry (1980) *The Absent Father. Virginia Woolf and Walter Pater*. New Haven: Yale University Press.

Millett, Kate (1969) *Sexual Politics*. London: Virago, 1977.

Mitchell, Juliet (1971) *Woman's Estate*. Harmondsworth: Penguin.

—— (1974) *Psychoanalysis and Feminism*. Harmondsworth: Penguin.

—— (1984) *Women: The Longest Revolution. Essays in Feminism, Literature and Psychoanalysis*. London: Virago.

—— and Jacqueline Rose (eds) (1982) *Feminine Sexuality. Jacques Lacan and the École Freudienne*. London: Macmillan.

Moers, Ellen (1976) *Literary Women: The Great Writers*. New York: Doubleday. Reprinted (1977) London: The Women's Press.

Moi, Toril (1981) 'Representation of patriarchy: sexuality and epistemology in Freud's "Dora"', *Feminist Review*, 9, Autumn, 60–74.

—— (1994) *Simone de Beauvoir: The Making of an Intellectual Woman*. Oxford: Blackwell.

—— (1999) *What Is a Woman? And Other Essays*. Oxford: Oxford University Press.

—— (2002) 'A woman's desire to be known: Expressivity and silence in *Corinne*', in McDayter, Ghislaine (ed.) *Untrodden Regions of the Mind: Romanticism and Psychoanalysis, Bucknell Review* 45.2: 143–75.

Montrelay, Michèle (1977) *L'Ombre et le nom. Sur la féminité*. Paris: Minuit.

Morgan, Robin (ed.) (1970) *Sisterhood is Powerful: an anthology of writings from the women's liberation movement*. New York: Vintage Books.

Neusüss, Arnhelm (1968) 'Schwierigkeiten einer Soziologie des utopischen Denkens', in Neusüss, Arnhelm (Hrsg) *Utopie. Begriff und Phänomen des Utopischen*. Neuwied: Luchterhand, 13–112.

Newton, Judith Lowder (1981) *Women, Power, and Subversion. Social Strategies in British Fiction 1778–1860*. Athens, Georgia: University of Georgia Press.

Norris, Christopher (1982) *Deconstruction. Theory and Practice*. London: Methuen.

Olsen, Tillie (1980) *Silences*. London: Virago.

Ortner, Sherry B. (1974) 'Is female to male as nature is to culture?', in Rosaldo, Michelle Zimbalist and Lamphere, Louise (eds) *Woman, Culture and Society*. Stanford: Stanford University Press, 67–87.

Pajaczkowska, Claire (1981) 'Introduction to Kristeva', *m/f*, 5 and 6, 149–57.

Plaza, Monique (1978) '"Phallomorphic power" and the psychology of "woman"', *Ideology and Consciousness*, 4, Autumn, 4–36.

Prokop, Ulrike (1976) *Weiblichen Lebenzusammenhang. Von der Beschränktheit der Strategien und den Unangemessenheit der Wunsche*. Frankfurt: Suhrkamp.

Questions féministes (collective) (1980) 'Variations on common themes', in Marks, Elaine and Courtivron, Isabelle de (eds), *New French Feminisms*. Brighton: Harvester, 212–30.

Ramonet, Ignacio (1998) 'Politics of hunger', translated by Barry Smerin, *Le monde diplomatique* November: 1. (Supplement to *Manchester Guardian Weekly*, 22 November, 1998.)

Register, Cheri (1975) 'American feminist literary criticism: a bibliographical introduction', in Donovan, Josephine (ed.), *Feminist Literary Criticism. Explorations in Theory*. Lexington: The University Press of Kentucky, 1–28.

Rich, Adrienne (1979) *On Lies, Secrets and Silence. Selected Prose 1966–1978*. Reprinted (1980) London: Virago.

—— (1980) 'Compulsory heterosexuality and lesbian existence', *Signs*, 5,4. Reprinted as a separate pamphlet (1981), London: Onlywomen Press.

Rigney, Barbara Hill (1978) *Madness and Sexual Politics in the Feminist Novel. Studies in Brontë, Woolf, Lessing and Atwood.* Madison: The University of Wisconsin Press.

Robinson, Lillian S. (1978) 'Dwelling in decencies', in Brown, Cheryl L. and Olson, Karen (eds), *Feminist Criticism: Essays on Theory, Poetry and Prose.* Metuchen: Scarecrow Press, 21–36. First published (1971) in *College English,* 32, May, 879–89.

—— (1978) *Sex, Class and Culture.* Bloomington: Indiana University Press.

—— and Vogel, Lise (1972) 'Modernism and history', in Cornillon, Susan Koppelman (ed.), *Images of Women in Fiction: Feminist Perspectives.* Bowling Green, Ohio: Bowling Green University Popular Press, 278–307.

Rochefort, Christiane (1972) *Archaos ou le jardin étincelant.* Paris: Grasset.

Rogers, Katharine M. (1966) *The Troublesome Helpmate. A History of Misogyny in Literature.* Seattle: University of Washington Press.

Roudiez, Léon S. (1980) 'Introduction', in Kristeva, Julia, *Desire in Language: A Semiotic Approach to Literature and Art.* Oxford: Blackwell, 1–20.

Rule, Jane (1975) *Lesbian Images.* Garden City, N.Y.: Doubleday.

Ruthven, K. K. (1984) *Feminist Literary Studies: An Introduction.* Cambridge: Cambridge University Press.

Said, Edward W. (1975) *Beginnings: Intention and Method.* New York: Basic Books.

Schweickart, Patrocinio (1982) 'Comment on Jehlen', *Signs,* 8, 1, 170–6.

Showalter, Elaine (1971) 'Women and the literary curriculum', *College English,* 32, May.

—— (1977) *A Literature of Their Own. British Women Novelists from Brontë to Lessing.* Princeton, N. J.: Princeton University Press.

—— (1979) 'Towards a feminist poetics', in Jacobus, Mary (ed.), *Women Writing and Writing About Women.* London: Croom Helm, 22–41.

—— (1981) 'Feminist criticism in the wilderness', *Critical Inquiry,* 8, 1, 179–205. Reprinted in Abel, Elizabeth (ed.) (1982) *Writing and Sexual Difference.* Chicago: University of Chicago Press, 9–36.

—— (1982) 'Comment on Jehlen', *Signs,* 8,1, 160–4.

Signs (1981) 7, 1, Autumn.

Smith, Barbara (1980) *Towards a Black Feminist Criticism.* Pamphlet, 19 pp. New York: Out and Out Books. First published in 1977 in *Conditions: Two.*

Spacks, Patricia Meyer (1976) *The Female Imagination. A Literary and Psychological Investigation of Women's Writing.* London: Allen & Unwin.

Spender, Dale (1980) *Man Made Language*. London: Routledge & Kegan Paul.
—— (1982) *Women of Ideas and What Men Have Done to Them*. London: Routledge & Kegan Paul.
Spivak, Gayatri Chakravorty (1981) 'French feminism in an international frame', *Yale French Studies*, 62, 154–84.
Stanton, Donna C. (1980) 'Language and revolution: the Franco-American dis-connection', in Eisenstein, Hester and Jardine, Alice (eds), *The Future of Difference*. Boston, Mass.: G. K. Hall, 73–87.
Stone, Jennifer (1983) 'The horrors of power: a critique of Kristeva', in Barker, Francis *et al.* (eds), *The Politics of Theory. Proceedings of the Essex Conference on the Sociology of Literature, July 1982*. Colchester: University of Essex, 38–48.
Stubbs, Patricia (1979) *Women and Fiction. Feminism and the Novel 1880–1920*. Brighton: Harvester; London: Methuen, 1981.
Taylor, Barbara (1983) *Eve and the New Jerusalem: Socialism and Feminism in the Nineteenth Century*. London: Virago.
Thorne, Barrie and Henley, Nancy (1975) 'Difference and dominance: an overview of language, gender, and society', in Thorne, Barrie and Henley, Nancy (eds), *Language and Sex: Difference and Dominance*. Rowley, Mass.: Newbury House, 5–42.
Vološinov, V. N. (1929) *Marxism and the Philosophy of Language*, Trans. Matejka, Ladislav and Titunik, I. R. (1973). New York: Seminar Press.
Wenzel, Hélène Vivienne (1981) 'Introduction to Luce Irigaray's "And the one doesn't stir without the other"', *Signs*, 7,1, Autumn, 56–9.
White, Allon (1977) *'L'éclatement du sujet'*: The Theoretical Work of *Julia Kristeva*. Birmingham: University of Birmingham Centre for Contemporary Studies. Stencilled Occasional Paper no. 49.
Whitman, Walt (1855) *Leaves of Grass*, in *The Portable Walt Whitman*. Harmondsworth: Penguin, 1977.
Wittgenstein, Ludwig (1953) *Philosophical Investigations*. Anscombe, G. E. M. (trans.) 3rd edn. New York: Macmillan, 1968.
—— (1963) *Philosophical Investigations*, trans. Anscombe, G. E. M., Oxford: Blackwell.
Wolff, Janet (1981) *The Social Production of Art*. London: Macmillan.
Woolf, Virginia (1925) *Mrs Dalloway*. Harmondsworth: Penguin, 1964.
—— (1927) *To the Lighthouse*. London: Dent, 1977.
—— (1929) *A Room of One's Own*. London: Granada, 1977.
—— (1938) *Three Guineas*. Harmondsworth: Penguin, 1977.

Wright, Elizabeth (1984) *Psychoanalytic Criticism: Theory in Practice*. London: Methuen.

Yale French Studies (1981) 62.

Zimmerman, Bonnie (1981) 'What has never been: an overview of lesbian feminist literary criticism', *Feminist Studies*, 7, 3, 451–76.

INDEX